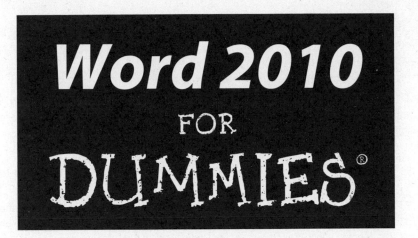

Word 2010 FOR DUMMIES®

by Dan Gookin

WILEY

John Wiley & Sons, Inc.

Word 2010 For Dummies®

Published by
John Wiley & Sons, Inc.
111 River Street
Hoboken, NJ 07030-5774

www.wiley.com

Copyright © 2010 by John Wiley & Sons, Inc., Hoboken, New Jersey

Published by John Wiley & Sons, Inc., Hoboken, New Jersey

Published simultaneously in Canada

For general information on our other products and services, please contact our Customer Care Department within the U.S. at 877-762-2974, outside the U.S. at 317-572-3993, or fax 317-572-4002.

For technical support, please visit www.wiley.com/techsupport.

Wiley publishes in a variety of print and electronic formats and by print-on-demand. Some material included with standard print versions of this book may not be included in e-books or in print-on-demand. If this book refers to media such as a CD or DVD that is not included in the version you purchased, you may download this material at http://booksupport.wiley.com. For more information about Wiley products, visit www.wiley.com.

Library of Congress Control Number: 2010923553

ISBN 978-0-470-48772-3 (pbk); ISBN 978-0-470-76998-0 (ebk); ISBN 978-0-470-76999-7 (ebk); ISBN 978-0-470-77000-9 (ebk)

Manufactured in the United States of America

10 9 8 7 6

WILEY

About the Author

After physically destroying three typewriters, **Dan Gookin** bought his first computer in 1982 at the urging of the guy in the typewriter repair shop. Contrary to his prejudices, Dan quickly discovered that computers were about more than math, and he quickly took to the quirky little devices.

Thirty years later, Mr. Gookin has written over 100 books about computers and high tech and gone through more than 50 computers, including a dozen or so laptops and portables. He has achieved fame as one of the first computer radio talk show hosts, the editor of a computer magazine, a national technology spokesman, and an occasional actor on the community theater stage.

Dan still considers himself a writer and computer "guru" whose job it is to remind everyone that computers are not to be taken too seriously. His approach to computers is light and humorous, yet very informative. He knows that the complex beasts are important and can do a great deal to help people become productive and successful. Dan mixes his vast knowledge of computers with a unique, dry sense of humor that keeps everyone informed — and awake. His favorite quote is "Computers are a notoriously dull subject, but that doesn't mean I have to write about them that way."

Dan Gookin's most recent books are *PCs For Dummies*, Windows 7 Edition, and *Laptops For Dummies*, 4th Edition. He holds a degree in communications/visual arts from the University of California, San Diego. Dan dwells in North Idaho, where he enjoys woodworking, music, theater, riding his bicycle, and spending time with his boys.

Publisher's Acknowledgments

We're proud of this book; please send us your comments through our online registration form located at http://dummies.custhelp.com. For other comments, please contact our Customer Care Department within the U.S. at 877-762-2974, outside the U.S. at 317-572-3993, or fax 317-572-4002.

Some of the people who helped bring this book to market include the following:

Acquisitions and Editorial

Senior Project Editor: Mark Enochs

Acquisitions Editor: Katie Mohr

Copy Editor: Rebecca Whitney

Technical Editor: James F. Kelly

Editorial Manager: Leah Cameron

Editorial Assistant: Amanda Graham

Sr. Editorial Assistant: Cherie Case

Cartoons: Rich Tennant
(www.the5thwave.com)

Composition Services

Project Coordinator: Lynsey Stanford

Layout and Graphics: Ashley Chamberlain, Samantha K. Cherolis, Christine Williams

Proofreaders: The Well-Chosen Word

Indexer: Steve Rath

Publishing and Editorial for Technology Dummies

    Richard Swadley, Vice President and Executive Group Publisher

    Andy Cummings, Vice President and Publisher

    Mary Bednarek, Executive Acquisitions Director

    Mary C. Corder, Editorial Director

Publishing for Consumer Dummies

    Kathleen Nebenhaus, Vice President and Executive Publisher

Composition Services

    Debbie Stailey, Director of Composition Services

Contents at a Glance

Table of Contents

Introduction

The only thing standing between you and your writing is your word processor. Yeah, I know: It's supposed to be helpful. Well, it tries. Computers can do only so much. But you, as a smart person, are capable of so much more. I'm guessing that's why you've opened this book.

Welcome to *Word 2010 For Dummies,* which takes the pain from using Microsoft's latest, greatest, most confusing word processing software ever! This book is your friendly, informative, and entertaining guide to the new-fangled way of processing words that is Word 2010.

Be warned: I'm not out to make you love Word. I don't even want you to enjoy the program. Use it, yes. Tolerate it, of course. The only promise I'm offering is that this book helps ease the pain that everyone feels from using Microsoft Word at the dawn of the 21st century. Along the way, I kick Word in the butt and you will, I hope, enjoy reading about it.

About This Book

I don't intend for you to read this book from cover to cover. It's not a novel, and if it were, it would be a political space opera with an antihero and a princess fighting elected officials who are in cahoots with a galactic urban renewal development corporation. The ending would be extremely satisfying, but it would be a long novel because I need something to balance out *Atlas Shrugged* on my bookshelf. Anyway.

This book is a reference. Each chapter covers a specific topic or task that Word does. Within a chapter, you find self-contained sections, each of which describes how to perform a specific task or get something done. Sample sections you encounter in this book include

- Save your stuff
- Moving a block of text
- Check your spelling
- How to format a paragraph
- Putting text into a table
- Inserting clip art
- Mail merge, ho!

I give you no keys to memorize, no secret codes, no tricks, no videos to sleep through, and no wall charts. Instead, each section explains a topic as though it's the first thing you read in this book. Nothing is assumed, and everything is cross-referenced. Technical terms and topics, when they come up, are neatly shoved to the side, where you can easily avoid reading them. The idea here isn't for you to learn anything. This book's philosophy is to help you look it up, figure it out, and get back to work.

How to Use This Book

You hold in your hands an active book. The topics between this book's yellow-and-black covers are all geared toward getting things done in Word 2010. Because nothing is assumed, all you need to do is find the topic that interests you and read.

Word uses the mouse and keyboard to get things done.

This is a keyboard shortcut:

Ctrl+P

This shortcut means that you should press and hold the Ctrl (control) key and type the letter *P,* just as you would press Shift+P to create a capital *P.* Sometimes, you must press more than two keys at the same time:

Ctrl+Shift+T

In this line, you press Ctrl and Shift together and then press the T key. Release all three keys.

Commands in Word 2010 exist as *command buttons* on the Ribbon interface. This book may refer to the tab, the command group, and then the button itself to help you locate that command button — for example, the Page Color button in the Page Background group on the Page Layout tab. Or, I might write, "the Page Color button found in the Page Layout tab's Page Background group."

Menu commands are listed like this:

Table⇨Insert Table

This command tells you to choose from the Table menu the command named Insert Table. The Table menu appears as a button on the Ribbon.

The main menu in Word 2010 is the File tab menu. It replaces the File menu from older versions of Word, and the Office Button menu, found in Microsoft Office 2007. Clicking the File tab displays the File tab menu, which fills the entire Word window. To return to Word, click the File tab menu again or press the Esc key.

When I describe a message or something you see onscreen, it looks like this:

```
Why should I bother to love Glenda when robots will
eventually destroy the human race?
```

If you need further help in operating your computer I can recommend my book *PCs For Dummies*. It contains lots of useful information to supplement what you find in this book.

Foolish Assumptions

Though this book was written with the beginner in mind, I still make a few assumptions. Foremost, I assume that you're a human being, though you might also be an alien from another planet. If so, welcome to Earth. When you conquer our planet, please do Idaho last. Thanks.

Another foolish assumption I make is that you use Windows as the computer's operating system, either Windows Vista or Windows 7 or any other version of Windows that can run Word 2010. Word and Windows have no specific issues as far as this book is concerned, but keep in mind that this book isn't about Windows.

Your word processor is Microsoft Word 2010. It is *not* Microsoft Works. It is not an earlier version of Word. It is not WordPerfect. It is not a version of Word that runs on a Macintosh.

Throughout this book, I use the term *Word* to refer to the Microsoft Word program. The program may also be called Word 2010 or even Microsoft Office Word 2010. It's all Word as far as this book is concerned. Word 2010 is a part of the Microsoft Office 2010 suite of programs. This book doesn't cover any other part of Microsoft Office, though I mention Excel and Outlook wherever they encroach upon Word's turf.

How This Book Is Organized

This book contains six major parts, each of which is divided into two or more chapters. The chapters themselves have been sliced into smaller, modular sections. You can pick up the book and read any section without necessarily knowing what has already been covered in the rest of the book. Start anywhere.

Here's a breakdown of the parts and what you can find in them:

Part I: Your Introduction to Word

This part provides a quick introduction to Word and word processing. You can find information on how to start and quit Word and a simple overview of the typical word processing day.

Part II: Your Basic Word

The chapters in this part of the book cover the seven basic tasks of any word processor: move around a document, edit text, search and replace, work with blocks of text, proof documents, save and open, and, finally, publish. (Publishing has replaced printing as the final result of your word processing efforts, though printing is still covered as part of the whole publishing milieu.)

Part III: Formatting

This part deals with formatting, from the smallest iota of text to formatting commands that span an entire document and more. Formatting is the art of making your document look less ugly.

Part IV: Spruce Up a Dull Document

This part is formatting dessert, or tasks you can do beyond regular formatting to help make your document look like more than a typical, boring document. Part IV covers lines, borders, tables, columns, lists, graphical goodness, and all sorts of stuff that makes Word more than a typical word processor.

Part V: Even More Word

This part covers a few dangling details that I consider myself fortunate to write about, such as outlining, collaboration, mail merge, label-making, and other interesting things that Word does.

Part VI: The Part of Tens

The traditional last part of any *For Dummies* book contains chapters with lists of ten items. You'll find lots of helpful information there, some weird things you may not know about, plus even more useful tips, tricks, and good suggestions.

What's Not Here

Word is one heck of a program. Covering the entire thing would fill a book several thousand pages long. (I kid you not.) My approach in this book is to cover as much basic word processing as possible. Because of that, some advanced features got pushed off the table of contents.

I give you some information about macros, though it's not meaty. Covering macros without a technical description is difficult. If the publisher ever lets me increase this book's size to more than 400 pages, I'd be happy to add a macro chapter; the publisher's address is in this book's front matter, in case you want to lobby on my behalf.

Some of the more esoteric features are touched on lightly here. For example, I could spend about 70 pages detailing what can be done with graphics in Word, but I limited myself to only a dozen pages.

Finally, this book doesn't cover using Word to make a blog post, create a Web page, or how to use Word as your e-mail program.Word does those things, but I consider this a word processing book rather than a Word-does-everything book.

Icons Used in This Book

This icon flags useful, helpful tips or shortcuts.

This icon marks a friendly reminder to do something.

This icon marks a friendly reminder *not* to do something.

This icon alerts you to overly nerdy information and technical discussions of the topic at hand. The information is optional reading, but it may enhance your reputation at cocktail parties if you repeat it.

Where to Go from Here

Start reading! Observe the table of contents and find something that interests you. Or, look up your puzzle in the index.

If you've been using an older version of Word, you're probably somewhat surprised at the look of Word 2010. Therefore, I recommend that you start reading at Chapter 1.

Read! Write! Let your brilliance shine!

My e-mail address is dgookin@wambooli.com. Yes, that's my real address. I reply to all e-mail I receive, and you'll get a quick reply if you keep your question short and specific to this book or to Word itself. Although I enjoy saying "Hi," I cannot answer technical support questions or help you troubleshoot your computer. Thanks for understanding.

You can also visit my Web page for more information or as a diversion: www.wambooli.com.

Enjoy this book. And enjoy Word. Or at least tolerate it.

Part I
Your Introduction to Word

The 5th Wave   By Rich Tennant

"I wrote my entire cookbook in Word. The other programs I saw just didn't look fresh."

In this part . . .

Word processing may seem routine these days, but that hasn't always been the case. Being able to dance your fingers across a computer keyboard and have your prose lit up by teensy dots of light on a screen is, well, sort of magic. It most certainly beats the pants off using a typewriter. For me, it's better than trying to communicate using my nearly illegible handwriting. Routine or not, word processing is a blessing.

Historically speaking, word processing is the culmination of an evolution that began 10,000 years ago, when the first humans started scrawling those "Look what I killed! Aren't I cool?" cave paintings. Today, you can communicate these simple messages with technological power unrivaled in human history. This part of the book introduces you to that technology.

Chapter 1

Hello, Word!

You can't do squat with a computer until you start the thing. Likewise, you can't even write the word *squat* on a computer until you start a word processing program. Because you bought *this* book and not *Pencils For Dummies,* the program you need to start is Microsoft Word. This chapter tells you how to get Word started and begin your word processing day. Let me also mention that reading this chapter is a far more enriching experience than reading *Pencils For Dummies,* which is barely a pamphlet, albeit one that's charmingly illustrated.

Getting Word Started

There is no single way to start Word. The Windows operating system is all about offering many different (and, often, confusing) ways to get things done. Rather than bore you by listing all those ways, I figure you just want to find the best way to start Word for how you use the computer. This section offers three solid choices.

- ✔ Before you can use Word, your computer must be on and toasty. Log in to Windows. Start your computer day. (But — seriously — don't put bread into your computer and expect toast to appear.)

- ✔ Make sure you're seated, with a nice, upright, firm posture as you use your computer. They tell me that your wrists should be even with your elbows and that you shouldn't have to tilt your head forward. Shoulders are back and relaxed.

✔ Don't freak out because you're using a computer. You are in charge! Keep that in mind. Chant silently to yourself, over and over: "I am the master."

✔ If you need help starting your computer, refer to my book *PCs For Dummies* for quick and accurate turning-on-the-computer instructions.

✔ You can stop chanting "I am the master" now.

The good, yet unimaginative, way to start Word

Without fail, the place to start any program in Windows is at the fabled Start button. It may not be the fastest or the most interesting or most convenient way to start a program, but it's consistent and reliable — both good qualities to have in a computer. Obey these steps:

1. Click the Start button.

Use your computer mouse to click the Start button, which is often found on the left side of the taskbar and at the bottom of the screen, adorned with the Windows logo.

Clicking the Start button displays the Start menu.

2. Choose Microsoft Word 2010 from the list of programs.

As luck may have it, you might find the Microsoft Word 2010 program icon (shown in the margin) right there on the Start menu. Click the icon to run the program. Otherwise, keep plowing away in Step 3.

3. Choose All Programs to pop up the All Programs menu and choose Microsoft Word 2010.

If you don't see the Microsoft Word 2010 icon or program name, you must obey Step 4, which is almost certain to work.

4. Choose the Microsoft Office item (submenu) to display its contents, and then choose Microsoft Word 2010.

Behold! Word starts! Watch in amazement as the program unfurls its sails on your computer's monitor.

Don't let Word's appearance overwhelm you! I describe what you're looking at in the section "Looking at Word," later in this chapter.

✔ If you can't find Word anywhere on the All Programs menu, it may not be installed on your computer. This book is specific to Microsoft Word, not the Microsoft Works word processor or any other word processor. (See the section "Foolish Assumptions" in this book's Introduction.)

✔ Supposedly, every program ever installed on your computer has installed its icon in a spot somewhere on the All Programs menu.

✔ I refer to the program as *Word,* though its icon may be labeled Microsoft Word, Microsoft Office Word, Microsoft Word 2010, or another variation.

The better way to start Word

When you use Word a lot, it helps to have quick access to its program icon; opening that icon is the way you start Word and then start your work. A better way than keeping Word hidden on the All Programs menu is to create a Word shortcut icon on the desktop. Heed these steps:

1. **Locate the Word icon on the Start button's All Programs menu.**

   Don't start Word now! Just point the mouse at the Word icon on the Start button's All Programs menu or wherever else it may be found. (Refer to the preceding section.)

2. **Right-click the Microsoft Word 2010 menu item.**

   A pop-up menu appears.

3. **Choose Send To⇨Desktop (Create Shortcut).**

4. **Press the Esc key to hide the Start button menu and view the desktop.**

 You haven't changed anything, but you have added the Word program icon to the desktop (shown in the margin). You can use that icon to start Word: Just double-click the icon and Word starts.

The best way to start Word

The *best* way to start Word, and the way I do it every day, is to place the Word icon on the taskbar in Windows 7, or what's called the Quick Launch toolbar in older versions of Windows. To do so, follow these steps:

1. **Find the Word icon on the Start button's All Programs menu.**

   Don't click the icon — just find it!

2. **Right-click the Word icon on the All Programs menu.**

3a. **In Windows 7, choose the command Pin to Taskbar.**

3b. **In Windows Vista, choose the command Add to Quick Launch.**

   The Word icon is *pinned* (permanently added to) the taskbar in Windows 7; in Windows Vista, the Word icon is slapped on the Quick Launch Toolbar.

To start Word, you merely click the Word icon placed on the taskbar. *Click!* And then Word starts. That's the fastest and bestest way to begin your word processing day.

Another way to have the Word icon always handy is to pin it to the Start menu directly. In Step 3, choose the item named Pin to Start Menu. That way, the Word icon always appears at the top of the list on the Start button menu.

Start Word by opening a document

You use the Word program to create *documents,* which are stored on your computer in much the same way as people pile junk into boxes and store them in their garages. But that's not important. What is important is that you can use those documents to start Word: Opening a Word document causes Word to start *and* to display that document for editing, printing, or just giving others the impression that you're doing something.

What's your point, Dan?

My point is that you can also start Word by opening a Word document. Simply locate the Word document icon (shown in the margin) in a folder window. Double-click to open that document and Word starts up on the screen, instantly (more or less) displaying that document for editing, reading, modifying, perusing, cussing, mangling, and potentially fouling up beyond all recognition.

- ✔ The Word document you open can be on the desktop, in the My Documents or Documents folder, or in any other folder or location where a Word document icon can lurk.

- ✔ The document name appears beneath or to the right of the icon. You can use the name to determine the document's contents — as long as the document was properly named when it was saved to disk. (More on that elsewhere in this book.)

- ✔ In Windows 7, you can see a Jump List of recently opened documents by either right-clicking the Word icon on the taskbar or clicking the right-pointing arrow next to the Word icon on the Start button menu. Choose a document from the list to start Word and open that document.

- ✔ Word is capable of opening other types of documents, including documents from previous versions of Word, Rich Text Format documents, and others. Each of these documents has its own icon, though the icon looks similar to the standard Word document icon. See Chapter 24 for more information on opening alien documents in Word.

Looking at Word

Like all programs in Windows, Word offers its visage in a program window. It's the electronic version of a blank sheet of paper — and more. It's the *more* part that you might find daunting. The dee-dads and goo-bobs that surround the Word program window all have specific names that you need to know to get the most from the program. Figure 1-1 shows the big picture.

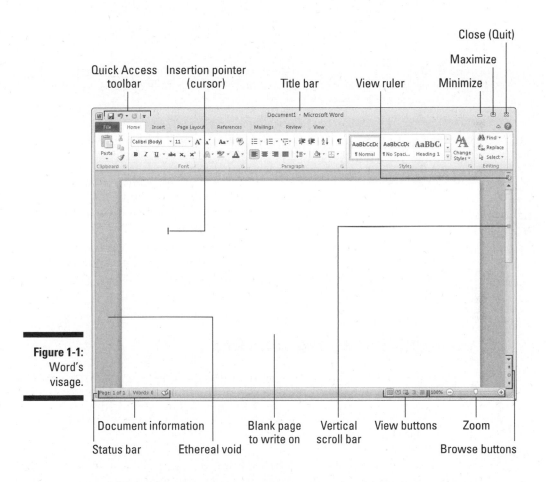

Quick Access toolbar   Insertion pointer (cursor)   Title bar   View ruler   Minimize   Maximize   Close (Quit)

Document information   Blank page to write on   Vertical scroll bar   View buttons   Zoom   Status bar   Ethereal void   Browse buttons

Figure 1-1:
Word's
visage.

Figure 1-2 highlights the gizmos at the top of the Word window, showcasing the Ribbon interface.

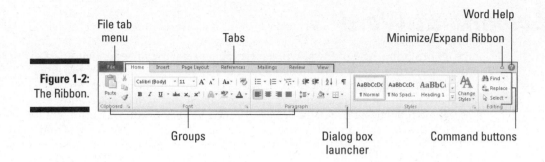

Figure 1-2:
The Ribbon.

The details of how all the dee-dads and goo-bobs in the Word window work are covered elsewhere in this book. Use this book's index to help you find topics you might be curious about.

✔ The *very* first time you start Word, you may be asked some questions: Enter your name and initials, set up Word security, and set Microsoft update options. I recommend the updates.

✔ To get the most from Word's window, change the window size: As with any window, you can use the mouse to drag the window's edges in or out or click the window's Maximize button (the middle button in the window's upper right corner) to have the window fill the screen.

✔ Word's window size affects what you see in the Ribbon command groups. When the Word window is smaller, fewer buttons show up, or they may show up in three rows. When the window is larger, you see more buttons, usually in two rows.

Around the Word window

Word processing is about writing, so the things you see in the Word window are all there for your writing pleasure. Or, if you find writing a pain, the items festooning the Word window are there for your agony. The word for the whole of those items is *interface,* which is how a computer program presents itself to the human world.

The largest portion of the Word screen is for composing text. It's blank and white, just like a fresh sheet of paper. (Refer to Figure 1-1.) That's where you compose and format your text, and I cover that area specifically in the next section.

Surrounding the text-composing area is a host of goobers that are as bewildering as an exhibit in a modern art museum, as intimidating as the cockpit of a jet fighter, and almost as dangerous as a plate of sushi. Despite their intimidating presence, those items exist to help you write. The following list gives you a quick top-to-bottom explanation. Use Figure 1-1 for reference. And, please: Do not memorize anything!

- ✔ **The title bar** lists the document's title, or merely `Document1` until you give the document a title by saving it to disk. (See Chapter 8 for information on saving documents — very important!)

- ✔ **The File tab** replaces the traditional File menu of older Windows programs. Clicking the File tab replaces the contents of the Word window with a full-screen menu full of commands and their descriptions. To return to the Word window, click the File tab or any other tab on the Ribbon. Speaking of which:

- ✔ **The Ribbon** contains all Word commands, which appear as buttons, input boxes, and menus. The Ribbon is divided into tabs (refer to Figure 1-2). The commands on the Ribbon are separated into groups. Some tabs may appear and disappear depending on what you're doing in Word. And the commands in groups change as you change the window's size.

- ✔ **The Ruler** may or may not be visible. When it's visible, it helps you set margins and tabs. The View Ruler button (refer to Figure 1-1) shows and hides the Ruler.

Below the writing area dwells the status bar. This informative strip of graphical goodness contains trivial information about your document as well as the following ornaments:

- ✔ **Document information** lists optional data that's specific to your document.

- ✔ **The View buttons** specify how the blank page appears in the window (also refer to the next section).

- ✔ **The Zoom thing** specifies how large or small your document appears inside the window. (See Chapter 29 for more information on zooming.)

Don't fret over these things! What's important now is that you recognize the names so that you don't get lost later.

- ✔ You can hide the Ribbon if you would rather have more room to write: Use the Expand the Ribbon button (refer to Figure 1-2).

- ✔ The Windows taskbar, located at the bottom of the screen, is a part of Windows itself and not Word. However, as you open documents in Word, buttons representing those documents appear on the Windows taskbar.

✔ Unlike in previous versions of Word, the tabs, groups, and command buttons *cannot* be changed. You can customize the Quick Access Toolbar (refer to Figure 1-1), and you can add your own, custom groups and tabs, a topic I cover in Chapter 29.

The blank place where you write

Word's equivalent of the mind-numbing, writer's-block-inducing blank page can be found in the center part of the Word program window (refer to Figure 1-1). That's where the text you write, edit, and format appears. Unlike with a sheet of paper, however, the text you create in Word can be viewed in five different ways.

Relax. Of all the different ways to view text in Word, only these two are useful enough to describe here:

✔ **Print Layout:** Word's native mode is named Print Layout, shown in Figure 1-1. In this view, the entire page of text is displayed on the screen just as it prints. Print Layout view shows graphical images, columns, and all sorts of other fancy effects. You even see the blank space between pages, described as the ethereal void in Figure 1-1.

✔ **Draft:** I prefer using Word in Draft view, which shows only basic text and not all the fancy features. Because Draft view doesn't show any fancy formatting (graphics, columns, or page breaks, for example), you can more easily concentrate on writing.

The three other ways to view your document are Full Screen Reading, Web Layout, and Outline. None of these views has anything to do with basic word processing.

Switch between views by using the View buttons found in the lower right corner of the Word program window (refer to Figure 1-1). Clicking a button with the mouse changes the view.

✔ When you're working in Draft view and you want to edit a header or insert a picture, Print Layout view is activated. You can switch back to Drafts view by clicking the Drafts button when you're done going graphical.

✔ One thing that's visible in Draft view that you don't find in Print Layout view is a thick, horizontal bar on the left side of the page, just below a document's last line of text. That heavy bar marks the end of your document's text.

✔ Draft view may also be referred to as *Normal view,* as it was in previous versions of Word.

✔ Any weird stuff you see onscreen (a ¶, for example) is a Word secret symbol. Chapter 2 tells you why you may want to view those secret symbols and how to hide them if they annoy you.

The mouse pointer in Word

Though word processing is a keyboard thing, you'll find that the computer mouse does come in handy. You use the mouse to choose commands, move around the document you're editing, and do something called *selecting text*. This book explains all those topics elsewhere. For now, it helps to understand how the mouse pointer changes its look as you work in Word:

For editing text, the mouse pointer becomes the I-beam.

For choosing items, the standard 11 o'clock mouse pointer is used.

For selecting lines of text, a 1 o'clock mouse pointer is used.

The mouse pointer may change its look when *click-and-type* mode is active: Lines appear to the left and right of, and below, the I-beam mouse pointer. Refer to Chapter 32 for more information on using click-and-type.

✔ You can use the mouse to see what some of the little buttons and items with pictures on them do in Word. Just hover the mouse pointer over the button, and — voilà! — it's like Folgers instant information crystals.

✔ Chapter 4 discusses how to use the mouse pointer to move around a document to edit different parts of your text.

Cajoling Word to help you

Like most programs in Windows, a Help system is available in Word. You can summon it by pressing the F1 key, which displays the Word Help window. There you can type a topic, a command name, or even a question into the box to search for help. Or, you can browse the table of contents for helpful information.

The F1 key also works any time you're deep in the bowels of Word and doing something specific. The Help information that's displayed tends to be specific to whatever you're doing in Word. Little buttons that look like question marks in blue circles also summon Word Help.

Though it's nice to have the help available, the information offered is little more than the "Word manual," which is as cryptic and unforgiving as the computer manuals that were once printed on paper.

Ending Your Word Processing Day

It's the pinnacle of etiquette to know when and how to excuse oneself. Leaving can be done well or poorly. For example, the phrase "Well, I must be off," works lots better than "Something more interesting must be happening somewhere else" — especially at Thanksgiving.

Just as there are many ways to start Word, there are several ways to quit. You can quit the program outright, you can pause and start over, or you can set Word aside. These options are covered in the following sections.

To quit Word

When you're done word processing and you don't expect to return to it anytime soon, you can quit the Word program. Quitting a computer program is like putting away a book on a shelf. In the electronic world of the computer, this is how you do such a thing:

1. **Click the File tab.**

   The Word screen is replaced by the File tab menu screen. Do not be alarmed.

2. **Choose the Exit command.**

   Word vanishes from the screen.

The only time Word doesn't vanish is during that shameful circumstance when you have unsaved documents. If so, you're prompted to save the document, as shown in Figure 1-3. My advice is to click the Save button to save your work.

Figure 1-3:
Better click
that Save
button!

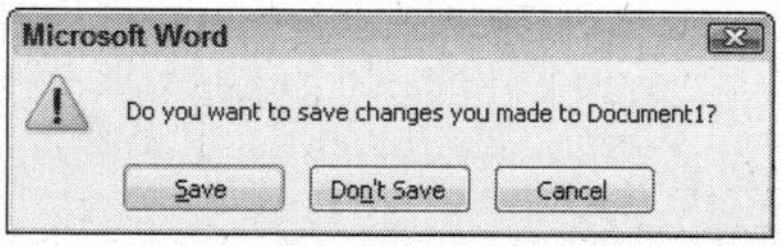

Microsoft Word

⚠ Do you want to save changes you made to Document1?

Save   Don't Save   Cancel

If you click the Don't Save button, your work isn't saved, Word quits. If you click the Cancel button, Word doesn't quit and you can continue working.

✔ See Chapter 8 for more information on saving documents.

✔ Also see Chapter 8 on how to recover drafts of documents you failed to save.

✔ You don't have to quit Word just to start editing another document. Refer to the next couple of sections for helpful, time-saving information!

✔ After quitting Word, you can continue to use Windows, by starting up any other program, such as Spider Solitaire, or perhaps something more calming, such as *Call Of Duty*.

Quit what you're doing without quitting Word

You don't always have to quit Word. For example, if you're merely stopping work on one document to work on another, quitting Word is a waste of time. Instead, you can *close* the document.

To close a document in Word, click the File tab and choose the Close command. Word banishes the document from its window, but then the program sits there and waits for you to do something else, such as start working on a new document or open a document you previously saved.

Bottom line: There's no point is quitting Word when all you want to do is start editing a new document.

✔ When you try to close a document before it has been saved, Word displays a warning dialog box. Click the Save button to save your document. If you want to continue editing, click the Cancel button and get back to work.

✔ There's no need to close a document, really. In fact, I work on a document over a period of days and keep it open (and my PC turned on) the entire time. Doesn't hurt a thing. (I occasionally save it to disk, which *is* important.)

✔ See Chapter 8 for more information about starting a new document.

✔ The keyboard shortcut for the Close command is Ctrl+W. That command may seem weird, but it's used to close documents in many programs.

Set Word aside

There's no need to quit Word if you know that you will use it again soon. In fact, I've been known to keep Word open and running on my computer for *weeks* at a time. The secret is to use the Minimize button.

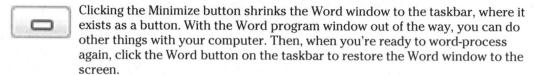 Clicking the Minimize button shrinks the Word window to the taskbar, where it exists as a button. With the Word program window out of the way, you can do other things with your computer. Then, when you're ready to word-process again, click the Word button on the taskbar to restore the Word window to the screen.

The Minimize button is the first of the three buttons in the window's upper right corner. Refer to Figure 1-1.

Chapter 2

The Typing Chapter

Word processing is about using the computer keyboard. It's typing. That's the way computers were used for years, long before the mouse and all the fancy graphics became popular. Yep, ask a grizzled old-timer and you'll hear tales of ugly text screens and keyboard commands that would tie your fingers in knots. Though things aren't that bad today, I highly recommend that you bone up on using your computer's keyboard to get the most from your word processing duties. This chapter tells you what you need to know.

Behold the PC Keyboard!

Typing happens on a computer keyboard. Though I'm sure you can easily recognize a computer keyboard, you should know how to refer to the various keys. To assist you, I've illustrated a typical, generic computer keyboard in Figure 2-1.

Function keys   Numeric keypad

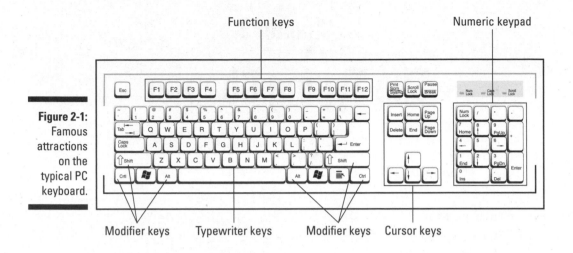

Figure 2-1:
Famous
attractions
on the
typical PC
keyboard.

Modifier keys   Typewriter keys   Modifier keys   Cursor keys

Here's a summary of what you see:

- **Function keys:** Labeled F1 through F12 and used alone or in cahoots with the Ctrl, Alt, and Shift keys.

- **Typewriter keys:** The standard alphanumeric keys that the computer inherited from the ancient typewriter: *a* through *z* and the number keys plus symbols and other exotic characters.

- **Cursor keys:** Also called *arrow keys;* they control the cursor. Also included are the non-arrow keys: Home, End, PgUp (or Page Up), PgDn (or Page Down), Insert, and Delete.

- **Mon key:** A cute little primate that you don't want to have as a pet.

- **Numeric keypad:** Keys that serve sometimes as cursor keys and sometimes as number keys. The split personality is evident on each key cap, which displays two symbols. The Num Lock key and its corresponding light are on if the numeric keypad (1, 2, 3) is active. If the cursor keys (arrows, Home) are active, Num Lock is off.

- **Modifier keys:** Don't do anything by themselves. Instead, the Shift, Ctrl, and Alt keys work in combination with other keys.

Here are some individual keys worth noting:

- **Enter:** Marked with the word *Enter* and sometimes a cryptic, left-arrow thing: ⌐. You use this key to end a paragraph of text.

- **Esc:** The "escape" key doesn't exactly do anything in Word. However, pressing the Esc key in a dialog box is the same as clicking the Cancel button with the mouse.

- **Spacebar:** The only key with no symbol; inserts spaces between the words.

- **Tab:** Inserts the tab "character," which shoves the next text you type over to the next tab stop; an interesting and potentially frustrating formatting key (and nicely covered in Chapter 12).

- **Backspace:** Your backing-up-and-erasing key — very handy.

- **Delete:** Also labeled Del; works like Backspace but doesn't back up to erase. Read more on that in Chapter 4.

Every character key you press on the keyboard produces a character on the screen, on the blank part where you write. Typing those character keys over and over is how you write text on a word processor.

- The Shift key is used to produce capital letters; otherwise, the text you see is in lowercase.

- The Caps Lock key lets you type text in UPPERCASE letters. After you press Caps Lock, the Caps Lock light on your keyboard comes on, indicating that you're entering ALL CAPS mode. Press the Caps Lock key again to return to normal.

- Ctrl is pronounced "control." The variety of names that people give to the Ctrl key before they know it as *the control key* is amazing.

The Old Hunt-and-Peck

After starting Word, you'll most likely type these words next:

Clackity-clack-clack-clack.

The text you type on the keyboard appears on the screen — even the typos and mistakes and bad grammar: It all falls into place regardless of your intent, posture, or good looks. This section offers some basic typing tips, suggestions, and advice.

Depressing the keys

You don't actually depress a key on a computer keyboard. Nope. Instead, you press and release. Any swift tapping motion will do. Some keyboards even generate a pleasing *click* sound when a key is pressed.

Now, if you really want to depress a key, just stare at it and say, "You're one ugly, good-for-nothing key!" If that doesn't work, continue the insults. Eventually, any well-adjusted key will succumb to your verbal taunts and find itself sufficiently depressed.

"Do I need to learn to type?"

No one needs to learn to type to use a word processor, but you do yourself a favor when you learn. My advice is to get a computer program that teaches you to type. I can recommend the *Mavis Beacon Teaches Typing* program, even though I don't get any money from her and none of her children resembles me. I just like the name Mavis, I suppose.

Knowing how to type makes a painful experience like using Word a wee bit more enjoyable.

Follow the blinking cursor

The key to writing in Word is to look for the *insertion pointer* in your text. It's a flashing vertical bar:

|

Text you type appears *before* the insertion pointer, one character at a time. After a character appears, the insertion pointer hops to the right, making room for more text.

For example, type this line:

```
Let's go see the clowns!
```

The insertion pointer moves to the right, marching along as you type. It's called *insertion* pointer for a reason: Press the left-arrow key a few times to move the insertion pointer back before the word *go*.

Type the word *not* and a space. The word (and the space) is inserted into your text. The text to the right is pushed off to make room for the new text. Now the sentence should read:

```
Let's not go see the clowns!
```

Chapter 4 covers moving the insertion pointer around in more detail.

When to whack the spacebar

The spacebar isn't the same thing as the right-arrow key on the keyboard. Pressing the spacebar doesn't just move the insertion pointer; it inserts a *space character* into the text. Spaces are important between words and sentences. Withoutthemreadingwouldbedifficult.

The most important thing to remember about the spacebar is that you need to whack it only once. In word processing, as in all typing done on a computer, only *one* space appears between words and after punctuation. That's it!

- ✔ I'm serious! If you're an old-timer, you're probably used to putting two spaces after a period, which is what they once taught in typing class. This extra space is wrong on a computer; typing it doesn't really add more space between words or sentences. Trust me on that.

- ✔ Anytime you feel like using two or more spaces, what you need is a tab. Tabs are best for indenting text as well as for lining up text in columns. See Chapter 12 for more information.

- ✔ The reason that only one space is needed between sentences is that computers use proportionally spaced type. Old-fashioned typewriters used monospace type, so pressing the spacebar twice after a sentence was supposed to aid in readability (though it's debatable). Computer type is more like professionally typeset material, and both typesetters and professional-document folk now put only one space after a period or a colon.

- ✔ If you want to type two spaces after a period and actually see them, choose a monospace font, such as Courier.

Backup and erase keys

When you make a typo or another type of typing error, press the Backspace key on the keyboard. The Backspace key is used to back up and erase. The Delete key can also be used to erase text, though it gobbles up characters to the *right* of the insertion pointer.

- ✔ Refer to Chapter 4 for more information on deleting text with Backspace and Delete.

- ✔ The Backspace key is named Backspace on your keyboard, or it may have a long, left-pointing arrow on it: ←.

- ✔ Backspace backs up and *erases.* If you merely want to move the insertion pointer to the left, press the left-arrow key. See Chapter 3.

When to press that Enter key

In word processing, you press the Enter key only when you reach the end of a paragraph. Though pressing Enter at the end of a line of text might seem logical, there is no need: Word takes the text that hangs over at the end of a line and wraps that text down to the next line. Therefore, you press Enter only to end a paragraph.

To practice pressing the Enter key at the end of a paragraph, type the following text:

```
It was the scratching at the front door that alerted us.
For a second I thought it might be Jasper, showing up
late. It wasn't. You see, around these parts, during the
full moon, we have an issue: The dead won't stay buried.
Still, it was a good stew, so we decided to finish eating
before getting busy with the axes and shovels.
```

Now that you're done typing the paragraph, press the Enter key. There. You did it right.

- There's no need to use the Enter key when you want to double-space your text. Double-spacing uses a text formatting command in Word. See Chapter 11 for more information.

- Neither do you need to press the Enter key twice to add extra space between your paragraphs. Word can automatically add space before or after paragraphs, which is also covered in Chapter 11.

- If you want to indent a paragraph, press the Tab key after pressing Enter. This can also be done automatically; refer to (you guessed it) Chapter 11.

- The process of taking text from the end of one line and placing it at the start of the next line is named *word wrap*.

Curse you, StickyKeys!

As your mind wanders, your fingers absently press and release the Shift key. Suddenly, you see the warning: StickyKeys! By pressing the Shift, Ctrl, or Alt key five times in a row, you activate the Windows StickyKeys function, a tool designed to make a computer keyboard more accessible to people. If you don't need the help, you'll probably find the intrusion annoying.

Don't panic! You can easily turn off the StickyKeys feature: Open the Windows Control Panel and choose the Ease of Access link. On the next screen, find and click the link labeled Change How Your Keyboard Works. Remove the check mark by Turn On Sticky Keys. Click OK and you'll never be bothered again!

Stuff That Happens While You Type

As you madly compose your text, fingers energetically jabbing the buttons on the keyboard, you may notice a few things happening on the screen. You might see spots. You might see lines and boxes. You may even see lightning! All are side effects of typing in Word. They're normal, and they're explained in this section.

The left end of the status bar

The reason it's the *status* bar is that it can show you the status of your document, lively updating the information as you type, as shown in Figure 2-2.

Document proofing

Page location

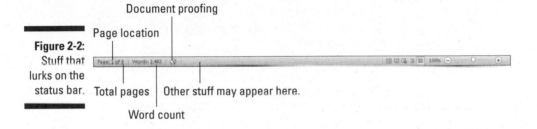

Figure 2-2:
Stuff that
lurks on the
status bar.

Total pages   Other stuff may appear here.

Word count

The type of information that's displayed, as well as how much information is displayed, depends on how you configured Word. Chapter 29 explains which features the status bar can display.

- ✔ The status bar also displays information when you initially open a document, giving the document's name and character count. The info disappears quickly, however.

- ✔ When a document is saved, the status bar displays information about the save, though often the information disappears too fast to see.

Between the pages

Word tries its best to show you where one page ends and another page begins. This feature is most helpful because often times you want to keep elements on one page, or maybe folks just like to know when the text they're writing flows from one page to the next.

The status bar helps you discover which page you're working on. For example, the Page Number indicator changes from 6 to 7 when you start a new page. Word also shows you graphically where one page ends and another begins.

In Print Layout view, you see virtual pages and a space between them, as shown in Figure 2-3.

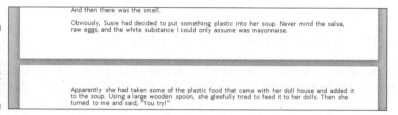

Figure 2-3:
Page break
in Print
Layout view.

> And then there was the smell.
>
> Obviously, Susie had decided to put something plastic into her soup. Never mind the salsa, raw eggs, and the white substance I could only assume was mayonnaise.
>
> Apparently she had taken some of the plastic food that came with her doll house and added it to the soup. Using a large wooden spoon, she gleefully tried to feed it to her dolls. Then she turned to me and said, "You try!"

In Draft mode, the visual break between pages is shown as a faint line of dots, like ants marching across the page:

Text appearing above the line of dots is on one page, and text below it is on the next page.

- Refer to Chapter 1 for more information on Print Layout and Draft views.

- You can change the gap between pages in Print Layout view. Point the mouse at the gap. When the mouse pointer changes, as shown in the margin, double-click to either close or open the gap.

- Because the page break is, technically, a *soft* page break, one page is full of text and Word must start putting text on a new page. See Chapter 13 for information on forcing page breaks and other types of page breaks in Word.

Spots and clutter in your text

There's no cause for alarm if you see spots — or dots — amid the text you type, such as

```
This·can·be·very·annoying.¶
```

What you're seeing are *nonprinting characters*. Word uses various symbols to represent things you normally don't see: spaces, tabs, the Enter key, and more.

To turn these items on or off, click the Show/Hide button on the Home tab in the Paragraph group. Click once to show the goobers; click again to hide them.

Why bother? Sometimes it's useful to see the marks to check out what's up with formatting, find stray tabs visually, or locate missing paragraphs, for example. (*WordPerfect users:* It's as close as you can get to the Reveal Codes command in Word.)

Strange underlines and colored text

Adding underlining to your text in Word is cinchy; Chapter 10 tells you all about that character format. Yet sometimes Word may do some underlining and add strange-colored text on its own.

Red zigzag: Spelling errors in Word are underlined with red zigzags. See Chapter 7.

Green zigzag: Grammatical errors in Word are underlined with green zigzags. See Chapter 7.

Blue zigzag: Word-choice errors are grammatical errors, but Word flags them with a special blue zigzag regardless. The blue underlined word is most likely not the best word to use given the sentence structure. Again, see Chapter 7.

Purple dots: Word's Smart Tags feature uses purple dots to highlight information such as names, dates, places, and similar data that can be shared with other programs in Microsoft Office. Smart tags are briefly discussed in Chapter 32.

Blue underlines: Word courteously highlights Web page addresses using blue, underlined text in your document. You can Ctrl+click the blue underline text to visit the Web page.

Red underlines and strikethrough: The red text that appears either underlined or in strikethrough means that you're using Word's Track Changes feature. It can drive you nuts when you don't know what's going on, so see Chapter 26 to keep your sanity.

Part II
Your Basic Word

In this part . . .

Word is a massive program, almost too huge to comprehend. If you try, your head will explode. I don't recommend it.

You'll find that, in all of Word's bulk, you need to use only the bare minimum for the typical, basic word processing chore. I'd estimate that the typical user never takes advantage of 90 percent of what the Word program can do. That's okay. You'll find that the 10 percent that remains is truly the most useful part, your basic Word. That's the topic for this part of the book.

Chapter 3

To and Fro in a Document

1 like the word *fro*. I like the word *yon*. They're archaic in the English language, referring to a direction and a location, respectively. *Fro* doesn't make sense by itself, so it's used in the phrase *to and fro,* which refers to going somewhere and then back again. *Yon* is often seen with its friends *hither* and *thither,* meaning "here" and "there." In that context, *yon* is a place beyond *there* (wherever *there* is). It's also short for *yonder,* which is another cool word that few people use any more.

As you work in Word, you find yourself moving to and fro and hither, thither, and yon. That's because writing text isn't always a linear task. You need to move that little insertion pointer guy around the document. It's basic movement. It's the topic of this chapter.

Scroll Through a Document

It's ironic that the word *scroll* is used to refer to an electronic document. The scroll was the first form of recorded text, existing long before bound books. On a computer, scrolling is the process by which you view a little bit of big document in a tiny window. This section explains how scrolling is relevant in Word.

Using the vertical scroll bar

On the right side of the Word program window you find the vertical scroll bar, illustrated in Figure 3-1. Its operation is similar to the scroll bar in any Windows program:

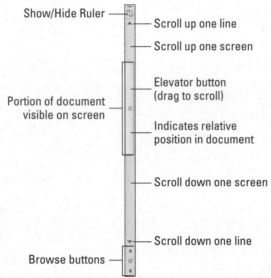

Show/Hide Ruler —

— Scroll up one line

— Scroll up one screen

Elevator button
(drag to scroll)

Portion of document
visible on screen —

Indicates relative
position in document

— Scroll down one screen

Figure 3-1:
The vertical
scroll bar.

— Scroll down one line

Browse buttons —

✔ Click the up- or down-arrow buttons at the top and bottom of the vertical scroll bar to scroll your document up or down. The document scrolls one line of text for each time you click those up- or down-arrow buttons.

✔ An *elevator button* appears inside the scroll bar. You can drag this button with the mouse, up or down, to scroll the document.

✔ You can click above or below the elevator button to scroll up or down one screen of text at a time.

The elevator button's size reflects how much of your document you can see at a time. When the button doesn't show up, or is dimmed, the whole document appears onscreen. Otherwise, the elevator button becomes smaller as your document grows longer.

The elevator button's position also helps show you which part of your document is visible. When the elevator button is at the top of the scroll bar, you're viewing text near the start of the document. When the elevator button is toward the bottom of the scroll bar, you're seeing text near the document's end.

Special bonuses are involved when you drag the elevator button to scroll through your document. As you drag the button up or down, you see a page number displayed, as shown in Figure 3-2. When a document is formatted with heading styles, you also see the heading title below the page number.

Figure 3-2:
Scroll bar
page-
number info.

Page: 4
Oscar's First Nude Play

Scrolling through your document doesn't move the insertion pointer. If you start typing, don't be surprised when Word jumps back to where the insertion pointer lurks. (Refer to the later section "Commanding the insertion pointer with the mouse" for help if such a thing bugs you.)

✔ Scrolling a document doesn't move the insertion pointer!

✔ Refer to the section "The Browse Buttons," later in this chapter, for information on using the browse buttons, which are located below the vertical scroll bar.

Using the horizontal scroll bar

The horizontal scroll bar appears just above the status bar at the bottom of the Word window — but only when your document is wider than the window. When that happens, you can use the horizontal scroll bar to shift the page back and forth and left and right.

When the horizontal (left-right) shifting bugs you, consider using Word's Zoom tool to adjust the size of your document on the screen. See Chapter 29.

Scrolling your document with the mouse

Aside from manipulating the scroll bars, you can use your computer mouse to scurry and scamper about your document. Sadly, this suggestions works only when you have one of those wheel mice. Coincidentally, you do all these tricks by manipulating that unique wheel button:

✔ Roll the wheel up or down to scroll your document up or down.

✔ Press and hold the wheel button to activate scrolling mode. With the wheel button down, you can move the mouse up or down to *pan* your document in that direction.

✔ If the mouse's wheel button also tilts from side to side, you can use it to pan left and right.

Move the Insertion Pointer

The beauty of the word processor is that you can edit any part of your document; you don't always have to work at "the end." The key to pulling off that trick is to know how to move the insertion pointer to the exact spot you want.

Moving the insertion pointer is important! Scientific studies have shown that merely looking at the computer screen does no good. As hard as you wish, new text appears only at the insertion pointer. And, the text you edit or delete? Yup, the insertion pointer's location is important there as well. Obviously, knowing how to move the insertion pointer is a big deal.

Commanding the insertion pointer with the mouse

The easiest way to put the insertion pointer exactly where you want it is to point the mouse at that spot in your text and then click the mouse button. Point, click, move insertion pointer. Simple.

Moving in small increments (basic arrow keys)

For short hops, nothing beats using the keyboard's arrow keys to quickly move the insertion pointer around a document. The four basic arrow keys move the insertion pointer up, down, right, and left:

Press This Key	To Move the Insertion Pointer
↑	Up to the preceding line of text
↓	Down to the next line of text
→	Right to the next character
←	Left to the preceding character

Moving the cursor doesn't erase characters. See Chapter 4 for information on deleting stuff.

If you press and hold the Ctrl (Control) key and then press an arrow key, you enter Jump mode. The invigorated insertion pointer leaps desperately in all four directions:

Press This Key Combo	To Move the Insertion Pointer
Ctrl+↑	Up to the start of the previous paragraph
Ctrl+↓	Down to the start of the next paragraph
Ctrl+→	Right to the start (first letter) of the next word
Ctrl+←	Left to the start (first letter) of the previous word

You can use either set of arrow keys on the computer keyboard, but when using the numeric keypad, ensure that the Num Lock light is off. Do this by pressing the Num Lock key. If you don't, you see numbers in your text rather than the insertion pointer dancing all over — like444this.

Moving from beginning to end

The insertion pointer also bows to pressure from those cursor keys without arrows on them. The first couple consists of End and Home, which move the insertion pointer to the start or end of something, depending on how End and Home are used:

Press This Key or Combination	To Whisk the Insertion Pointer
End	To the end of a line of text
Home	To the start of a line of text
Ctrl+End	To the end of the document
Ctrl+Home	To the tippy-top of the document

The remaining cursor keys are the Page Up or PgUp key and the Page Down or PgDn key. As you would guess, using these keys doesn't move up or down a page in your document. Nope. Instead, they slide through your document one screen at a time. Here's the round-up:

Press This Key or Combination	To Whisk the Insertion Pointer
PgUp	Up one screen or to the tippy-top of your document, if you happen to be near it
PgDn	Down one screen or to the end of the document, if you happen to be near it
Ctrl+Alt+PgUp	To the top of the current screen
Ctrl+Alt+PgDn	To the bottom of the current screen

The key combinations to move to the top or bottom of the current screen are Ctrl+Alt+PgUp and Ctrl+Alt+PgDn. That's Ctrl+Alt, not just the Ctrl key. And yes, few people use those commands.

You may be tempted to use Ctrl+PgUp and Ctrl+PgDn, but don't: Those commands don't work as you would expect. Refer to the following section for the details.

The Browse Buttons

Lurking at the bottom of the vertical scroll bar are three buttons, as shown in the margin. These *browse* buttons allow you to scroll through your document in leaps and bounds of various sizes.

The top button is the *Browse Up* button, which is linked to the Ctrl+PgUp key combination.

The bottom button is the *Browse Down* button, which is linked to the Ctrl+PgDn key combination.

The center button is the What-the-heck-am-I-browsing-for? button, which is linked to the Ctrl+Alt+Home key combination.

When you click the center button, a pop-up palette of items to browse for appears, as shown in Figure 3-3. Pointing the mouse at any one of the items displays text that explains the item in the bottom part of the palette.

Figure 3-3:
Things to
browse for.

Unless you've chosen another item from the browsing palette (refer to Figure 3-3), the browse buttons (and Ctrl+PgUp and Ctrl+PgDn) leap through your document by full pages.

Whenever an option other than Page is chosen from the browsing palette, the browse buttons change color. So, when the buttons are black, you know that you're browsing by page. When the browse buttons turn blue, they're searching for something else. (Alas, the browsing palette doesn't tell you which option is chosen.)

Get Back to Where You Once Edited

Considering all the various commands for moving the insertion pointer, it's quite possible to make a mistake and not know where you are in a document. Yea, verily, the insertion pointer has gone where no insertion pointer has gone before.

Rather than click your heels together three times and try to get back the wishful way, just remember this keyboard combination:

Shift+F5

Pressing the Shift+F5 keys forces Word to return you to the last spot you edited. You can do this as many as three times before the cycle repeats. But the first time should get you back to where you were before you got lost.

✔ The Shift+F5 command is the same as the Browse by Edits option, found on the Browse palette. Refer to the preceding section.

✔ Sadly, the Shift+F5 keyboard shortcut works only in Word; you can't use this command in real life.

Go to Wherever with the Go To Command

Word's Go To command allows you to send the insertion pointer to a specific page or line or to the location of a number of interesting elements that Word can potentially cram into your document. The Go To command is your word processing teleporter to anywhere.

To use the Go To command, click the Find button in the Home tab's editing group. Choose the Go To command from the menu. Or, you can use the Ctrl+G keyboard shortcut. Either way, the Go To tab portion of the Find and Replace dialog box appears, as shown in Figure 3-4.

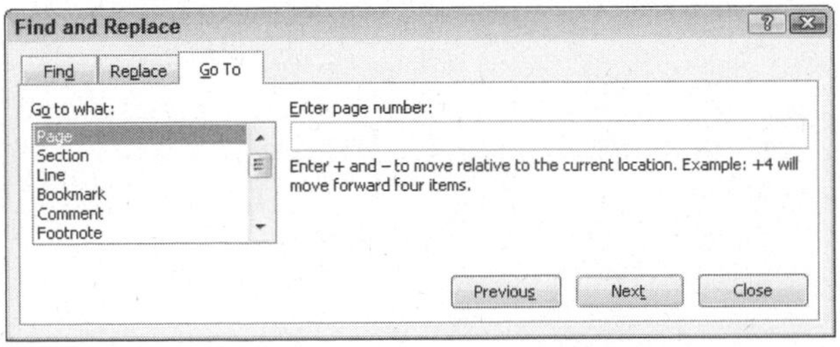

Figure 3-4:
Telling
Word to
Go To
you-know-
where.

Find and Replace

Find | Replace | Go To

Go to what:

Page
Section
Line
Bookmark
Comment
Footnote

Enter page number:

Enter + and – to move relative to the current location. Example: +4 will move forward four items.

Previous | Next | Close

Choose which element to go to, such as a page, from the scrolling list on the left side of the dialog box. Then type the relevant information, such as a page number, in the box on the right side of the dialog box. Click the Go To button to go to that location.

For example, type **14** in the box and press Enter, and you go to page 14 — if you have a page 14 to go to.

✔ You can also summon the Go To command by clicking the page number on the status bar.

✔ Note that you can go to a page *relative* to the current page. For example, to go three pages forward, choose Page and type **+3**. To go 12 pages backward, type **-12** in the box.

Chapter 4

Text Editing

1 believe that writing involves two parts of your brain: The wild, creative burst part is the typing part. Then there's the tame, controlled editing part. You need both parts in order to write anything good. In fact, I'd wager that people who become frustrated with writing are too quick to enter the controlled editing part. Don't fall into that trap: Write! Spew forth your words! Editing your text is easier when you have lots of words than when you have only a scant few.

When you're ready to edit, you'll use Word's text editing commands. They all basically delete the stuff you've written. That's right: Editing text is basically the same task as ruthlessly slashing away words from your text. Word comes with ample tools to make that happen. Use them freely, as described in this chapter. But get your abundance of words down on paper before you enter the vicious slashing mode.

Remove Text You Don't Want

Credit the guy who put the eraser on the end of the pencil: It's a given that human beings make mistakes. The round, soft eraser counterbalances the sharp point of the pencil in more ways than one.

The ability to erase text is just as valuable and necessary as the ability to create text. Deleting text is part of writing text, part of thinking and rethinking, and part of self-editing. Writing. Deleting. Rewriting. Redeleting. That's how it goes!

Both creating and destroying text are accomplished by using the computer keyboard. The majority of keys are used to create text. Only two keys delete text: Backspace and Delete. How these keys work, and how much of your text they can delete, depends on how the keys are used, as described in this section.

Deleting single characters

By themselves, the Backspace and Delete keys are used to delete single characters:

✔ **Backspace key:** Deletes the character to the left of the insertion pointer

✔ **Delete key:** Deletes the character to the right of the insertion pointer

In the following example, the insertion pointer is "flashing" (okay, it *would* be flashing on a computer screen) between the *h* and the *a* in *that.* Pressing the Backspace key deletes the *h;* pressing the Delete key deletes the *a.*

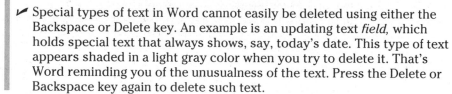

```
Bob proudly announced th|at he feels safe
enough in his neighborhood to leave his home
unlocked, but he added that his neighbor has
nicer stuff.
```

✔ After you delete a character, any text to the right or below the character shuffles over to fill the void.

✔ You can press and hold Backspace or Delete to continuously "machine-gun-delete" characters. Release the key to halt such wanton destruction, although I recommend using other delete commands (covered in this chapter) rather than the machine-gun approach.

✔ Special types of text in Word cannot easily be deleted using either the Backspace or Delete key. An example is an updating text *field,* which holds special text that always shows, say, today's date. This type of text appears shaded in a light gray color when you try to delete it. That's Word reminding you of the unusualness of the text. Press the Delete or Backspace key again to delete such text.

Deleting a word

To gobble up an entire word, add the Ctrl key to the Backspace or Delete key's destructive power:

✔ Ctrl+Backspace deletes the word in front (to the left) of the insertion pointer.

✔ Ctrl+Delete deletes the word behind (to the right) of the insertion pointer.

These keyboard shortcuts work best when the insertion pointer is at the start or end of a word. When you're in the middle of the word, the commands delete only from that middle point to the start or end of the word.

After you delete a word, the insertion pointer sits at the end of the preceding word (or paragraph) when you use Ctrl+Backspace. Deleting a word by using Ctrl+Delete puts the cursor at the beginning of the next word. This is done to facilitate the rapid deletion of several words in a row.

After deleting the text, Word neatly wraps up the remaining text, snuggling it together in a grammatically proper way; deleting a word doesn't leave a "hole" in your text.

No mere pencil eraser can match Ctrl+Delete or Ctrl+Backspace for sheer speed and terror!

Deleting more than a word

Beyond deleting a word or character, Word lacks keyboard-specific commands to delete lines or paragraphs of text. Word has ways to delete these things — those ways just aren't obvious. Before the details come some definitions:

- ✔ A **line of text** is merely a line across the page (not really a grammatical issue).

- ✔ A **sentence** is a sentence. You know: Start with a capital letter and end with a period, a question mark, or an exclamation point. You probably learned this concept in grammar school, which is why they call it *grammar* school anyway.

- ✔ A **paragraph** is one or more sentences, or a heading, ending with a press of the Enter key.

- ✔ A **page** of text is just that — all the text from where the page starts to where the page ends.

Word can also delete odd-size chunks of text by marking that text as a *block*. Refer to Chapter 6 for more information on blocks of text.

Deleting a line of text

The easiest way to delete a line of text is to use the mouse:

1. **Move the mouse into the left margin of your document.**

   You know you've found the sweet spot when the mouse pointer changes into a northeast arrow.

2. **Point the mouse pointer arrow at the line of text you want to obliterate.**

3. **Click the mouse.**

   The line of text is highlighted, or *selected*.

4. **Press the Delete key to send that line into oblivion.**

Deleting a sentence

Making a sentence go bye-bye is cinchy:

1. **Point the mouse at the offending sentence.**

2. **Press and hold the Ctrl key and click the mouse.**

   The sentence is selected.

3. **Press the Delete key.**

   Oomph! It's gone.

Deleting a paragraph

Here's the fastest way to delete a full paragraph:

1. **Point the mouse at the paragraph.**

2. **Click the mouse button thrice.**

   Thrice means "three times."

3. **Press the Delete key.**

If clicking thrice is befuddling you, move the mouse pointer into the left margin next to the offending paragraph. When the mouse pointer changes to a northeasterly-pointing arrow, click twice. That action selects the entire paragraph, which you can now whack by pressing the Delete key.

Deleting a page

Pages aren't things that Word deals with offhand. In fact, pages are a printer issue. Even so, to delete a page, mind these steps:

1. **Press Ctrl+G to summon the Go To tab in the Find and Replace dialog box.**

   See Chapter 3 for more information on the Go To command.

2. **Type the number of the page you want to delete.**

3. **Click the Close button to dismiss the Go To dialog box.**

4. **Press the F8 key.**

   The F8 key is used to enter a special selection mode in Word, which I cover in detail in Chapter 6.

5. **Press Ctrl+G.**

   Once again, the Find and Replace dialog box appears, with the Go To tab ready for action.

6. **Type the next page number.**

   If you're deleting page 6, for example, type **7**.

7. **Press Enter.**

   The entire page is now selected.

8. **Press the Delete key.**

   The page is gone.

Refer to Chapter 9 for special information on deleting that annoying extra blank page at the end of your document.

Split and Join Paragraphs

For some people, a paragraph in a word processor is a strange thing. It's basically a chunk of text. Like most things that come in chunks — cheese, meat, large men named Floyd — it's often necessary to split or combine them. Well, maybe not for Floyd.

Making two paragraphs from one

To split a single paragraph in twain, locate the point where you want them to break — say, between two sentences. Move the insertion pointer to that location and then press the Enter key. Word splits the paragraph in two; the text above the insertion pointer becomes its own paragraph, and the text following it then becomes the next paragraph.

Depending on where you placed the insertion pointer, you may need to delete an extra space at the beginning of the second paragraph or at the end of the first paragraph.

Making one paragraph from two

To join two paragraphs and turn them into one, you delete the Enter character between the paragraphs. To do that, move the insertion pointer to the start of the second paragraph and then press the Backspace key. Removing the Enter character joins two paragraphs.

Depending on how neatly the paragraphs were joined, you may need to add a space between the sentences at the spot where the paragraphs were glued together.

The Soft and Hard Returns

Pressing the Enter key in Word ends a paragraph. It's officially known as typing a *hard return*. Yes, it's *return* even though the key is known as Enter on a PC. Don't blame me for this odd nomenclature. I only write the books — not the programs.

The problem with the hard return is that it adds a bit of "air" after a paragraph. That's a good thing; as I explain in Chapter 11, you should have air around paragraphs in a document. Those times when you don't want air, when you need to put lines of text close together, you use a soft return.

The *soft return,* or *line break,* is used primarily in titles and headings; when you have a long title and need to split it up between two lines, you press Shift+Enter to insert the soft return. For example, type this line:

```
Enjoying the Ballet
```

Press Shift+Enter. A new line starts. Continue typing:

```
A Guide for Husbands and Boyfriends
```

The soft return keeps the title text together (in the same paragraph), but on separate lines.

You should also use the soft return when typing an address, either on an envelope or in a letter. Press Shift+Enter after typing each of these lines:

```
Mr. President
1600 Pennsylvania Ave.
Washington, DC 20500
```

If you try typing the same text and press Enter instead, you see more space between the lines, which isn't what you want. Nope, that soft return can sure come in handy.

Undo Mistakes with Undo Haste

That quaffing and drinking will undo you.

— Richard II, William Shakespeare

The Undo command undoes anything you do in Word, which includes formatting text, moving blocks, typing and deleting text, formatting — the whole quesadilla. You have two handy ways to unleash the Undo command:

- ✔ Press Ctrl+Z.
- ✔ Click the Undo command button on the Quick Access Toolbar.

 I prefer using the Ctrl+Z key combination, but an advantage of the Undo command button is that it sports a drop-down menu that helps you review the past several things you've done, or that can be undone.

- ✔ Word's Undo command is handy, but don't use it as an excuse to be sloppy!
- ✔ Regrettably, you cannot pick and choose from the Undo command button's drop-down menu; you can merely undo multiple instances of things all at one time.
- ✔ Undo works sporadically sometimes. Before this happens, Word warns you. For example, you may see a message such as "There is not enough memory to undo this operation, Continue?" Proceed at your own peril.
- ✔ The Undo command doesn't work when there's nothing to undo or if something just cannot be undone. For example, you cannot undo a save-to-disk operation.
- ✔ To undo an Undo, choose Redo. See the next section.

Redo, the Undo-Undo command

If you undo something and — whoops! — you didn't mean to, you must use the Redo command to set things back to the way they were. For example, you may type some text and then use Undo to "untype" the text. You can use the Redo command to restore the typing. You have two choices:

- ✔ Press Ctrl+Y.
- ✔ Click the Redo command button on the Quick Access Toolbar.

The Redo command does exactly the opposite of whatever the Undo command does. So, if you type text, Undo untypes the text and Redo recovers the text. If you use Undo to recover deleted text, Redo deletes the text again.

Redo, the Repeat Typing command

 When the Redo command has nothing left to redo, it changes functions and becomes the Repeat Typing command. Boy, can the Repeat Typing command be a timesaver!

For example, type these lines in Word:

```
Knock, knock.
Who's there?
Knock.
Knock who?
```

Now press Ctrl+Y or choose the Repeat Typing command button from the Quick Access Toolbar. Word repeats the last few things you typed. (If you had to press the Backspace key to back up and erase, Ctrl+Y repeats only from that point on.)

 The Repeat Typing command can also used to reapply formatting. When you're working through a document and changing styles on various chunks of text, using the Repeat key or Redo command can save oodles of time, especially in applying formatting. (See Part III of this book for information on formatting.)

Chapter 5

Search for This, Replace It with That

Pity poor Lebnb Nook. He's lost his *Imperial Fleet* in the Galactic Empire and now Darth Vader is on the other line, requesting an update. One must not keep Lord Vader on hold. Too bad for Lebnb that he doesn't have Word. If so, he could use the Find command to instantly locate the absent armada. Not only that, but he could also use the Replace command to swap out some of those rusty old *Corellian*s for some *Super Star Destroyers*. That would certainly impress the Dark Lord of the Sith! Could Word rival the Force as the strongest power in the galaxy?

Text Happily Found

Finding text is the domain of the Editing group, found on the far right end of the Home tab on Word's Ribbon interface. The Editing command button group may appear in its full glory, as shown in Figure 5-1, or, when Word's window is too narrow, you simply see an Editing button. When it's a button, you must click the button first to see the palette of commands, which (surprisingly) looks like the one shown in Figure 5-1.

Figure 5-1:
The Editing
group.

Using the Find command

Word can quickly and graphically locate text in your document, from the tee-niest tidbit of text to the world's longest run-on sentence. It's handled by the Find command. Abide by these steps:

1. On the Home tab, click the Find button in the Editing group.

You can also use the keyboard shortcut: Ctrl+F, which is one of the few keyboard shortcuts that make sense.

Clicking the Find button or pressing Ctrl+F summons the Navigation pane, illustrated in Figure 5-2.

Search text   Close Navigation pane

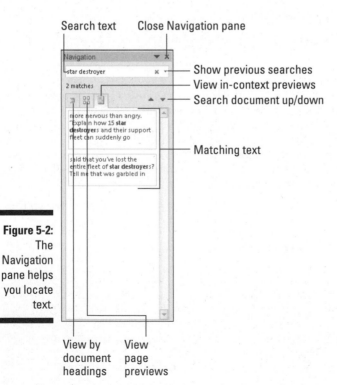

Show previous searches

View in-context previews

Search document up/down

Matching text

Figure 5-2:
The
Navigation
pane helps
you locate
text.

View by   View
document   page
headings   previews

2. Type the text you want to find.

As you type, matching text is highlighted in the document. Depending on which tab is chosen in the Navigation pane, you see matching results beneath the text box (refer to Figure 5-2).

Be exact. For example, if you want to find fame and glory, type **fame and glory** — no period or spaces or quotes. Type only the text you're looking for.

3. Page through the search results until you find the exact chunk of text you want.

As you page, the document scrolls to find the next matching bit of text.

4. Close the Navigation pane when you're done hunting down text.

If you'd rather use the more traditional Find dialog box to locate text in Word, see the next section.

✔ When text can't be found, the Navigation pane's text box briefly shows red. You see the text No Matches displayed. Try again.

✔ The Navigation pane may already display text in the Find What box. If so, you can delete the text by pressing the Backspace key.

✔ Do not end the text with a period unless you want to find the period too.

✔ The Find command can find elements that you can't readily type in, such as the Tab or Enter key. See the section "Finding stuff you can't type in," later in this chapter.

✔ If you're not sure whether the text is typed in uppercase or lowercase letters, use lowercase.

✔ If the text isn't found and you're *certain* that it's in there, check your spelling. If it's correct, try searching for a single word rather than two or more words or a sentence.

✔ Word finds text only in the current document (the one you see on the screen). To find text in another document, switch to that document's window and try searching again.

✔ After using the Find command, you can use the Browse Down button to continue your finding foray. Simply close the Find and Replace dialog box and then click the Browse Down button (or press Ctrl+PgDn). So, if you've already searched for and found *nothing,* clicking the Browse Down button finds even more *nothing.*

Using the traditional Find command

Word's traditional Find command isn't as fancy as using the Navigation pane, but it offers more features. Oddly, you cannot easily summon the old Find command dialog box directly. Instead, you have to use a "work-around." Here's how to do it:

1. **Press Ctrl+G.**

   The Ctrl+G keyboard shortcut summons the Find and Replace dialog box, with the Go To tab forward. (Go To is covered in Chapter 4.)

2. **Click the Find tab in the Find and Replace dialog box.**

   And there you are, looking at something similar to Figure 5-3.

Figure 5-3:
The Find tab
of the Find
and Replace
dialog box.

3. **Type the text you want to find into the Find What box.**

4. **Click the Find Next button.**

   Word searches your document from the insertion pointer's position to the end of the document.

   You can continue to click the Find Next button until the text you want is located.

5. **Click the Cancel button to close the Find and Replace dialog box.**

If the text you're looking for isn't found, Word lets you know; click the OK button to dismiss the dismal warning.

- ✔ The advantage of using the traditional Find command in the Find and Replace dialog box is that you have many more options for finding text. See the next section.

- ✔ As with the newfangled Find command (see the preceding section), you can use the Browse buttons on the vertical scroll bar to hop through a document to find text in either the up or down direction, depending on which Browse button you click.

✔ You can use the drop-down arrow gizmo (to the right of the Find What text box) to display a scrolling list of text you've previously searched for. To search again for a bit of text you've already searched for, click the drop-down arrow and click the text you want to find again. Click the Find Next button, and Word frantically begins searching.

Finding more than text

The Find command is powerful. It can do more than hunt down chunks and chunklettes of text. The Find command can find text *exactly* as it's typed, text you cannot type, text formatting, and just about anything in a document. Yes, it's still the same Find command, but it's *more*.

To unleash the Super Find command, you need to summon the traditional Find and Replace dialog box: Press Ctrl+G and then click the Find tab (described in the preceding section). You unveil the Find command's über-abilities by clicking the More button. The Find and Replace dialog box grows taller, with a bunch of options and doodads at the bottom, as illustrated in Figure 5-4.

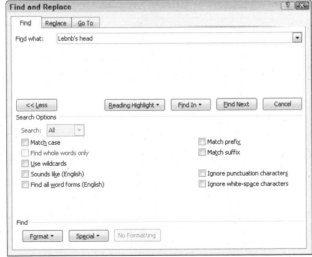

Figure 5-4: The more detailed Find and Replace dialog box.

The following sections explain how you can use the Find and Replace dialog box with its More part hanging open.

Finding an exact bit of text

There's a difference between *Pat* and *pat.* One is a name, and the other is to lightly touch something. To use the Find command to find one and not the other, select the Match Case option under Search Options. That way, *Pat* matches only words that start with an uppercase *P* and have lowercase *at* in them.

Finding a whole word

Use the Find Whole Words Only option to look for words such as *elf* and *ogre* without also finding words like *shelf* and *progress.*

Finding text that you know only a small part of (by using wildcards)

Here's a can-o-worms for you. You can use wildcards to find words that you know only a part of or a group of words with similar letters. This trick is a highly technical operation, so I advise you not to operate heavy machinery or sign a long-term lease or marriage contract when reading the following text.

The two basic wildcard characters are ? and *, where ? represents any single letter and * represents a group of letters. Suppose that you type the following line in the Find What box:

```
?ove
```

If you select the Use Wildcards option (in the More part of the Find and Replace dialog box), Word searches for any four-letter word that starts with any old letter but must end with "oh vee ee" — *dove, love,* and *wove,* for example.

The asterisk finds a group of characters, so the following wildcard locates any word starting with *w* and ending with *s* (there are lots of them):

```
w*s
```

Finding text that sounds like something else

The Sounds Like (English) option allows you to search for *homonyms,* or words that sound the same as the search word. You know: *their* and *there* or *deer* and *dear* or *hear* and *here.* How this is useful, I'll never know.

Oh! This isn't a rhyming search command. If you try to use it to find everything that rhymes with *Doris,* for example, it doesn't find *Boris, chorus, pylorus,* or anything of the like.

Finding variations of a word

Your editor informs you that no one will believe how the protagonist in your novel uses a pogo stick to travel the South. So you make him a biker. That involves changing every variation of the word *hop* (*hopping* and *hopped,* for example) to *ride.* In Word, you put a check mark by the option Find All Word Forms (English) in the über Find command's dialog box (refer to Figure 5-4) and type the word **hop** in the Find What box. Click the Find Next button and you're on your way.

Searching this way or that

Word normally searches from the insertion pointer's position to the end of a document and then back 'round the top again. You can override that stubbornness by placing your hand on the Find command's tiller in the Search drop-down list, found in the More part of the Find and Replace dialog box. You have three options:

- ✔ **All:** When this option is chosen, Find searches the entire document, from the insertion pointer's location down to the end of the document, back up to the beginning, and then back to where you started searching.

- ✔ **Down:** Find searches from the insertion pointer's location to the end of your document and then it stops.

- ✔ **Up:** Find searches — backward — from the insertion pointer's location to the start of your document. Then it stops.

You can also use the Browse buttons on the vertical scroll bar to repeat the Find command up or down, depending on which Browse button you press.

Finding stuff you can't type in

You can search for certain items in a document that you just cannot type at the keyboard. No, I'm not talking about nasty things — this isn't a censorship issue. Instead, I'm referring to items such as tabs, Enter keys (paragraphs), page breaks, graphics, and other, similar nontypable things.

To find a special, unprintable character, click the More button to see the super-duper Find and Replace dialog box (refer to Figure 5-4), and then click the Special button. Up pops a list of various items that Word can search for but that you would have a dickens of a time typing, similar to the ones shown in Figure 5-5.

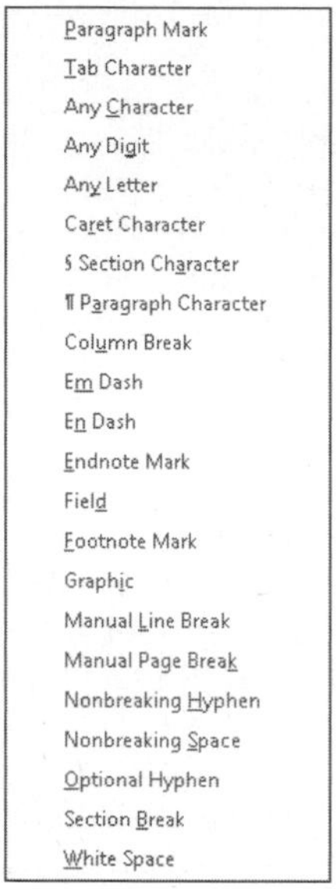

Paragraph Mark
Tab Character
Any Character
Any Digit
Any Letter
Caret Character
§ Section Character
¶ Paragraph Character
Column Break
Em Dash
En Dash
Endnote Mark
Field
Footnote Mark
Graphic
Manual Line Break
Manual Page Break
Nonbreaking Hyphen
Nonbreaking Space
Optional Hyphen
Section Break
White Space

Figure 5-5:
Items to
search for
that you
can't type.

Twenty-two items are on the list, and you probably don't recognize any of them. That's fine; I've used maybe six of them in my entire word processing career. Here are some of the handier options you can use from the Special pop-up menu:

- ✔ **Any Character, Any Digit,** and **Any Letter** are special characters that represent, well, just about anything. These items can be used as wild-cards for matching lots of stuff.

- ✔ **Caret Character** allows you to search for a caret (^) symbol, which may not seem like a big deal, but it is: Word uses the ^ symbol in a special way for finding text; see the third bullet in this section.

- ✔ **Paragraph Mark** (¶) is a special character that's the same as the Enter character — the one you press to end a paragraph.

- ✔ **Tab Character** moves the cursor to the next tab mark.

- ✔ **White Space** is any number of blank characters: one or more spaces, tabs, empty lines, or a combination of each one.

Choose an item from the list to search for that special character. When you do, a special, funky shorthand representation for that character (such as ^t for Tab) appears in the Find What box. Click the Find Next button to find that character.

- ✔ To search for the Enter keypress, which marks the end of a paragraph, choose Paragraph Mark. To search for the paragraph character, ¶, choose Paragraph Character.

✔ Yes, you can mix special characters with plain text. For example, to find a Tab character followed by *Hunter,* you use the Special button to insert the tab character (^t on the screen) and then type **Hunter**. It looks like this:

```
^tHunter
```

✔ It's possible, although nerdy, to type the special characters manually. Although this method avoids using the Special menu, which can be big and baffling, it means that you need to memorize the character codes. Each one starts with the caret character, ^, and some of them are logical, such as ^p for Paragraph Mark (Enter) or ^t for Tab. Here are a few other handy shortcuts, for reference:

Paragraph mark	^p
Tab character	^t
Any character	^?
Any digit	^#
Any letter	^$
Caret character	^^
Em dash	^+
En dash	^=
Manual line break	^1
Manual page break	^m
White space	^w

Finding formatting

In its most powerful superhero mode, the Find command can scour your document for formatting information. For example, if you want to find only those instances of the word *lie* in boldface type, you can do that. Before you attempt this task, I recommend that you understand Word's formatting abilities and commands, which are covered in Part III of this book.

The formatting options you can search for are revealed to you after a click of the Format button, which appears in the Find and Replace dialog box when the More button is clicked (refer to Figure 5-4). Clicking the Format button displays a pop-up menu of Word's primary formatting commands, as shown in Figure 5-6. Choosing any item from that list displays a corresponding dialog box, from which you can choose the formatting attributes to search for.

Figure 5-6:
Searching
for
formatting.

Suppose that you want to find a *red herring* in your document. Follow these steps:

1. **Summon the Find and Replace dialog box.**

   Press Ctrl+G and then click the Find tab in the Find and Replace dialog box.

2. **Type** red herring **in the Find What box.**

3. **If needed, click the More button to display the bottom part of the Find and Replace dialog box.**

4. **If the No Formatting button is available, click it.**

   This button is used to clear any previous formatting attributes you may have searched for. If the button can be clicked, click it to clear out those attributes and start afresh.

5. **Click the Format button.**

6. **Choose Font from the pop-up list.**

   The Find Font dialog box appears, which is where you set or control various text attributes. Say that the red herring you're searching for is 24 points tall.

7. **Choose 24 from the Size list.**

   Look in the upper right corner of the Find Font dialog box.

8. **Click OK.**

   The Font dialog box goes away and you return to the Find and Replace dialog box.

   Notice the text just beneath the Find What box: Format: Font: 24 pt. That bit of text is telling you that Word is now geared up to find only text that's 24 points tall — about twice the normal size.

9. **Click the Find Next button to find your formatted text.**

If you want to search only for a format, leave the Find What text box blank (refer to Step 2). That way, you can search for formatting attributes without caring what the text reads.

✔ To find specific text attributes (bold or underline, for example), use the Find Font dialog box to choose those attributes.

✔ You can use this technique to look for specific occurrences of a font, such as Courier or Times New Roman, by selecting the font from the selection list. Scroll through the font menu to see what you can choose.

✔ You can also search for paragraph formatting, such as an indented paragraph, by choosing Paragraph rather than Font from the Format pop-up list in the Find and Replace dialog box.

✔ Yes, you can search for more than one formatting attribute at a time. Just keep choosing format options from the Format button.

✔ Word remembers your formatting options! The next time you want to search for plain text, you click the No Formatting button. Doing so removes the formatting options and allows you to search for text in any format. If you forget to clear out the formatting before you begin your next search, don't be surprised if Word cannot find your text.

Replace Found Text and Stuff

The Find command is good only for finding stuff. Using Find and Replace, Little Bo Peep's dream of becoming a real estate mogul reaches full fruition. You can quite easily in Word change every instance of *sheep* in a document to *real estate*. How that makes the document read, of course, is anyone's guess. But it can be done!

You may opt for a more practical use of the Find and Replace command. For example, you may want to change all instances of *ungulates* in your document to *ruminants*. Here's how that's done:

1. **On the Home tab, click the Replace command button, found nestled in the Editing group on the far right side.**

   When the Replace command button isn't visible in the Editing group (refer to Figure 5-1), click the Editing button and then choose the Replace command button from the pop-up group of command buttons that appears.

   Choosing the Replace command button displays the Find and Replace dialog box, shown in Figure 5-7. This place should be familiar if you've often used the Find command. After all, finding stuff is the first part of using Find and Replace.

2. **In the Find What box, type the text you want to find.**

   You want to replace this text with something else. So, if you're finding *misery* and replacing it with *company,* type **misery**.

   Press the Tab key when you're done typing.

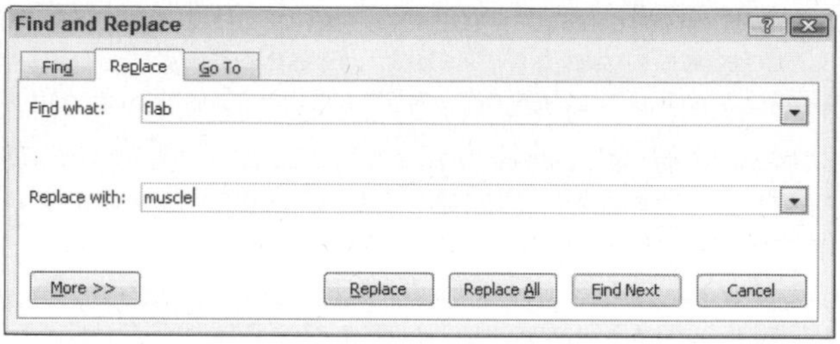

Figure 5-7:
The Replace
part of the
Find and
Replace
dialog box.

3. **In the Replace With box, type the text you want to use to replace the original text.**

   To continue from the example in Step 2, you type **company** here.

4. **Click the Find Next button.**

   At this point, the Replace command works just like the Find command: Word scours your document for the text you typed in the Find What dialog box. When that text is found, you move on to Step 5; otherwise, the Replace command fails because there's nothing to replace.

5. **Click the Replace button.**

   Word replaces the found text, highlighted onscreen, with the text typed in the Replace With box.

6. **Continue replacing.**

   After you click the Replace button, Word immediately searches for the next instance of the text, at which point you repeat Step 5 until the entire document has been searched.

7. **Read the summary that's displayed.**

   After the last bit of text is replaced, a dialog box appears and lists a summary for you. For example, it might say, "Word has completed its search of the document and has made 9 replacements." Of course, the number of replacements depends on what you were searching for and yadda-yadda.

8. **Click the Close button.**

You're done!

✔ All the restrictions, options, and rules for the Find command also apply to finding and replacing text. Refer to the section "Text Happily Found," at the start of this chapter.

✔ The keyboard shortcut for the Replace command is Ctrl+H. The only way I can figure that one out is that Ctrl+F is the Find command and Ctrl+G is the Go To command. F, G, and H are found together on the computer keyboard, and Find, Replace, and Go To are found together in the Find and Replace dialog box. Go figure.

✔ The Replace command's dialog box also sports a More button, which can be used exactly as the More button for the Find command. See the section "Finding more than text," earlier in this chapter.

✔ Word may find your text in the middle of another word, such as *use* in *causes*. Oops! Click the More button and select the Find Whole Words Only option to prevent such a thing from happening.

✔ If you don't type anything in the Replace With box, Word replaces your text with *nothing!* It's wanton destruction!

✔ Speaking of wanton destruction, the Undo command restores your document to its preceding condition if you foul up the Replace operation. See Chapter 4 for more information.

Replacing it all at once

The steps in the previous section work well to find and replace tidbits of text around your document. But it can often be tedious to keep pressing that Replace button over and over. That's why the Replace command's dialog box sports a handy Replace All button.

The Replace All button directs the Replace command to find all instances of the Find What text and — without question — replace it with the Replace With text. To use this button, simply click the Replace All button in Step 5 in the previous section. Then skip to Step 8.

Finding and replacing formatting

Just as the Find command can search for text with specific formatting, you can use the Replace command to replace text and apply formatting or to replace one type of formatting with another. Needless to say, this process can be tricky: Not only do I recommend that you be familiar with Word's formatting commands, but you should also be well practiced in using the Replace command.

Suppose that you want to replace all instances of underlined text with italic. Underlined text reeks so much of typewriter, and that's just too 20th century for these modern times. By replacing underline with italic, you're searching for one text format and replacing it with another; you're not even searching for text. So be careful. Do this:

1. **Press Ctrl+H to summon the Find and Replace dialog box.**

2. **Click the More button, if necessary, to display the full dialog box.**

3. **Click to select any text in the Find What box, and then delete that text by pressing the Backspace key.**

4. **Click the Format button and choose Font from the pop-up menu that appears.**

   The Find Font dialog box appears.

5. **In the Find Font dialog box, choose the single underline graphic from the Underline style drop-down list.**

6. **Click OK.**

   Back in the Find and Replace dialog box, the text `Format: Underline` appears below the Find What box.

7. **Click to select any text in the Replace With box and press Backspace to delete that text.**

8. **Choose Font from the Format button's pop-up list.**

9. **In the Find Font dialog box, choose (None) as the underline style.**

   This step is necessary because otherwise Word wouldn't remove the first style; it would merely add to that style. Likewise, text attributes such as Not Bold and Not Italic are found in the Replace Font dialog box.

10. **Choose Italic from the Font Style list.**

11. **Click OK to close the Replace Font dialog box.**

    Below the Replace With box, it should say `Format: Font: Italic, No underline`. That means Word will search for underlined text and replace it with italic text *and* remove the underline.

12. **Click the Replace All button.**

    Word scours your document and replaces any underlined text with italic.

13. **Click OK when the find-and-replace is done.**

As long as you set things up carefully, searching and replacing text formatting is a quick and easy way to spiff up a boring document.

✔ To replace one format with another, such as underline with italic, be sure to leave the Find What and Replace With text boxes empty. That way, only the text formatting is replaced.

✔ An easier way to update formatting in a document is to use and apply *styles*. Refer to Chapter 15 for details.

✔ Don't forget about the No Formatting button! You need to click it if you want to change the formats or replace text without paying attention to formats.

Chapter 6

Blocks o' Text

. . . .

. . . .

There are plenty of interesting blocks when it comes to writing: those moveable blocks that the ancient Chinese used for printing, the inevitable writer's block, and, finally, the blocks of text in a document. I believe that you'll find, of these three examples, working with blocks of text in a document not only the most useful but also the easiest to understand. That's because working with blocks in Word is like playing with blocks as a kid: Mix in some cut, copy, and paste and you have this engaging chapter on working with blocks of text.

Understanding Blocks

A *block* is simply a portion of text in your document, from a single character to the entire document. The block has a beginning and an end, and the block itself consists of all the text between them.

You create a block by selecting text. You *select* text by using the keyboard or the mouse or one of various other text-selection techniques covered in this chapter.

On the screen, the block appears highlighted, as shown in Figure 6-1.

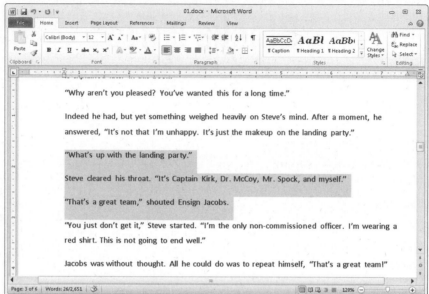

"Why aren't you pleased? You've wanted this for a long time."

Indeed he had, but yet something weighed heavily on Steve's mind. After a moment, he answered, "It's not that I'm unhappy. It's just the makeup on the landing party."

"What's up with the landing party."

Steve cleared his throat. "It's Captain Kirk, Dr. McCoy, Mr. Spock, and myself."

"That's a great team," shouted Ensign Jacobs.

"You just don't get it," Steve started. "I'm the only non-commissioned officer. I'm wearing a red shirt. This is not going to end well."

Jacobs was without thought. All he could do was to repeat himself, "That's a great team!"

Figure 6-1:
A block
of text is
selected.

By marking off text as a block, you can perform certain actions, or use various Word commands, that affect only the text in that block. Or, you can copy or move the block of text.

✔ A block of text in Word includes all letters and characters *and* the text formatting.

✔ Graphics and other nontext elements can also be selected as a block. In fact, you can select graphics along with text in the same block.

✔ When the status bar is displaying a word count, the number of words selected in the block of text is displayed, next to the total number of words in the document. (Refer to Figure 6-1.)

✔ When the Find command locates text, the text is selected as a block. Refer to Chapter 5 for more information on the Find command.

✔ Selecting text also means selecting characters such as tabs and the Enter keypress that marks the end of a paragraph. Fortunately, Word shows the Enter "character" as an extra blank space at the end of a paragraph. When you select that blank, you select the whole paragraph as a paragraph. To avoid selecting the Enter character, don't select the blank space at the end of a paragraph.

Selecting Blocks of Text

Word offers you many ways to *mark* text as a block in your document. This section mulls over the possibilities.

Using the keyboard to select text

The secret to using the keyboard to select text is the Shift key. By holding down the Shift key, you can use the standard keyboard commands that move the insertion pointer to select blocks of text. Table 6-1 has some suggestions for you.

Table 6-1	Shifty Selection Wizardry
To Select This	*Press This*
A character at a time to the right of the insertion pointer	Shift+→
A character at a time to the left of the insertion pointer	Shift+←
A block of text from the insertion pointer to the end of the line	Shift+End
A block of text from the insertion pointer to the beginning of the line	Shift+Home
A block of text from the insertion pointer to a line above	Shift+↑
A block of text from the insertion pointer to a line below	Shift+↓

You can use any keyboard cursor-movement command (I list them in Chapter 3), but I recommend using this Shift key method for selecting only small chunks of text. Otherwise, you may end up tying your fingers into knots!

Either Shift key works, although I prefer to use the left Shift key and then work the arrow keys on the right side of the keyboard.

Out, damn Mini toolbar!

When the mouse is used to select text, Word displays the Mini toolbar, looking like this:

The *Mini toolbar* is a *palette* of common formatting commands that Word supposes you need for a quick format on that selected text. After initially disliking the Mini toolbar, I've grown to enjoy it. But I recognize that you may find it more annoying than useful. If so, you can suppress its display. Follow these steps:

1. **Choose the Options command from the File tab's menu.**

2. **If necessary, choose General from the list on the left side of the Word Options window.**

3. **Remove the check mark by the item Show Mini Toolbar on Selection.**

4. **Click OK.**

If you would rather not eternally banish the Mini toolbar, note that it hides itself whenever you move the mouse beyond the selected chunk of text.

Marking a block with the mouse

Forget cheese. The computer mouse was born to mark text, by selecting vast swaths of words with a wide sweep of your hand, by clicking a number of times, or by using the old click-and-drag routine. Mickey may rule a kingdom, but your computer mouse rules over text selection in your computer.

Dragging over text to select it

The most common way to select text is by using the computer mouse thus:

1. **Point the mouse at the start of the text block.**

2. **Click and drag the mouse over the text you want to select.**

   As you drag, text becomes highlighted, or *selected*. (Refer to Figure 6-1.)

3. **Release the mouse — stop the dragging — to mark the end of the block.**

You can use these steps to select any old block size in your document.

✔ This selection technique works best when you use the mouse to drag over only the text you can see on the screen. When you try to select text beyond what you see on the screen, you have to select and scroll — which can be unwieldy; the mouse scrolls the text up and down quickly and, well, things get out of hand.

✔ When you find yourself becoming frustrated over not selecting all or part of a word, refer to the nearby sidebar, "Would you rather select text by letter or by word?"

Would you rather select text by letter or by word?

When you're selecting more than a single word, the mouse tends to grab text a full word at a time. If you want Word to select text by characters rather than by words (which is what I prefer), follow these steps:

1. **Choose the Options command from the File tab's menu.**

2. **Choose Advanced from the list on the left side of the Applications Settings window.**

3. **Under the Editing Options heading, remove the check mark by the item labeled When Selecting Automatically Select Entire Word.**

4. **Click OK.**

Selecting text by clicking the mouse

A speedy way to select specific sizes of chunks of text is to match the power of the mouse with the dexterity of your index finger. Table 6-2 explains some clicking-and-selecting techniques worth noting.

Table 6-2	Mouse Selection Arcana
To Select This Chunk of Text	*Click the Mouse Thus*
A single word	Point at the word with your mouse and double-click.
A line	Move the mouse pointer into the left margin beside the line you want to select. The mouse pointer changes to an arrow pointing northeastward. Click the mouse to select a line of text or drag the mouse up or down to select several lines.
A sentence	Point the mouse at the sentence and Ctrl+click. (Press the Ctrl key and click the mouse.)
A paragraph	Point the mouse somewhere in the paragraph's midst and triple-click.

Selecting text with the old poke-and-point

Here's the best way to select a chunk of text of any size, especially when that chunk of text is larger than what you can see on the screen at one time:

1. **Click the mouse to set the insertion pointer wherever you want the block to start — the anchor point.**

2. **Scroll through your document using the scroll bar.**

   You must use the scroll bar to scroll through your document. If you use the cursor-movement keys, you reposition the insertion pointer, which isn't what you want.

3. **To mark the end of the block, press and hold the Shift key and click the mouse where you want the block to end.**

   The text from the insertion pointer to wherever you clicked the mouse is selected as a block.

Using the F8 key to mark a block

If you can remember that the F8 key on the computer's keyboard can be used to mark text, you can exploit one of the most powerful but seldom used text-marking tools that Word has to offer.

Yes, wacky as it sounds, the F8 key is used to mark a block of text. Pressing F8 once enters *extended selection* mode. That's where Word drops anchor at the insertion pointer's location and then lets you use either the mouse or the cursor keys to select text. In fact, you cannot do anything but select text in extended selection mode (unless you press the Esc key to exit this mode).

Don't let the F8 key weirdness boggle you. Instead, consider these steps the next time you need to mark a block of text:

1. **Position the insertion pointer at the start of the block of text.**

2. **Press the F8 key.**

   The F8 key drops anchor and marks one end of the block.

3. **Use the keyboard's cursor keys to select the block of text.**

   The cursor-navigation keys are discussed in Chapter 3.

   Press a letter key to select text up to and including that letter. If you press N, you select all text up to and including the next *N* in your document. Nice. Nifty. Neat-o.

   Word highlights text from the point where you dropped anchor with F8 to wherever you move the insertion pointer.

4. **Do something with the selected block of text.**

   Word remains in extended selection mode until you do something with the block.

Doing something with a block of text is covered in the second half of this chapter.

To cancel the extended selection, press the Esc key. That action ends extended selection mode and keeps the block of text marked.

✔ You can use the mouse and the F8 key to get fancy. Position the cursor at either end of the block you want to mark and press the F8 key. Then position the mouse cursor at the other end of the block and press the left mouse button. Everything from there to there is marked.

✔ After pressing the F8 key, you can use the Find command to locate a specific bit of text. Word marks all text between the spot where F8 was pressed (the anchor) and the text that the Find command locates.

✔ Press the F8 key twice to select the current word (the one the insertion pointer is blinking inside of).

✔ Press the F8 key thrice (three times) to select the current sentence.

✔ Press the F8 key four times to select the current paragraph as a block of text.

✔ Press the F8 key five times to select the entire document, from top to bottom.

✔ No matter how many times you press F8, be aware that it always drops anchor. So, pressing F8 once or five times means that Word is still in extended selection mode. Do something with the block or press Esc to cancel that mode.

Blocking the whole dang-doodle document

The biggest block you can mark is an entire document. Word has a specific command to do it, to select all text in a document: From the Home tab, locate the Editing area. (Click the Editing button when the entire Editing area isn't visible.) Then choose Select⇨Select All. Instantly, the entire document is marked as a single block o' text.

From the keyboard, you can use Ctrl+A to select an entire document or just press the F8 key five times. Or, you can even use the obscure Ctrl+5 (the 5 on the numeric keypad) key combo.

Deselecting a Block

When you mark a block of text and change your mind, you must unmark, or *deselect,* the text. Here are a few handy ways to do it:

- **Move the insertion pointer.** It doesn't matter how you move the insertion pointer, with the keyboard or with the mouse — doing so unhighlights the block. Note that this trick doesn't exit the F8 key's extended selection mode.

- **Press the Esc key and then the ← key.** This method works to end extended selection mode.

- **Press Shift+F5.** The Shift+F5 key combo is the "go back" command (see Chapter 3), but it also deselects a block of text *and* returns you to the text you were editing before making the selection.

Manipulating Blocks of Text

You can block punches, block hats, block and tackle, play with building blocks and engine blocks, take nerve blocks, suffer from mental blocks, jog for blocks, and, naturally, block text. But what can you do with those marked blocks of text?

Why, plenty of things! You can apply a format to all text in the block, copy a block, move a block, search through a block, proof a block, print a block, and even delete a block. The information in this section explains those tricks.

- Blocks must be selected before you can manipulate them. See the first half of this chapter.

- When a block of text is marked, various Word commands affect only the text in that block.

Copying a block

After a block is marked, you can copy it into another part of your document, to duplicate the text. The original block remains untouched by this operation. Follow these steps to copy a block of text from one place to another:

1. **Mark the block.**

   Detailed instructions about doing this task are offered in the first part of this chapter.

2. **From the Home tab, choose the Copy tool from the Clipboard area.**

   Or, you can use the common Ctrl+C keyboard shortcut for the Copy command.

   You get no visual clue that the text has been copied; it remains selected.

3. **Move the insertion pointer to the position where you want to place the block's copy.**

   Don't worry if there's no room! Word inserts the block into your text.

4. **Choose the Paste tool from the Clipboard area.**

   Or, you can use the common Ctrl+V keyboard shortcut for the Paste command.

The block of text you copy is inserted into your text just as though you had typed it there by yourself.

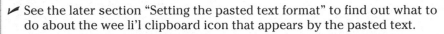

✔ See the later section "Setting the pasted text format" to find out what to do about the wee li'l clipboard icon that appears by the pasted text.

✔ After you copy a block, you can paste it into your document a second time. That's because whenever a block of text is cut or copied, Word remembers it. You can yank that block into your document again at any time — sort of like pasting text again after it has already been pasted in. You use Ctrl+V, the Paste shortcut. Pasting text again simply pastes down a second copy of the block, spit-spot (as Mary Poppins would say).

✔ You can paste the block into another document you're working on or even into another application. (This is a Windows trick, which most good books on Windows discuss.)

✔ Refer to the section "Collecting and Pasting," near the end of this chapter, for more copy and paste choices.

Moving a block

To move a block of text, you select the text and then *cut* and paste. This process is almost exactly the same as copying a block, described in the previous section, although in Step 2 you choose the Cut tool rather than the Copy tool or press the Ctrl+X keyboard shortcut for the Cut command. Otherwise, all steps are the same.

Don't be alarmed when the block of text vanishes! That's cutting in action; the block of text is being *moved,* not copied. You see the block of text again when you paste it in place.

Don't panic! If you screw up, remember that the Ctrl+Z Undo shortcut undoes a block move.

Setting the pasted text format

When you paste text in Word, the Paste Options icon appears near the end of the pasted block of text, as shown in the margin. Don't let it annoy you! That button allows you to select formatting for the pasted block because occasionally the block may contain formatting that, well, looks quite ugly after it's pasted in.

To work the Paste Options button, click it with the mouse or press and release the Ctrl key on the keyboard. You see a menu of options, illustrated in Figure 6-2.

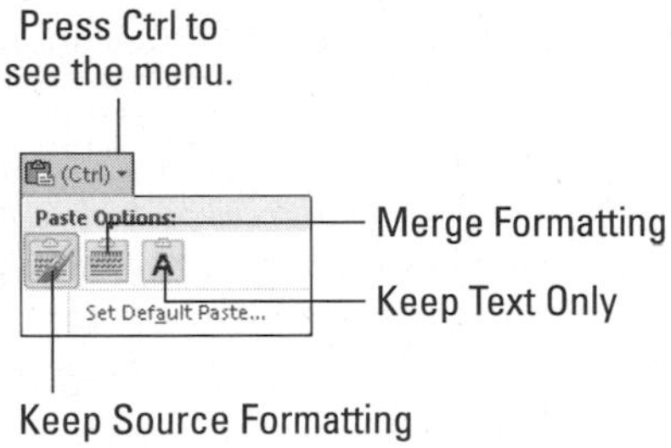

Press Ctrl to
see the menu.

Figure 6-2:
Pasting
options.

Merge Formatting

Keep Text Only

Keep Source Formatting

Table 6-3 summarizes the available paste options.

Table 6-3		Paste Option Options	
Icon	*Keyboard Shortcut*	*Name*	*Description*
	K	Keep Source Formatting	The formatting is fine; don't do a thing.
	M	Merge Formatting	Reformat the pasted block so that it looks like the text it's being pasted into.
	T	Keep Text Only	Just paste in the text — no formatting.

To keep only text with a copied or cut block (no formatting), you can press the Ctrl key and then the T key after pasting. That's two separate keys, not Ctrl+T.

Using the Paste Options icon is utterly optional. In fact, you can continue typing or working in Word and the icon bows out, fading away like some nebbish who boldly asked a power blonde to go out with him and she utterly failed to recognize his existence. Like that.

You can choose the Set Default Paste command after clicking the Paste Options icon to direct Word on how to permanently deal with pasted text. That's a handy trick, especially when you find yourself repeatedly choosing the same Paste Options format.

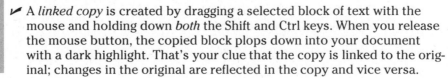

Copying or moving a block with the mouse

When you have to move a block only a short distance, you can use the mouse to drag-move or drag-copy the block. This feature works best when you're moving or copying a block to a location that you can see right on the screen. Otherwise, you're scrolling your document with the mouse while you're playing with blocks, which is like trying to grab an angry snake.

To move any selected block of text with the mouse, just drag the block: Point the mouse cursor anywhere in the blocked text and then drag the block to its new location. Notice how the mouse pointer changes, as shown in the margin. That means you're moving the block of text.

Copying a block with the mouse works just like moving the block, except that you press the Ctrl key as you drag. When you do that, a plus sign appears in the mouse pointer (see the margin). That's your sign that the block is being copied and not just moved.

 ✔ The Paste Options icon appears after you "drop" the chunk of text. Refer to the preceding section for more information on the Paste Options icon.

 ✔ When you drag a block of text with the mouse, you're not copying it to the Clipboard. You cannot use the Paste (Ctrl+V) command to paste in the block again.

 ✔ A *linked copy* is created by dragging a selected block of text with the mouse and holding down *both* the Shift and Ctrl keys. When you release the mouse button, the copied block plops down into your document with a dark highlight. That's your clue that the copy is linked to the original; changes in the original are reflected in the copy and vice versa.

Collecting and Pasting

When you cut or copy a block of text, the block is placed into a storage area known as the *Clipboard.* The block of text remains on the Clipboard until it's replaced by something else — another block of text or a graphic or anything cut or copied in Windows. (The Clipboard is a Windows feature, which is how you can copy and paste between Windows applications.)

In Word, however, the Clipboard can hold more than one thing at time. You can copy, copy, copy and then use the special Clipboard pane to selectively paste text back into your document. The technique, *collect and paste,* is discussed in this section.

Looking at the Clipboard pane

To view the Clipboard pane, click the dialog box launcher found in the lower right corner of the Clipboard group on the Home tab, right next to the word *Clipboard.* The Clipboard pane then appears in the writing area of the Word window, perhaps looking similar to the one shown in Figure 6-3.

Figure 6-3:
The
Clipboard
task pane.

The scrolling list contains the last several items you copied, not only from Word but perhaps from other programs as well.

Pasting items from the Clipboard task pane is covered in the next section.

✔ You can use the Copy command multiple times in a row to collect text when the Clipboard task pane is visible.

✔ Word's Clipboard can hold only 24 items. If any more than that number is copied or cut, the older items in the list are "pushed off" to make room for the new ones. The current number of items is shown at the top of the task pane.

✔ Other programs in Microsoft Office (Excel and PowerPoint, for example) also share this collect-and-paste feature.

✔ You can close the task pane when you're done with collect and paste: Click the X in the upper right corner of the task pane window.

Pasting from the Clipboard pane

To paste any collected text from the Clipboard pane into your document, simply click the mouse on that chunk of text. The text is copied from the Clipboard and inserted into your document at the insertion pointer's location, just as though you typed it yourself.

After you paste, the Paste Options icon appears next to the pasted text. Refer to the section "Setting the pasted text format," earlier in this chapter, to find out what do to with that thing.

✔ You can click the Paste All button to paste every item from the Clipboard into your document.

✔ Click only once! When you double-click, you insert *two* copies of the text.

Cleansing the Clipboard pane

You're free to clean up Word's Clipboard whenever the Clipboard pane is visible. To remove a single item, point the mouse at that item and click the downward-pointing triangle to the right of the item. Choose Delete from the shortcut menu and that lone item is zapped from the Clipboard.

To whack all items on the Clipboard, click the Clear All button at the top of the Clipboard task pane.

You cannot undo any clearing or deleting that's done in the Clipboard task pane.

Chapter 7

Spell It Write

. . . .

. . . .

There's no such thing as spelling in English. Spelling in English evolved over time. Even the venerable Bard, William Shakespeare, spelled his own name several different ways. It wasn't until the notion of the "dictionary" that spelling became more or less standardized.

The same feeling of randomness can be applied to English grammar. Despite all those schoolteachers and editors out there, English is *not* Latin. English grammar has more exceptions than it has rules. That makes English a remarkably flexible and poetic language, but also makes it frustrating to discern meaning or ply some type of consistency from our mother tongue.

Word tries its best to remedy the situation: It comes with document proofing tools. They include on-the-fly and in-your-face spelling and grammatical checkers. This chapter describes how they work, when to use them, and when to ignore them.

Hue Right Grate

Word's document proofing tools are as technologically advanced as the programmers at Microsoft can make them. As the title of this section suggests, however, there's something to be said about *context*.

Just because it appears that your document contains no errors doesn't mean that everything is perfect. You have no better way to proof a document than to read it with human eyes.

Check Your Spelling

Spell-checking in Word works the second you start typing. Offending or unknown words are immediately underlined with the red zigzag of shame. Word can also be employed to scan the entire document word-by-word for your attempts at mangling the English language, Word can be trained to use the AutoCorrect feature to automatically correct your common typos and misspellings. This section describes the details.

Dealing with on-the-fly spell checking

Word has an internal library consisting of tens of thousands of words, all spelled correctly. Every time you type a word, it's checked against that dictionary. When the word isn't found, it's marked as suspect in your document. The mark is a red zigzag underline, as shown in Figure 7-1. What to do, what to do?

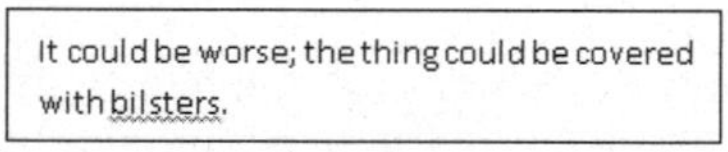

Figure 7-1:
The word
bilsters is
flagged as
misspelled.

> It could be worse; the thing could be covered with bilsters.

My advice: Keep typing. Don't let the "red zigzag of a failed elementary education" perturb you. Focus on getting your thoughts up on the screen rather than on stopping and fussing over inevitable typos.

When you're ready, say, during one of those inevitable pauses that takes place as you write, go back and fix your spelling errors. Here's what to do:

1. **Locate the misspelled word.**

   Look for the red zigzag underline.

2. **Right-click the misspelled word.**

   Up pops a shortcut menu and the Mini toolbar, shown in Figure 7-2.

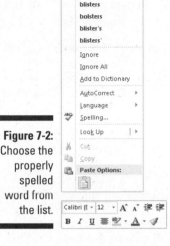

Figure 7-2:
Choose the
properly
spelled
word from
the list.

3. **Choose from the list the word you intended to type.**

    In Figure 7-2, the word *blisters* fits the bill. Click that word and it's auto-matically inserted into your document, to replace the spurious word.

If the word you intended to type isn't on the list, don't fret. You may have to use a real dictionary or take another stab at spelling the word phonetically and then correct it again.

✔ When the word is spelled correctly and Word is just too stupid to recog-nize it, you can add the word to its dictionary. See the next section.

✔ Word turns off automatic proofing when your document grows over a specific size. For example, on my computer, when the document is more than 100 pages long, automatic spell checking is disabled. A warning appears to alert you when this happens. Note that you can still manu-ally spell-check, which is covered in the section "All-at-Once Document Proofing," later in this chapter.

Dealing with words incorrectly flagged as being misspelled

Occasionally, Word's spell checker bumps into a word it doesn't recognize, such as your last name or perhaps your city. Word dutifully casts doubt on the word, by underlining it with the notorious red zigzag. Yes, this case is one of those where the computer is wrong.

Two commands are on the spell-checker's right-click menu (refer to Figure 7-2) to deal with those false negatives: Ignore All and Add to Dictionary.

Ignore All: Select this command when the word is properly spelled and you don't want Word to keep flagging it as misspelled.

For example, your science fiction short story has a character named Zadlux. Word believes it to be a spelling error, but you (and all the people of the soon-to-be-conquered planet Drebulon) know better. After you choose the Ignore All command, all instances of the suspect word are cheerfully ignored, but only in that one document.

Add to Dictionary: This command adds words to Word's custom dictionary, which is a supplemental list of spelled-correctly words used to proof a document.

For example, I once lived on Pilchuck Avenue, which Word thinks is a misspelling of the word *Paycheck*. If only. So, when I right-click the incorrectly flagged word, I choose the Add to Dictionary command. Presto — the word *Pilchuck* is added to Word's custom dictionary. I'll never have to spell-check that word again.

- ✔ If the word looks correct but is red-wiggly-underlined anyway, it could be a repeated word. They're flagged as misspelled by Word, so you can either choose to delete the repeated word or just ignore it.

- ✔ Word ignores certain types of words — for example, words with numbers in them or words written in all capitals, which are usually abbreviations. For example, Pic6 is ignored because it has a 6 in it. The word *NYEP* is ignored because it's in all caps.

- ✔ You can adjust how spell-checking works, especially if you feel that it's being too picky. See the section "Control Word's Proofing Options," later in this chapter.

Undoing the Ignore All command

Choosing the Ignore All command means that all instances of a given misspelled word or typo are ignored in your document. This statement holds true even when you save that document and open it again later. So, if you make a mistake and would rather have the ignored word regarded once more, do this:

1. **Choose the Options command from the File tab's menu.**

   The Word Options window appears.

2. **Choose Proofing on the left side of the window.**

3. **Scroll down the right side of the window (if necessary) until you can see the Recheck Document button; click that button.**

   A warning dialog box appears, reminding you of what you're about to do.

4. **Click the Yes button.**

   Everything you've told Word to ignore while proofing your document is now ignored. It's the ignore-ignore command!

5. **Click the OK button to return to your document.**

By following these steps, you direct Word to not only un-ignore all previously ignored words but also any grammatical errors you've chosen to ignore. You have no way to undo this command.

The steps for undoing the Ignore All command affect only the current document. The Ignore All command affects only the current document.

Removing words from the custom dictionary

When you choose the Add to Dictionary command, the given word is placed into the custom dictionary. Recognizing that people may change their minds, Word allows you to edit its custom dictionary, to remove words you may have added accidentally.

To remove unwanted words from the custom dictionary, follow these steps:

1. **Click the Word Options button on the File tab's menu.**

   The Word Options window shows up.

2. **From the left side of the window, choose Proofing.**

3. **Click the button labeled Custom Dictionaries.**

   The Custom Dictionaries dialog box appears.

4. **Select the CUSTOM.DIC dictionary file.**

   It's probably the only item in the list.

5. **Click the button labeled Edit Word List.**

   You see a scrolling list of words you've added to the custom dictionary.

6. **Find and select the word you want to remove from the dictionary.**

   The word is selected by clicking it once.

7. **Click the Delete button.**

8. **Repeat Steps 6 and 7 if you want to remove more words.**

9. **Click the OK button when you're done editing the dictionary.**

   Close any other open windows.

The 25 most frequently misspelled words

a lot	atheist	grammar	maneuver	ridiculous
accidentally	collectible	gauge	no one	separate
acquire	consensus	independent	occurrence	supersede
amateur	definite	kernel	realize	their
argument	embarrass	liaison	receive	weird

AutoCorrect Your Common Typos

Some typos and spelling errors are never graced by the red zigzag. That's because Word quickly fixes hundreds of common typos and spelling errors on the fly. It's done by the AutoCorrect feature, and you have to be quick to see it.

Understanding AutoCorrect

There's nothing to using AutoCorrect; it happens automatically. In Word, try to type the word *mispell*. You can't! Word uses AutoCorrect and suddenly you see *misspell*.

Most commonly misspelled words can be found in AutoCorrect's repertoire: *believe, suposed, recieve,* and so on. Try a few. See whether you can baffle Word!

In addition to fixing spelling errors, AutoCorrect helps you enter special characters. For example, type **(C)** and AutoCorrect properly inserts the © copyright symbol. Ditto for **(TM)** for the trademark. Typing–> is translated into an arrow, and even **:)** becomes a happy face.

Beyond spelling, AutoCorrect fixes some common punctuation. It automatically capitalizes the first letter of a sentence. AutoCorrect capitalizes *I* when you forget to, properly capitalizes the names of days, fixes the iNVERSE cAPS lOCK pROBLEM, plus other common typos.

Creating your own AutoCorrect entries

One joy of using AutoCorrect is that you can add your own commonly mis-spelled words to its list. For example, I'm always goofing up the word *brief. I* before *E? E* before *I?* Never mind! I need to fix the spelling error only once by placing my typo and the proper spelling into AutoCorrect's repertoire. This task is cinchy:

1. **Right-click the misspelled word.**

   Normally, you choose the proper spelling from the list. But that fixes the word only once. Instead:

2. **Click the AutoCorrect item.**

   Up pops a submenu containing various corrections, as shown in Figure 7-3.

3. **Choose the properly spelled word from the AutoCorrect submenu.**

   The word is added to the AutoCorrect list, and Word, as a special favor, corrects the word in your text as well.

Figure 7-3:
Auto-
Correcting a
werd.

Whenever your typo is encountered, Word automatically corrects it for you. But you must remember to use the AutoCorrect item from the spell-check-thingy pop-up menu on your first sighting of the misspelled word rather than just choose the corrected word from the list.

If possible, try to add only lowercase words with AutoCorrect. When you add a word with an initial capital letter, such as *Werd,* AutoCorrect replaces only words with an initial capital letter. When you use AutoCorrect on a word that's in all lowercase, the word is fixed every time.

Undoing an AutoCorrect correction

weird

You can reverse AutoCorrect instant changes, but only when you're quick. The secret is to press Ctrl+Z (the Undo command) immediately after AutoCorrect makes its correction. The change is gone, but also note the blue rectangle under the first letter of the still-corrected word, as shown in the margin.

The AutoCorrect blue rectangle is your key to access AutoCorrect options and change the way AutoCorrect behaves: Point the mouse at the rectangle to see a button, which you can then click to see various AutoCorrect options, shown in Figure 7-4.

Figure 7-4:
Adjusting
an Auto-
Correction.

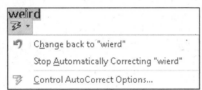

Here are your options:

- **Change Back to "*whatever*":** Undo the AutoCorrection.

- **Stop Automatically Correcting "*whatever*":** Remove the word from the AutoCorrect dictionary so that it's not corrected automatically again. (But it may still be flagged as incorrect by the spell checker.)

- **Control AutoCorrect Options:** Display the AutoCorrect dialog box, which is used to customize various AutoCorrect settings and to edit or create new entries in the AutoCorrect library. Refer to the section "Control Word's Proofing Options," later in this chapter.

Grammar Be Good

Mark Twain once referred to spelling in the English language as "drunken." If that's true, English grammar must be a hallucination. To help you to detox, Word comes with a grammar checker. It's just like having your eighth grade English teacher inside your computer — only it's all the time and not just third period.

Word's grammar checker works on the fly, just like the spelling checker. The main difference is that words are underlined with a green, not red, zigzag underline. The grammar checker also flags improperly used words with a blue zigzag underline. Either way, you're getting a hint of Word's sense of grammatical justice, which, as I've written elsewhere, is merely a suggestion, given the illusionary nature of English grammar in the first place.

As with a spelling error, right-click the green-underlined text. The pop-up menu that appears either explains why the sentence is wrong or offers an alternative sentence you can choose. You also have an option to ignore the error, which I find myself using quite a bit.

- ✔ When you select About This Sentence from the pop-up menu, the Office Help system attempts to explain which part of the *English Language Book of Rules* you offended.

- ✔ Sometimes you may be puzzled about a word that the grammar checker finds wrong. Don't give up! Always check the entire sentence for a potential error. For example, the grammar checker may suggest *had* in place of *have.* Chances are good that *have* is correct but another word in the sentence has an unwanted *s* attached.

- ✔ You can customize or even turn off grammar checking. Refer to the section "Control Word's Proofing Options," later in this chapter.

All-at-Once Document Proofing

You can cheerfully ignore all of Word's on-the-fly document proofing, and instead opt to do a once-over scan for spelling and grammatical errors. This process can take place when you're done writing, just before printing or publishing your document. I consider it a final scan, kind of like ironing out the wrinkles in a freshly laundered shirt. Here's how it works:

1. **Click the Review tab.**

2. **In the Proofing group, click the Spelling & Grammar button.**

   The Spelling and Grammar dialog box appears, as shown in Figure 7-5. It displays English language offenses one at a time, flagging the spelling or grammar errors as they occur in your document.

   Here's what you can do:

   - To fix the error, edit the text in the box.

   - Use the Ignore button (or buttons) to skip the error, or click the Next Sentence button to continue moving through the document.

   - Choose a proper spelling from the list and then click the Change button.

3. **Continue checking your document until Word says that you're done.**

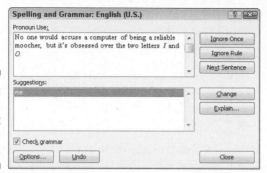

Figure 7-5:
Proofing a
document
one mistake
at a time.

If you find this method easier, and more gentle to your spelling-challenged
ego, you can turn off on-the-fly spelling and grammar checking. The next section explains how to do it. If you choose that option, don't forget to proof
your document before you finish your work.

REMEMBER

✔ You can easily enter a trancelike state while you're document proofing. You might find yourself clicking the Ignore button too quickly. My
advice: Use the Undo button. It lets you go back and change some text
you may not have paid attention to.

✔ A proofing button (an animation, actually) is on the status bar. If you
click the button, shown in the margin, Word takes you to the next man-
gled chunk of English in your document. Using that button is another
way to hop through and proof your document.

Control Word's Proofing Options

All document proofing options and settings are kept in one place, buried
deep in Word's bosom. Here's how to get there:

1. **Click the File tab.**

2. **Choose Options from the File tab's menu.**

3. **In the Word Options window, choose Proofing from the left side.**

The right side of the window contains options and settings for document
proofing. The following sections describe what you can do there.

When you're done working in the Word Options window, click the OK button
to lock in whichever changes you've made.

Changing spell-check and grammar settings

After you find yourself in the Word Options window, the Proofing corner, you can peruse and change the way Word reacts to your mangling of the mother tongue. Here are some highlights:

✔ To turn off on-the-fly spell checking, remove the check mark by the item Check Spelling As You Type.

✔ To disable grammar checking, remove the check mark by the item Mark Grammar Errors As You Type.

✔ Click the Settings button by the Writing Style drop-down list to customize and hone the grammatical transgressions that Word marks. (I typically disable the Fragments warning because Word is often wrong when flagging fragments.)

Perusing AutoCorrect options

You can click the AutoCorrect Options button in the Word Options window to view the AutoCorrect dialog box and its slew of automatic word-correcting and typo-fixing options, as shown in Figure 7-6.

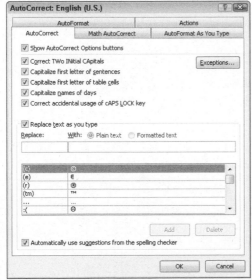

Figure 7-6: Oodles of AutoCorrect options.

Here are some things you can do:

✔ The AutoCorrect tab lists all problems that AutoCorrect fixes for you, plus common typo corrections. That's also where you can remove the AutoCorrect entries you detest.

✔ If you don't like how Word changes Web page addresses in your document into real hyperlinks, remove the check mark by the option Internet and Network Paths with Hyperlinks on the AutoFormat tab.

✔ The AutoFormat tab also harbors those insidious options that automatically create bulleted lists and heading styles in Word; remove the appropriate check marks to disable those unwanted features.

✔ Also refer to the AutoFormat As You Type tab to kill off additional automatic numbering and bulleted list features in Word.

Chapter 8

Documents and Such

· ·

· ·

1 like the word *document*. It's elegant. It's much better than saying "a file" or "that thing I created with my word processor." It makes everything from a shopping list to a note excusing little Jimmy's absence because you thought he might have impetigo but it turned out to be jelly stuck to his chin from the night before — it makes all that trivial text somehow seem more important.

The thing you create in Word, from a tiny note to a Pulitzer prize-winning autobiography, is a *document.* It starts off new, and then a document is saved for long-term storage on the PC's mass storage system. You can also retrieve documents already saved, even if they're created by other folks, and open them in Word for more editing, reviewing, and printing, for example.

What Is a File?

To understand documents, you must first recognize the importance of *files.* This concept is vital to grasp if you ever want your computer experience to be a pleasant one. In fact, most of the trouble people have with computers comes from not understanding what a file is.

Your computer stores all kinds of information. In addition to storing word processing documents, the computer can store graphical images, music and video, and all sorts of things. It also stores the programs you run, games, and even Windows itself. Those items are all stored inside the digital container known as a *file*.

Most of what the computer does is to help you access and organize the files — the stuff you collect and create. Oh, I could go into a good, long diatribe about files and computer storage, and utterly bore you with computer science. I won't.

After a Word document is saved, it exists as a file. Documents are files. They exist as unique and separate from other items on the computer, including the word processor. Word is merely the device you use to create the document or file; Word itself is not the document.

Think of the relationship this way: A pianist uses sheet music to play a tune, but the sheet music isn't part of the piano. Just as you can store or mail sheet music, you can store a Word document file (on an optical disc, for example) or send it via e-mail. The Word document that exists on your computer's hard drive as a file is its own, unique thing.

✔ Working with files is a task you do in Windows, not in Word. That topic includes renaming files, deleting them, moving and copying them, as well as doing other nerdy things.

✔ For more information on understanding files as well as mass storage and other basic computer concepts, I highly recommend reading my book *PCs For Dummies*. The more you know about your computer, the happier you are as a computer user.

A New Document

When you start your word processing day, Word automatically presents you with a blank sheet of paper — a blank *document* — on which you can start writing. That's what most folks do.

After Word has already started and you're ready to begin another new document, you summon the electronic equivalent of a fresh, blank sheet of paper. Here's how to do it, to start a new document, in Word:

1. **Click the File tab.**

   The Word window changes to display the File tab menu.

2. **Choose the New command from the left side of the window.**

   Word lists a slew of options for starting a new document, many of which may appear confusing to you, which is, I believe, the program's intent.

What you want is the Blank Document item, which is conveniently chosen for you, as shown in Figure 8-1.

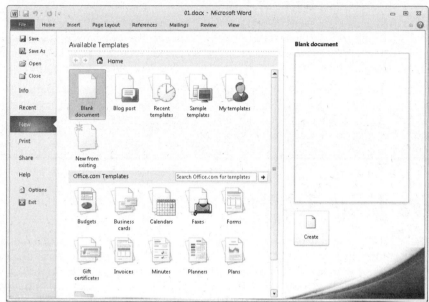

3. Click the Create button to start a new, blank document.

The Create button is found on the right side of the window, beneath that obnoxiously large, blank sheet of paper.

After you click the Create button (or press the Enter key), the Word window returns to normal and you see a blank page, ready for typing.

You can repeat these steps as often as you need new documents; Word lets you work with several documents at a time. See Chapter 24 for information on multiple-document mania.

- ✔ Ah, the shortcut: Press Ctrl+N to quickly summon a new, blank document in Word.

- ✔ Another way to start your work is to open a document on disk. To do this, use the Open command from the File tab menu, covered later in this chapter.

- ✔ The New Document window contains numerous options for starting something new in Word. Rather than use the Blank Document choice, lots of folks use templates to start documents. *Templates* help save time by predefining document layout and formatting (and sometimes even text). See Chapter 16 for more information.

How big can a Word document be?

There's no upper limit on how many pages you can have in your document. Theoretically, a Word document can be thousands of pages long. Even so, I don't recommend that you make your documents that big.

The longer a document is in Word, the more apt the computer is to screw things up. So, rather than advise you to make a single long document, I recommend that you split your work into smaller, chapter-size documents. Those documents can then be organized into a single *master document* in Word, where page numbers and references can be used as though the smaller documents were one larger document.

See Chapter 25 for more information on managing several smaller documents into a single large document.

Save Your Stuff!

It doesn't matter whether you've written a masterpiece — the most important thing you can do to a document is *save it.* Create a permanent copy of what you see onscreen by saving the document as a file on the PC's storage system. That way, you can use the document again, keep a copy for business reasons, publish it electronically, or just keep the thing for sentimental reasons. All those tasks require saving!

Saving a document the first time

Don't think that you have to wait until you finish a document to save it. In fact, you should save almost immediately — as soon as you have a few sentences or paragraphs. Save! Save! Save!

To save a document that hasn't already been saved to disk, follow these steps:

1. **Click the File tab.**

2. **Choose the Save As command.**

    The Save As dialog box appears, similar to the one shown in Figure 8-2.

3. **Type a name for your document in the File Name box.**

    Word automatically selects the first line or first several words of your document as a filename and puts it in the Save dialog box. If that's okay, you can move to Step 4. Otherwise, type a name in the File Name box.

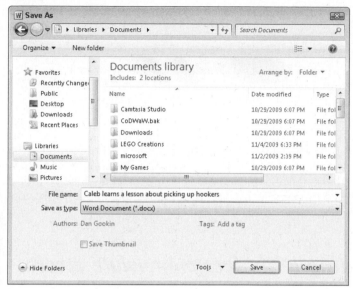

Figure 8-2:
The Save As
dialog box.

Be descriptive! The more concisely you name your document, the easier it is to recognize it by that name in the future.

4. **Choose a location for your file (optional).**

   Use the various gizmos in the Save As dialog box to choose a specific folder for your document. (Folders are a part of file organization. My book *PCs For Dummies* explains how to use folders, if you're unfamiliar with the concept.)

5. **Click the Save button.**

   The file is now safely stored in the PC's storage system.

At this point, you can keep working. As you work, continue to save; refer to the section "Saving or updating a document," later in this chapter.

✔ There's no need to quit after you save a document. Indeed, the idea is to save as you go.

✔ The only time you need to use the Save As dialog box is when you first create a document. After that, you can use the Save command merely to update your document, by storing the latest modifications as you write.

✔ Your clue that the file has been successfully saved is that the name you've given it (the *filename*) now appears on the document's title bar, near the top of the screen.

✔ Always save your document, even after you type only a few lines of text.

✔ The Save As command can also be used to save a document with a new name or to a different location on disk.

✔ Some older versions of Windows use a type of Save As dialog box that's different from the one shown earlier (refer to Figure 8-2). Though the dialog box looks different, it has the same features and is used in the same way.

✔ Do not save a document to removable media, such as an optical disc or memory card. Instead, save the document to the computer's main storage devices, the hard drive. Then, using Windows, copy that document to the removable media. Otherwise, Word may lose your document or the computer may crash if you remove the media before you're done working on the document.

Dealing with document-save errors

Saving a document involves working with both Word and the Windows operating system. This process doubles the chances of something going wrong, so it's high time for an error message. A potential message you may see is

```
The file whatever already exists
```

You have three choices:

✔ **Replace Existing File:** Nope.

✔ **Save Change with a Different Name:** Yep.

✔ **Merge Changes into Existing File:** Nope.

After choosing the middle option, type a different file name in the Save As dialog box.

Another common problem occurs when a message that's displayed reads something like this:

```
The file name, location, or format 'whatever' is not valid
    . . .
```

That's Word's less-than-cheerful way of telling you that the filename contains a boo-boo character. To be safe, stick to letters, numbers, and spaces when you're naming a file. Check the nearby sidebar, "Complicated — but important — information about filenames." Then click OK and try again.

Complicated — but important — information about filenames

Word lets you be creative in your writing, but your creativity is limited in naming a document as it's saved to disk. Here are the rules:

✔ A filename can be longer than 200 ridiculous-something characters; even so, keep your filenames short but descriptive.

✔ A filename can include letters, numbers, and spaces and can start with a letter or number.

✔ A filename can contain periods, commas, hyphens, and even underlines.

✔ A filename cannot contain any of these characters: \ / : * ? " < > |

Word automatically appends a *filename extension* to all documents you save — like a last name. You may or may not see this extension, depending on how you've configured Windows. No matter: You don't need to manually type the extension yourself; just concern yourself with giving the document a proper and descriptive filename.

Saving or updating a document

Every so often as you continue to work on your document, you should save again. That way, any changes you've made since the last time you saved are remembered and recorded on the PC's storage system permanently. I generally save my documents dozens of times a day, usually when the phone rings or when I need to step away and the cat is lurking too closely to the keyboard or, often, when I'm just bored.

To resave a document that has already been saved to disk, choose the Save command from the File tab menu. You get no feedback, and the Save As dialog box doesn't show up. That's because you've already given the file a name; the Save command merely updates the existing file on disk.

✔ The fastest way to save a document is to use the Ctrl+S keyboard shortcut.

✔ You can also click the Save icon on the Quick Access toolbar to save a document to disk.

✔ The most bizarre command for saving a document? Shift+F12. Weird.

Forgetting to save before you quit

When you're done writing in Word, you close the document, close the window, or just quit Word outright. No matter how you call it quits, when the document hasn't yet been saved or was changed since the last save, you're asked to save again, as shown in Figure 8-3.

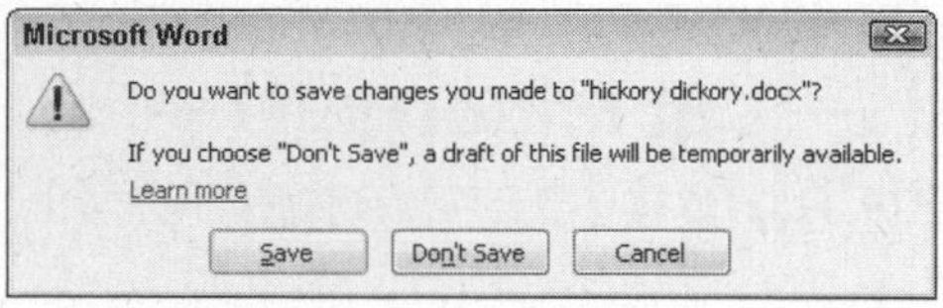

Figure 8-3:
Your last
chance to
save.

Microsoft Word

Do you want to save changes you made to "hickory dickory.docx"?

If you choose "Don't Save", a draft of this file will be temporarily available.
Learn more

[_S_ave]   [Don't Save]   [Cancel]

Here are your options:

Yes: The document is saved. If you've been bad and haven't saved the document even once, the Save As dialog box appears when you choose Yes. See the earlier section "Saving a document the first time."

No: Don't save the document. Any changes made since the document was last saved are lost, or if the document was never saved, the entire thing is lost forever.

Cancel: Word returns you to your document for more editing and stuff.

I recommend choosing the Yes option.

The text that appears about a temporary draft version may not show up every time. See the later section "Recover a Draft" for how to deal with the temporary draft versions of unsaved documents.

Open a Document

Saving a document to disk means nothing unless you have a way to retrieve it. You have several ways to _open_ a document that was previously saved as a file on disk. This section mulls the possibilities.

Using the Open command

Open is the standard computer command used to fetch a document that already exists on the PC's storage system. You use Open to hunt down documents that were previously saved and open them like you're unwrapping a present. The document is then displayed in Word's window as though it has always been there.

To grab a file from disk — to _open_ it — follow these steps:

1. **Choose the Open command from the File tab menu.**

   The Open dialog box materializes, as shown in Figure 8-4.

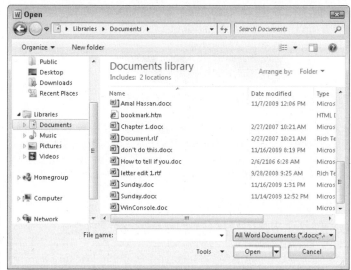

Figure 8-4:
The Open
dialog box.

2. **Choose the document's name with the mouse.**

   The Open dialog box — vast and wild as it is — contains a list of documents previously saved to disk (refer to Figure 8-4). Your job is to find the one you want to open.

   Using the Open dialog box, you can examine various folders on your PC's hard drive, and on any computer network your PC is connected to, to scour for files to open.

3. **Click the Open button.**

   Word opens the highlighted file, carefully lifting it from your PC's storage system and slapping it down on the screen.

After the document is open, you can edit it, just look at it, print it, or do whatever you want.

✔ Opening a document doesn't erase it from the PC's storage system. In fact, the original copy of the file stays on the storage system until you use the Save command to save the document again.

✔ When you open a document, there's no need to use the Save As command to save it again. Simply use the Save command (shortcut: Ctrl+S). That's because the document already has a filename.

- ✔ The shortcut key for the Open command is Ctrl+O.
- ✔ Avoid opening a file on any removable media, such as a digital memory card or an optical disc. Although it's possible, it can lead to headaches later if you remove the media before Word is done with the document. Because of that, I recommend that you use Windows to copy the document from the removable media to the PC's hard drive. Then open it in Word.

Opening a document icon

One way to work on a document is to find its icon in Windows and double-click to open the document. Merely locate a Word document icon in any folder window, from the desktop, or on the Start button's recently opened file list and then double-click, and Word loads that document for editing.

Accessing recently opened files

Word remembers the last several files you've been working on. It keeps them in the Recent list on the File tab menu, as shown in Figure 8-5. Chances are good that you probably need to open one of them, so choosing one from the File tab menu is a handy way to open that document quickly.

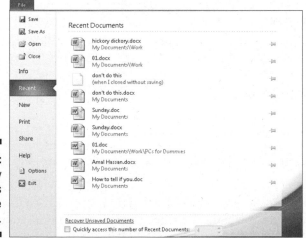

Figure 8-5:
Recently
opened files
on the File
tab menu.

Those pushpins by the document's name allow you to permanently pin a document to the File tab menu. Click a pushpin to "push it in." That makes the document stick around in the list. Clicking the pushpin again allows the document to fade away after a while.

A list of recently opened files appears in Windows 7 on a Jump List: Right-click the Word icon on the taskbar and you see the jump list pop up; choose a recently opened file from that list.

Opening more than one document at a time

Word places no limit on the number of documents you can have open at a time. For example, I'm writing this chapter in one window, and I have two more Word documents open in other windows. If you're like me and tend to work on multiple documents at a time, you can open them all by using the Open command. The secret is simply to select multiple documents and then open them.

For example, in the Open dialog box (refer to Figure 8-4), press and hold the Ctrl key as you click to select multiple documents to open. Click the Open button and they all open in their own, separate windows in Word.

Likewise, you can use the Ctrl key to select multiple Word documents in a folder window in Windows. Press the Enter key to instantly open all those documents.

Also see Chapter 24, which covers working with multiple documents in Word.

Opening one document inside another

A handy trick to pull with the Open command is to stick one document smack dab into the middle of another document. For example, you may have your biography, résumé, or curriculum vitae in a file on disk and want to add that information to the end of a letter begging for a job. If so, or in any other circumstances that I can't think of right now, follow these steps:

1. **Position the insertion pointer where you want the other document's text to appear.**

   The text is inserted at that spot.

2. **Click the Insert tab.**

3. **From the Text group, choose Object⇨Text from File.**

   A dialog box similar to the Open dialog box opens (refer to Figure 8-4).

4. **Choose the icon representing the document you want to insert.**

   You can also use the gadgets and gizmos in the dialog box to locate a file in another folder or on another disk drive or even on someone else's computer on the network. Such power!

5. **Click the Insert button.**

The document you selected is inserted into the current document, just as though you had typed (and formatted) the whole thing right there with your stubby little fingers.

✔ The resulting combined document still has the same name as the first document; the document you inserted remains unchanged.

✔ You can insert any number of documents into another document, one at a time. There's no limit.

✔ Inserting text from one document into another is often called *boilerplating*. For example, you can save a commonly used piece of text in a document and then insert it into other documents as necessary. This process is also the way sleazy romance novels are written.

✔ Biography. Résumé. *Curriculum vitae.* The more important you think you are, the more alien the language used to describe what you've done.

Close a Document

When you're done writing a document, you need to do the electronic equivalent of putting it away. That electronic equivalent is the Close command: Choose the Close command from the File tab menu, or use the handy Ctrl+W keyboard shortcut.

If you haven't saved your document recently, Word prompts you to save before you close; click the Yes button and the document is saved. (If it hasn't yet been saved — shame on you! — you see the Save As dialog box, as described earlier in this chapter).

When the document has been saved, closing it simply removes it from view. At that point, you can quit Word, start up a new document, open a document on disk, or just put away Word and hit another game of Spider Solitaire.

- Refer to Chapter 1 for more quitting options.

- You don't have to choose the Close command. You can choose the Exit command from the File tab menu if you're done with Word, which is almost the same thing: You're prompted to save your document if it needs saving; otherwise, the Exit Word command quits Word rather than keeps the window open.

- You can also just close the Word program window, which closes the document. When you close the last open Word program window, you also quit Word.

Recover a Draft

Computers crash. Users forget to save in a pinch. Or, perhaps some other type of disaster has befallen your unsaved Word document. When the planets are properly aligned and the word processing gods are smiling, it's possible to recover those lost documents, the ones that Word calls *drafts*. Here's how:

1. **Click the File tab.**

2. **Choose Recent from the list.**

    You see the list of recent documents (refer to Figure 8-5). When unsaved drafts are available, you see a link at the bottom of the list: Recover Unsaved Documents.

3. **Click the link Recover Unsaved Documents.**

    An Open dialog box appears.

4. **Choose from the list a document to recover.**

    The document may have an unusual name, especially when it has never been saved.

5. **Click the Open button to open and recover the document.**

The document you recover might not be the one you wanted it to be. If so, try again and choose another document. You might also find that the document doesn't contain all the text you typed or thought would be there. You can't do anything about it, other than *remember to save everything* in the first place!

The recovery of drafts is possible because of Word's AutoRecover feature. Refer to Chapter 31 for more information on AutoRecover.

Chapter 9

Publish Your Document

A long time ago, the final step in creating a document with a word processor was printing. After writing, editing, formatting, and proofing (with lots of document-saving along the way), you printed your masterpiece to show the world. The process was simply called "printing" because there was little else you could do with the document after you were done working on it. Times have changed.

Today, the final step in the word processing saga is *publishing*. No, it doesn't mean that you need to get an agent or shop your book to big New York publishers or face a slew of rejection letters. Publishing a Word document means printing, but it also includes other electronic ways of sharing your document: sending it by e-mail, posting it to a Web site, sticking it on a blog somewhere, or even good ol' printing. It's all publishing.

Your Document on Paper

Getting it down on paper has been the goal of writers ever since paper was invented. The word processor, the best writing tool ever invented, is also the first tool to utterly avoid paper. You can change that situation, however, by using the most traditional method to publish your document: Print it. You use a printer, either attached directly to your computer or available on a network, to create a *hard copy* of your document. You can use a thousand-dollar computer to accomplish what anyone else can do with a little ink and some paper.

Preparing the printer

Before you print a document, I recommend following these steps to ensure that the printer is ready to print something:

1. **Make sure that your printer is plugged in and properly connected to your computer.**

   Refer to my book *PCs For Dummies* for more information on connecting and using a printer and using various printer tips and stuff like that.

2. **Make sure that your laser printer has enough toner or that your ink printer's cartridges are brimming with ink.**

   Laser printers should have a good toner cartridge installed. If the laser printer's Toner Low indicator is on, replace the toner at once.

   Most ink printers let you know when they're out of ink, or you notice that the image appears streaked or faded or is missing information. Replace the ink cartridge at once.

3. **Check the printer for paper.**

   The paper can feed from the back or top or enter from a paper tray, or it can be manually fed one sheet at a time. However your printer eats paper, make sure that you have it properly stocked before you print.

4. **Turn on the printer.**

   You can try to print with the printer turned off, but it takes quite a long time.

5. **Your printer must be *online* or *selected* before you can print anything.**

   This is weird: Some printers can be on but not ready to print. The power is on, but unless the printer is online or selected, it ignores the computer. To force those types of printers to listen to the computer, you must press the Online, Ready, or Select (or similar) button.

When you're certain that the printer is up to the task, you can proceed with the printing operation in Word.

Previewing a document

Before you print, I recommend previewing the look of the final document. Yeah, even though the material you've written is supposed to look the same on the screen as it does on the paper, you may still see surprises: missing page numbers, blank pages, or half pages, for example. The best way to find those surprises before printing is to peruse your document in Full Screen Reading view.

 To get into Full Screen Reading view, click the Full Screen Reading button found on the taskbar (and shown in the margin). The screen changes to show your document, as depicted in Figure 9-1.

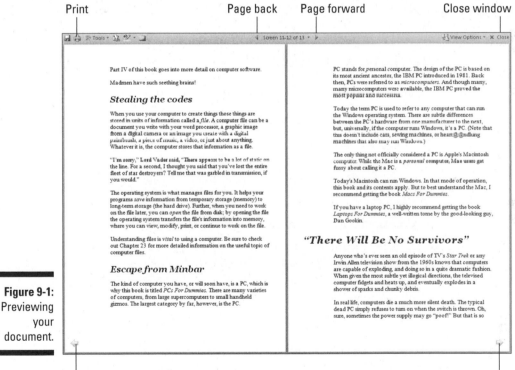

Print   Page back   Page forward   Close window

Page back   Page forward

Figure 9-1: Previewing your document.

Take note of how your text looks on the page. Look at the margins. If you're using footnotes, headers, or footers, look at how they lay out. The idea is to spot something dreadfully wrong *before* you print.

Click the Close button when you finish perusing and previewing your document.

✔ Though you can edit and do other things in Full Screen Reading view, I recommend that you switch back to either Print Layout or Draft view for editing; click the appropriate button on the status bar.

✔ Use the View Options button (refer to Figure 9-1) to control how your document appears in Full Screen Reading view.

✔ The Zoom tool on the status bar can also be used to zoom in or out. In fact, you can zoom out to where you see the entire document displayed as tiny pages on the screen.

✔ Sideways printing, paper sizes, and other document-related options are set when you format your document's pages. These are Word functions, not ones you set when you print. Refer to Chapter 13.

Printing the whole document

Printing the document is easy to do:

1. **Make sure that the printer is on and ready to print.**

2. **Save your document.**

   Ha! Surprised you. Saving before you print is always a good idea. Click the little Save button on the Quick Access toolbar for a quickie save.

3. **Click the File tab.**

4. **Choose the Print command from the File tab's window.**

   You see the document previewed in the File tab window, as shown in Figure 9-2. That's the Print Settings window, and the various interesting items available in that window are pointed out in the figure.

5. **Click the Print button.**

   The File tab window closes and the document spews from your printer.

Printing may take some time — a *long* time. Fortunately, you can continue working while the document prints.

✔ The keyboard shortcut to display the Print window (refer to Figure 9-2) is Ctrl+P.

✔ If nothing prints, don't use the Print command again! There's probably nothing awry; the computer is still thinking or sending information to the printer. If you don't see an error message, everything will probably print, eventually.

✔ The computer prints one copy of your document for every Print command you incant. If the printer is just being slow and you impatiently click the Print button ten times, you print ten copies of your document. (See the section "Canceling a print job," later in this chapter.)

✔ Information on printing only a page or block or another part of a document, is found in the next several sections.

✔ When your document is formatted using a unique paper size, the printer may prompt you to load that paper size. Printing on paper of different sizes is a printer-specific function, not something that Word does. But you set the paper size in Word as part of the page formatting. Refer to Chapter 13.

✔ Manual-feed printers beg for paper before they can print. The printer may say "Feed me paper!" or the ever-popular "PC Load Letter." Like a dutiful mother, you must comply: Stand by the printer, line up the paper, and shove it into the printer's gaping maw until your document has finished printing. Fortunately, there's no need to burp the printer after manually feeding it paper.

✔ Aside from saving your document, you may consider proofreading it before you print. See Chapter 7.

Print the document

Choose printer   Number of copies   Document preview

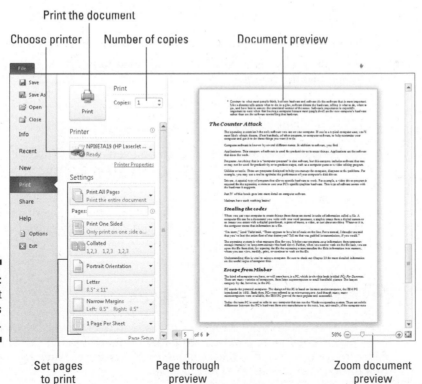

Figure 9-2: The Print Settings window.

Set pages   Page through   Zoom document
to print   preview   preview

Deleting that extra blank page at the end of a document

Occasionally, you may be surprised when your document prints and has one extra page — a blank page. And, it bothers you because you cannot get rid of it! Until now:

To remove the ugly blank page that often roots at the end of your document, press Ctrl+End.

With the insertion pointer at the end of your document, keep pressing the Backspace key until the extra page is gone. How can you tell? Keep an eye on the total page count on the status bar. When that page count decreases by one, you know that the extra page is gone.

Printing a specific page

Follow these steps to print only one page of your document:

1. **Move the insertion pointer so that it's sitting somewhere on the page you want to print.**

   Check the page number on the status bar to ensure that you're on the right page.

2. **Choose the Print command from the File tab menu or press Ctrl+P.**

3. **Click the button beneath the Settings heading and choose Current Page from the menu.**

   The button is illustrated in Figure 9-2.

4. **Click the Print button.**

The single page prints with all the formatting you applied, including footnotes and page numbers and everything else, just as though you plucked that page from a complete printing of the entire document.

Printing a single page in this manner is useful for when you goof up (or the printer goofs up) one page in a document and you need to reprint only that page. Printing only a single page doesn't waste paper.

Printing a range of pages

Word enables you to print a range of pages, odd pages, even pages, or a hodgepodge combination of random pages from within your document. To print a range or group of pages, summon the Printing window by choosing the Print command from the File tab menu.

Your key to printing a range (or hodgepodge) of pages is the Print What button (refer to Figure 9-2).

To print various pages, choose the command Print Custom Range from the button just beneath the Settings heading (refer to Figure 9-2). Then use the Pages text box to input the pages you want to print. For example:

> To print pages 3 through 5, for example, type **3-5**.
>
> To print pages 1 through 7, type **1-7**.
>
> To print pages 2 and 6, type **2,6**.
>
> To print page 3, pages 5 through 9, pages 15 through 17, and page 19 (boy, that coffee went everywhere, didn't it?), you type **3, 5-9, 15-17, 19**.

Click the big Print button when you're ready to print. Only the pages you specify churn from the printer.

Printing a block

After you mark a block of text onscreen, you can beg the Print command to print only that block. Here's how:

1. **Mark the block of text you want to print.**

   See Chapter 6 for all the block-marking instructions in the world.

2. **Choose the Print command from the File tab menu.**

3. **From the button beneath the Settings heading, choose the item Print Selection.**

   The Print Selection item is available only when a block is selected in your document.

4. **Click the Print button.**

The block you selected prints at the same position, with the same formatting (headers and footers) as though you had printed the entire document.

Printing more than one copy of something

Imagine how silly it would be to send your résumé to a company but add that you need your résumé returned because you have only one copy. No, I'm not trying to convince you that buying a photocopier is necessary. Why do that when Word can easily print multiple copies of any document? Here's how:

1. **Choose the Print command from the File tab menu.**

2. **Enter the number of copies in the Copies box.**

   For three copies, for example, click the box and type **3**.

3. **Click the big Print button to print your copies.**

Under normal circumstances, Word prints each copy of the document one after the other. This process is known as *collating*. However, if you're printing seven copies of a document and you want Word to print seven copies of page 1 and then seven copies of page 2 (and so on), choose the option Uncollated from the Collated menu button, found under the Settings heading in the Print Settings window.

Choosing another printer

Your computer can have more than one printer attached. Even small offices and home offices have computers networked and sharing printers. In any case, you can use the Print Settings window in Word to choose which printer to use to print your document.

In the Print Settings window, choose a different printer from the Printer button's drop-down menu. A list of available printers appears; simply choose a printer from the list. Make other settings in the window as well, and then click the big Print button. Your document prints on the printer you've chosen.

- ✔ Yes, you also should check to ensure that the printer you've chosen is on, selected, stocked with paper, and ready to print.

- ✔ Setting up or adding printers is a task you do in Windows, not in Word.

- ✔ Faxing works just like printing, although you're printing to a fax machine over a phone line. In Word, simply choose the fax printer from the list of printers. (You install a fax printer in Windows, not in Word.)

- ✔ For more information on printing and faxing, I recommend my book *PCs For Dummies*.

Canceling a print job

Because you might need to quickly cancel your printing, here goes:

1. **Double-click the li'l printer icon by the current time on the taskbar.**

That little icon appears whenever you print something in Windows. When you open the icon, the printer's window is displayed. It lists any documents waiting to be printed, as shown in Figure 9-3.

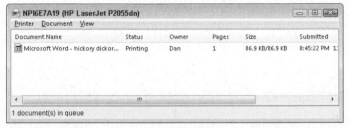

Figure 9-3:
The printer queue.

2. **Click the name of your Word document job on the list.**

3. **Choose Document⇨Cancel.**

   The command may be Document⇨Cancel Printing in some versions of Windows.

4. **Click Yes to terminate the job.**

   The command may be named OK in some versions of Windows.

5. **Close the printer's window when you're done.**

   Choose Printer⇨Close to make the window run away from the desktop. You're zapped back to Word, ready for more editing action.

Note that it may take a while for the printer to stop printing. That's because the printer has its own memory and a few pages of the document may be stored there *and* continue to print even after you tell the printer to stop. (Stupid printer — stupid.)

✔ Stopping a print job is a Windows task, not anything that Word has control over.

✔ If you're using a network printer, you may not be able to cancel printing. Oh, well.

✔ You can use your printer's window (refer to Figure 9-3) to cancel more jobs if you're in an especially vicious mood: Just repeat Steps 2 through 4 for each job you want to sack.

✔ To cancel all documents (the printer *jobs*) waiting to print, choose Printer⇨Cancel All Documents.

✔ Many printers feature a Cancel button. It may have the word *Cancel* on it, or it might just be a big red button or a button with a red X on it. Pressing that button does, after a spell, stop printing. In fact, if your printer has that button, follow the steps in this section first and then click the Cancel button on the printer.

Electronic Publishing

Mr. Bunny likes to live in the forest. It's his home. The forest is full of trees and friendly critters. It's also home to predators who would love to eat Mr. Bunny, but that's not my point. My point is that you can do your part to help save Mr. Bunny's home by publishing your documents electronically. Keep that statement in mind: It's not always necessary to print your documents.

Preparing a document for sharing

There are lots of interesting things you might have put in your Word document that you don't want published. Those items include comments, revision marks, hidden text, and other items useful to you or your collaborators, which would mess up a document you share with others. The solution is to use Word's Check for Issues tool, like this:

1. **Ensure that your document is finished, finalized, and saved.**

2. **Click the File tab.**

   In the File tab window, the Info area should be highlighted. If not, click the word *Info*.

3. **Click the Check For Issues button.**

4. **Choose Inspect Document from the Check for Issues button menu.**

   The Document Inspector window shows up. All items are checked.

5. **Click the Inspect button.**

   After a few moments, the Document Inspector window shows up again, listing any issues, as shown in Figure 9-4. The issues shown are explained, which allows you to cancel out of the Document Inspector to fix individual items.

6. **Click the Remove All button next to any issues you want to clear up.**

   Remember that this step is entirely optional. Now that you know what the issues are, you can always click the Close button and return to your document to manually inspect them.

7. **Click the Close button, or click Reinspect to give your document another once-over.**

8. **Click the Back button to return to your document.**

You can go forward with publishing your document or just continue working.

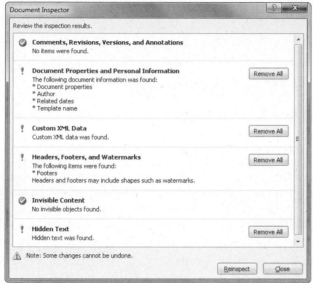

Figure 9-4:
Your
document is
inspected.

Sending a Word document by e-mail

E-mailing your Word document is a snap — as long as you're using Microsoft Outlook as your e-mail program. That opening statement also implies that your organization uses an "Exchange Server." If that's you, great — you can follow these steps to e-mail your document:

1. **Save your document one more time.**

2. **Click the File tab.**

3. **Choose the Save & Send command.**

4. **Choose Send Using E-Mail.**

5. **Click the Send As Attachment button.**

   At this point, Outlook takes over and you compose your e-mail message. When you send the message, your Word document is sent along as well.

If you don't use Outlook (and I don't blame you), you can always send a Word document just as you send any e-mail file attachment. The key is to save the document *and* remember its filename and location so that you can find it later. To attach a Word document to an e-mail message using just about any e-mail program, follow these general steps:

1. **Compose your e-mail message as you normally do.**

2. **Use the Attach command to find the Word document and attach it to the message.**

3. **Send the message.**

Also see the following section.

Saving a Word document in a sharable format

Not everyone can read Word documents. In fact, users of older versions of Word might not be able to read the Word documents you create in Word 2010. To ensure that the files are compatible, you can publish your documents in a more compatible or universal file format. Obey these steps:

1. **Finish your document.**

   Yes, that includes saving it one last time.

2. **Click the File tab.**

3. **Choose the Save & Send command from the File tab menu.**

4. **Choose Change File Type.**

   Use the options in the Save Document list to save your document using another file type, one that would be more compatible than Word's own document file format. Here are my suggestions:

   Word 97-2003 Document (*.doc): This is the most compatible Word file format, ideal for sharing your documents with anyone who has Word. Even Macintosh users can read Word documents saved in this file format.

   Rich Text Format (*.rtf): This file format is compatible with every word processing program now available. In fact, RTF was created so that documents can be shared between different computers and programs.

   Single File Web Page (*.mht, *.mhtml): You're basically creating a Web page document in Word. Almost anyone with a Web browser, which is just about everyone who uses a computer, can read documents saved in this format.

5. **Use the Save As dialog box to save your document in the special file format.**

   You can, if you want, change the document's filename and location. The Save As Type area of the Save As dialog box has preselected the file type you've chosen.

6. **Click the Save button to save your document.**

The document is now saved using the new file type. It's ready for sharing on the Internet, as a Web page attachment or however you need to get it out there.

✔ You can save the document in plain-text format in Step 4: Choose the option Plain Text (*.txt). Even so, rarely does anyone use the plain-text format any more. That format stores no formatting, no fonts, no images. It's just plain old text, but the option is there in case you're requested to save a document that way.

✔ After saving a document in the new file format, you will have changed the document's filename in Word. Check the window's title bar to confirm. To continue editing the original document, you need to close the current document and then reopen that original document.

✔ Yes, it's okay to save the document using the same filename as Word originally chose. That's because the file *type* is different; two files can share the same name as long as they are of different types.

✔ Also see Chapter 24 for more information on using and sharing documents with unusual file formats.

Saving a Word document as a PDF

Another common file format is PDF, the Adobe Acrobat Portable Document Format. It's quite popular, especially on the Internet. Word lets you publish PDF documents easily by following these steps:

1. **From the File tab menu, choose the Save & Send command.**
2. **Choose the option Create PDF/XPS Document.**
3. **Click the big button labeled Create a PDF/XPS.**

   The Publish As PDF or XPS dialog box appears.

4. **If necessary, choose PDF (*.pdf) from the Save As Type drop-down list.**

   You could also choose the XPS file format but, honestly, no one uses it.

5. **Give your document a new filename, if you want, or specify a new location for saving the PDF file.**
6. **Click the Publish button to create the PDF file.**

The document is saved as a PDF file, and then an Adobe Acrobat window opens to display the document.

✔ Unlike saving your document in another file format, saving it as a PDF doesn't change the document's name in Word. (See the preceding section.)

✔ You need a copy of the Adobe Reader program to view PDF files. Don't worry: It's free. Go to www.adobe.com/acrobat.

Part III
Formatting

The 5th Wave   By Rich Tennant

"All I know is I can't get the reflection tool to work in my Word document."

In this part . . .

It all began a long time ago, when someone decided to scratch a line beneath a word or two. I'm sure whoever did it was making a point. He added *emphasis,* but in reality he launched the vast and encompassing topic of text formatting. O what hath he wrought!

Part of composing text is formatting the text. You can format characters, paragraphs, margins, tabs, pages, and entire documents. There's so much to do, in fact, that some people spend more time on formatting than they do on writing. I suppose they think that as long as the document looks good, who cares what they have to say?

Chapter 10

Character Formatting

*J*ust as your body is composed of millions of cells, documents are composed of thousands of characters. Like a cell, a *character* is the basic building block of the document. Characters include letters, symbols, and Aunt Eunice, who claims to talk with squirrels and even knits sweaters for them.

The most basic element you can format in a document is text — the letters, numbers, and characters you type. You can format text to be bold, underlined, italicized, little, or big or in different fonts or colors — all sorts of pretty and distracting attributes. Word gives you a magnificent amount of control over the appearance of your text. This chapter contains the details.

How to Format Characters

You can change the format of your text in two ways:

✔ **Choose a text-formatting command first, and then type the text.** All the text you type is formatted as chosen.

✔ **Type the text first and then select the text as a block and apply the formatting.** This technique works best when you're busy with a thought and need to return to format the text later.

You use both methods as you compose text in your document. Sometimes, it's easier to use a formatting command and type the text in that format. For example:

1. **Type this line:**

   The cake was

2. **Press Ctrl+I to activate *italic text.***

3. **Type this word:**

   really

4. **Press Ctrl+I again, which turns off italic.**

5. **Continue typing:**

   disgusting.

The final sentence looks like this:

The cake was *really* disgusting.

For more complex formatting, type the text first, go back, mark the text as a block, and then apply the formatting. Even so, either way works.

See Chapter 6 for more information on marking blocks of text.

Basic Character Formatting

Word stores some of the most common text-formatting commands on the Home tab, in the Font group, as shown in Figure 10-1. The command buttons in that group carry out most of the basic text formatting you use in Word. This section mulls over the possibilities.

✔ Text can also be formatted by using the Mini toolbar, which appears whenever you select text. Refer to Chapter 6.

✔ The Font group can help you quickly determine which formatting is applied to your text. For example, in Figure 10-1, the text where the insertion pointer is blinking is formatted in the Calibri font. The number 11 tells you that the text is 11 points tall. If the B button were highlighted, you would also know that the text was formatted in bold. (These text formats are discussed throughout this section.)

Figure 10-1:
Text-
formatting
gizmos.

Changing the font

The most basic attribute of text is its *typeface,* or *font.* The font sets up the way your text looks — its overall text style. Although deciding on a proper font may be agonizing, and indeed many graphic artists are paid well to choose just the right font, the task of selecting a font in Word is quite easy. It generally goes like this:

1. **On the Home tab, in the Font group, click the down arrow to display the Font Face list.**

   A menu of font options appears, as shown in Figure 10-2.

Figure 10-2:
The Fonts
list.

The top part of the menu shows fonts associated with the document *theme*. The next section contains fonts you've chosen recently, which is handy for reusing fonts. The rest of the list, which can be quite long, shows all fonts in Windows that are available to Word.

2. Scroll to the font you want.

The fonts in the All Fonts part of the list are displayed in alphabetical order as well as in context (as they appear when printed).

3. Click to select a font.

You can also use the Font menu to preview the look of fonts. Scroll through the list to see which fonts are available and how they may look. As you move the mouse over a font, any selected text in your document is visually updated to show how that text would look in that font. (Note that no changes are made until you select the new font.)

- ✔ When no font is displayed in the Font group (the listing is blank), it means that more than one font is being used in the selected block of text.

- ✔ You can quickly scroll to a specific part of the menu by typing the first letter of the font you need, such as T for Times New Roman.

- ✔ Graphic designers prefer to use two fonts in a document — one for the text and one for headings and titles. Word is configured this way as well. The font you see with `Body` after its name is the current text, or *body,* font. The font marked as `Heading` is used for headings. These two fonts are part of the document theme.

- ✔ Refer to Chapter 16 for more information on document themes.

- ✔ Fonts are the responsibility of Windows, not Word. Thousands of fonts are available for Windows, and they work in all Windows applications.

Applying character formats

The Font group lists some of the most common character formats. They're applied in addition to the font. In fact, they enhance the font. Use them as you see fit:

To make text bold, press Ctrl+B or click the Bold command button.

Use **bold** to make text stand out on a page — for titles and captions or when you're uncontrollably angry.

To make text italic, press Ctrl+I or click the Italic command button.

Italic has replaced underlining as the preferred text-emphasis format. Italicized text is light and wispy, poetic and free.

Underline text by pressing Ctrl+U or click the Underline command button. You can click the down arrow next to the Underline command button to choose from a variety of underline styles or set an underline color.

 Strike through text by clicking the Strikethrough command button. (There's no keyboard shortcut for this one.)

I don't know why strikethrough text made it to the Font group. If I were king of Microsoft, I would have put small caps up there instead. But, who am I? Strikethrough is commonly used in legal documents, and when you mean to say something but then ~~change your mind~~ think of something better to say.

 Make text subscript by pressing Ctrl+= (equal) or clicking the Subscript command button.

Subscript text appears below the baseline, such as the 2 in H_2O. Again, I'm puzzled about how this formatting command ranks up there with bold and italic. I suppose that there's a lot of subscripting going on somewhere.

 Make text superscript by pressing Ctrl+Shift+= (equal sign) or clicking the Superscript command button.

Superscript text appears above the line, such as the 10 in 2^{10}.

More text formats are available in Word, such as small caps, outline, and shadow. These can be accessed from the Font dialog box. Refer to the section "Text Formatting with the Font Dialog Box," later in this chapter.

✔ Basic character formatting affects only selected text or any new text you type.

✔ To turn off a text attribute, use the command again. For example, press Ctrl+I to type in *italic*. Then press Ctrl+I again to return to normal text.

✔ You can mix and match character formats. For example, press Ctrl+B and then Ctrl+I to apply bold and italic text. You press Ctrl+B and Ctrl+I, or the command buttons, to turn off those attributes again.

✔ The best way to use superscript or subscript is to write text first. Then go back, mark as a block the text you want to superscript or subscript, and *then* use these commands. So 42 becomes 4^2 and CnH2n+1OH becomes $C_nH_{2n+1}OH$. Otherwise, when you apply super- or subscript, the text you modify tends to be rather teensy and hard to edit. Better to write it first and then format.

✔ If you can remember that Ctrl+= adds subscript, just press the Shift key to apply Ctrl+Shift+= for superscript — if you can remember.

✔ When will the Underline text attribute die? I'm baffled. Honestly, I think we're waiting for the last typewriter-clutching librarian from the 1950s to pass on before underlining is officially gone as a text attribute. And please don't fall prey to the old rule about underlining book titles. It's *Crime and Punishment,* not <u>Crime and Punishment.</u>

Using less-common character attributes

Here are a few more text attributes: Call them second-string players. You may not use these as often as bold or italics, but Word makes them available to you just as well:

To switch to all caps text, press Ctrl+Shift+A. This is a text format, not applied by pressing the Shift or Caps Lock key. In fact, like other formats, it can be removed.

To set double-underlined text, press Ctrl+Shift+D. <u>This text is double-underlined</u>.

You create hidden text by pressing Ctrl+Shift+H. Hidden text is good for what it says — hiding text in a document. Of course, you don't see the text onscreen, either. To show hidden text, click the Show/Hide command button (in the Paragraph Group on the Write tab) as described in Chapter 2, in the section about spots and clutter in your text. The hidden text shows up in the document with a dotted underline.

To get small caps, press Ctrl+Shift+K. Small caps is ideal for headings. I use it for character names when I write a script or play:

> Bill. That's a clever way to smuggle a live grenade into prison.

To underline just words, and not the spaces between words, press Ctrl+Shift+W. <u>Word</u> <u>underline</u> <u>looks</u> <u>like</u> <u>this</u>.

Text Transcending Teeny to Titanic

Text size is considered a text format in Word. You can choose the size of your text, from indecipherably small to monstrously huge. Of course, more common is the subtle text-size adjustment; rare is the student who hasn't fudged the length of a term paper by inching up the text size a notch or two.

Understanding points

Word (and Windows) deals with text size as measured in *points*. It's a typesetting term. One point is equal to $\frac{1}{72}$ inch. Don't bother memorizing it. Instead, here are some point pointers:

- The bigger the point size, the larger the text.
- Most printed text is either 10 or 12 points tall.

✔ Headings are typically 14 to 24 points tall.

✔ Most fonts can be sized from 1 point to 1,638 points. Point sizes smaller than 6 are generally too small for a human to read.

✔ Seventy-two points is equal (roughly) to 1-inch-high letters.

✔ The point size of text is a measure from the bottom of the descender to the top of the ascender — from the bottom of the lowercase *p* to the top of the capital *E,* for example. So, the typical letter in a font is smaller than its given font size. In fact, depending on the font design, text formatted at the same size but with different fonts *(typefaces)* may not appear to be the same size. That's just one of those typesetting oddities that causes regular computer users to start binge drinking.

Setting the text size

Text size is set in the Font group on the Home tab. Just to the right of the Font box is the Size box (refer to Figure 10-1). Clicking the down arrow displays a list of font sizes for your text, as shown in Figure 10-3.

Figure 10-3: Select a font size from this list.

The Size menu lists only common text sizes. To set the text size to a value that isn't listed or to a specific value, type the value into the box. For example, to set the font size to 11.5, click in the Size box and type **11.5**.

You can preview the new text size by pointing the mouse at an item on the Size menu. The word under the insertion pointer, or a selected block of text, is updated on the screen to reflect the new size. Click to choose a size or press Esc to cancel.

Nudging text size

Sometimes, choosing text size is like hanging a picture: To make the picture level on the wall, you have to nudge it just a little bit this way and that. Word has similar tools for nudging the text size larger or smaller, two of which are found in the Font group.

 To increase the font size, click the Grow Font command button or press Ctrl+Shift+>.

The Grow Font command nudges the font size up to the next value as listed on the Size menu (refer to Figure 10-3). So, if the text is 12 points, the Grow Font command increases its size to 14 points.

 To decrease the font size, click the Shrink Font command button or press Ctrl+Shift+<.

The Shrink Font command works in the opposite direction of the Grow Font command, by reducing the text size to the next-lower value as displayed on the Size menu (refer to Figure 10-3).

I remember the Grow and Shrink keyboard commands easily because the greater-than symbol is > and the less-than symbol is <. Just think, "I'm making my text *greater than* its current size" when you press Ctrl+Shift+> or "I'm making my text *less than* its current size" when you press Ctrl+Shift+<.

 When you want to increase or decrease the font size by smaller increments, use these shortcut keys:

Ctrl+] Makes text one point size larger

Ctrl+[Makes text one point size smaller

More Colorful Characters

Adding color to your text doesn't make your writing more colorful. All it does is make you wish that you had more color ink when it's time to print your document. Regardless, you can splash around color on your text and there's no need to place a drop cloth in the document's footer.

 Text color is applied by clicking the Font Color command button. The bar below the *A* on the Font Color command button indicates which color is applied to text.

To change the color, you must click the menu arrow just to the right of the Font Color command button. A color menu appears, as shown in Figure 10-4; as you move the mouse pointer over various colors, selected text in your document is updated to reflect that color. When you find the color you like, click it. That color then becomes the new text color associated with the Font Color command button.

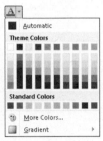

Figure 10-4:
Selecting a
color
for text.

✔ Theme colors are associated with the document theme. Refer to Chapter 16.

✔ Select the More Colors item to display the special Colors dialog box. Use the dialog box to craft your own, custom colors.

✔ The *Automatic* color refers to the color defined for the text style you're using. Refer to Chapter 15 for more information on styles.

✔ The Font Color command affects only the text color, not the background. To color the background, you use the Shading command, covered in Chapter 18.

✔ Colored text prints only when a color printer is available and readily stocked with color ink. Refer to Chapter 9 for more information on printing documents.

✔ Be careful with the colors you use! Faint colors can make your text extremely difficult to read. Choose your text color wisely.

✔ Be careful not to confuse the Font Color command button with the Text Highlight Color command button, to its left. Text highlighting is a text attribute, but it's best used for document markup. See Chapter 26.

Text Formatting with the Font Dialog Box

Word has a place where all your font-formatting delights are kept in a neatly organized fashion. It's the Font dialog box, shown in Figure 10-5.

To summon the Font dialog box, click the Dialog Box Launcher button in the lower-right corner of the Font group or press Ctrl+D.

The Font dialog box contains *all* the commands for formatting text, including quite a few that didn't find their way into the Font group. As with all text formatting, the commands you choose in the Font dialog box affect any new text you type or any selected text in your document.

When you're done setting up your font stuff, click the OK button. Or, click Cancel if you're just visiting.

✔ The best benefit of the Font dialog box is the Preview window, at the bottom. That window shows you exactly how your choices affect text in your document.

✔ The Font names *+Body* and *+Heading* refer to the fonts selected by the current document theme. This is done so that you can use Word's theme commands to quickly change body and heading fonts for an entire document all at one time.

✔ Use the festive attributes — such as Shadow, Outline, Emboss, or Engrave — for titles and headings.

✔ You can use the Advanced tab in the Font dialog box to set options for changing the size and position of text on a line.

✔ The Font dialog box can also be accessed from the Find dialog box or the Find and Replace dialog box. This feature helps you to search for, or search and replace, specific text formatting in a document.

✔ You can mark all similar text formatting in a document as a block by right-clicking a bit of text and choosing Styles⇨Select Text with Similar Formatting. That way, you can universally change similar text in a document without doing a search-and-replace for text formats. Also see Chapter 6 for more block-marking information.

✔ The Set As Default button in the Font dialog box is used to change the font that Word uses when you're creating a new document. If you prefer to use a specific font for all your documents, choose the font (plus other text attributes) in the Font dialog box and then click the Set As Default button. Click the Yes button to answer the question about changing the Normal template. Afterward, all documents start with the new default font you've selected.

Changing Text Case

Believe it or not, upper- and lowercase have something to do with a font. Back in the old days of mechanical type, a font came in a case, like a briefcase. The top part of the case, the upper case, held the capital letters. The bottom part of the case held the non-capital letters. So, in a way, changing the case of text is a font-formatting trick.

To change the case of text in Word, use the Change Case command button in the Font group. Choosing that button displays a menu of options, shown in Figure 10-6. Select the text you want to change, and then choose the proper item from the Change Case command button. Your text is modified to match the menu item that's selected.

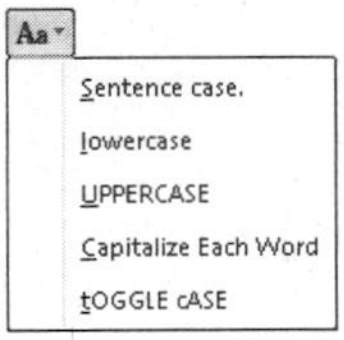

Figure 10-6:
Change
Case com-
mand button
menu.

You can also use the Shift+F3 command to change the case of selected text. But that keyboard shortcut cycles between only three of the menu options shown in the figure: ALL CAPS, lowercase, and Capitalize Each Word.

Removing Character Formatting

So many Word formatting commands are available that it's possible for your text to look more like a pile of formatting remnants than anything readable in any human language. Word understands this problem, so it created the Clear Formatting command to let you peel away all formats from your text, just like you peel the skin from a banana:

 To peel away formatting from a block of selected text, or the text the insertion pointer is on, or future text you type, use the Clear Formatting command button in the Font group or press Ctrl+spacebar.

The Clear Formatting command removes any formats you've applied to the text: font, size, text attributes (bold or italic), and color.

✔ Another key combination for Ctrl+spacebar is Ctrl+Shift+Z. Remember that Ctrl+Z is the Undo command. To undo formatting, all you do is add the Shift key, which may make sense — well, heck, if any of this makes sense.

✔ The Clear Formatting command removes the ALL CAPS text format but doesn't change the case of text you've created by using Shift, Caps Lock, or the Change Case command in Word.

 ✔ Technically, the Ctrl+spacebar command restores characters to the formatting defined by the *style* you're using. So, if the Body style is 12-point Calibri, pressing Ctrl+spacebar restores that font and size. Don't let this information upset or confuse you! Instead, turn to Chapter 15 for more information on Word styles.

Chapter 11
Paragraph Formatting

. . . .

. . . .

Paragraphs are goodly sized chunks of text. In school, you were probably taught that a paragraph must consist of one or more sentences expressing a thought. Or something. Anyway, I view a paragraph, formatting-wise, as a veritable text sandwich, bulky enough to qualify for its own round of formatting commands: A paragraph has left and right margins, a top and a bottom, a before and an after, plus space in the middle.

Word provides ample tools for formatting paragraphs of text. There's a simple way, for example, to automatically indent the first line of a paragraph. Imagine! That and other amazing formatting tricks, all designed to impress and inspire, are found in this handy chapter.

How to Format a Paragraph

You can format a paragraph in Word several ways:

✔ Use a paragraph-formatting command and then type a new paragraph in that format.

✔ Use the formatting command in a single paragraph to format that paragraph. (Place the insertion pointer in a paragraph, and then use a formatting command.)

✔ Use the formatting command on a block of selected paragraphs to format them all together.

Then again, what is a paragraph? It's a chunk of text larger than a character, word, or sentence, but a paragraph can be a single character, word, and sentence. The secret is the Enter key: A *paragraph* is a chunk of text that ends when you press the Enter key. So, as long as you type a single character, word, or sentence and then press Enter, you have a paragraph.

✔ Paragraph formatting commands affect either the paragraph the insertion pointer lurks in or any paragraphs marked as a block (selected).

✔ Refer to Chapter 6 for specific and entertaining block-marking instructions.

✔ You can format all paragraphs in a document by first selecting the entire document. The quick way to do it is to press the Ctrl+A key combination.

✔ To format individual characters or the text inside a paragraph, refer to Chapter 10.

✔ Some folks like to see the Enter key symbol (¶) in their documents, visually marking the end of each paragraph. You can do this in Word by choosing the Options command from the File tab menu. Click Display on the left side of the Word Options dialog box. On the right side, put a check mark by Paragraph Marks. Click OK. Now, every time you press the Enter key, a ¶ symbol appears at the end of the paragraph.

Where the Paragraph Formatting Commands Lurk

Word gathered some of the most popular paragraph-formatting commands into the Paragraph group, found on the Home tab. Figure 11-1 illustrates the Paragraph group, although you should note that Word may show a different arrangement of the command buttons depending on the Word window's width.

Figure 11-1:
Home tab
Paragraph
stuff.

Dialog Box
Launcher button

In an odd twist, indenting and paragraph spacing are found in another Paragraph group, this one on the Page Layout tab, shown in Figure 11-2.

Figure 11-2:
Page
Layout tab
Paragraph
things.

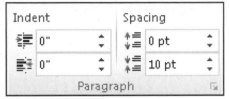

Because many of the paragraph-formatting commands require you to enter values, there also exists a Paragraph dialog box, shown in Figure 11-3. In it, you find some finer controls that the command buttons just don't offer.

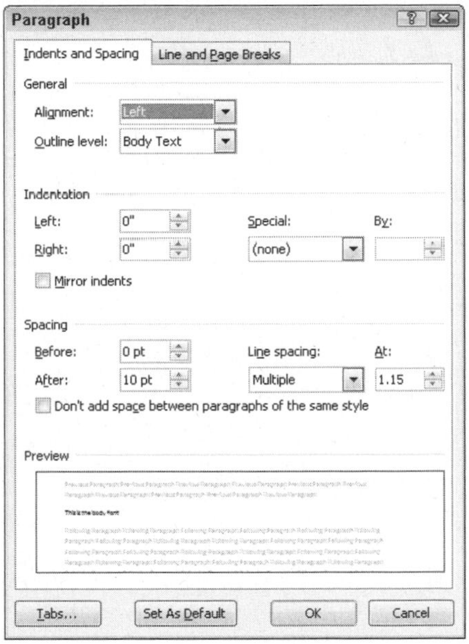

Figure 11-3:
The
Paragraph
dialog box.

To summon the Paragraph dialog box, click the Dialog Box Launcher button (shown in Figure 11-1), found in the lower-right corner of the Paragraph group. Or, you can use the forgettable keyboard shortcut Alt+H, P, G.

The commands in the various paragraph-formatting locations are covered throughout the rest of this chapter.

Click the Cancel button or press the Esc key to dismiss the Paragraph dialog box.

The Mini toolbar, which shows up after you select text, also contains a smattering of paragraph-formatting buttons. Refer to Chapter 6 for more information on the Mini toolbar.

Paragraph Justification and Alignment

Paragraph alignment has nothing to do with politics, and justification has nothing to do with the right or wrong of how paragraphs are formatted. Instead, both terms refer to how the left and right edges of the paragraph look on a page. The four options are Left, Center, Right, and Fully Justified, each covered in this section.

Line up on the left!

Much to the pleasure of southpaws the English-speaking world over, left-aligning a paragraph is considered normal: The left side of the paragraph is all even and tidy, and the right side is jagged, not lined up.

To left-align a paragraph, press Ctrl+L or click the Align Left command button.

- ✔ This type of alignment is also known as *ragged right*.
- ✔ Left-aligning a paragraph is how you "undo" the other types of alignment.

Everyone center!

Centering a paragraph places each line in that paragraph in the middle of the page, with an equal amount of space to the line's right or left.

To center a paragraph, press Ctrl+E or use the Center command button.

- ✔ Centering is ideal for titles and single lines of text. It's ugly for paragraphs and makes reading your text more difficult.
- ✔ You can center a single word in the middle of a line by using the center tab. Refer to Chapter 12 for the details.

Line up on the right!

A *right-aligned* paragraph has its right margin nice and even. The left margin, however, is jagged. When do you use this type of formatting? I have no idea, but it sure feels funky typing a right-aligned paragraph.

 To flush your text along the right side of the page, press Ctrl+R or click the Align Right command button.

✔ This type of alignment is also known as *ragged left* or *flush right*.

✔ You can right-justify text on a single line by using a right-align tab. Refer to Chapter 12 for more info.

Line up on both sides!

Lining up both sides of a paragraph is *full justification:* Both the left and right sides of a paragraph are neat and tidy, flush with the margins.

 To give your paragraph full justification, press Ctrl+J or click the Justify command button.

✔ Fully justified paragraph formatting is often used in newspapers and magazines, which makes the thin columns of text easier to read.

✔ Word makes each side of the paragraph line up by inserting tiny slivers of extra space between the words in a paragraph.

Make Room Before, After, or Inside Paragraphs

Word lets you add "air" to the space before or after or in the middle of your paragraphs. In the middle of the paragraph you have line spacing. Before and after the paragraph comes paragraph spacing. Figure 11-4 shows you where the spacing can be found. The following sections describe how to control that spacing.

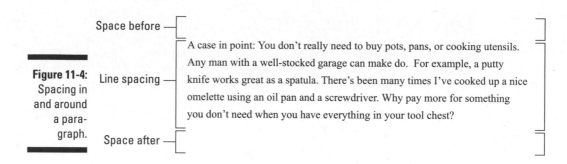

Space before —

Line spacing —

A case in point: You don't really need to buy pots, pans, or cooking utensils. Any man with a well-stocked garage can make do. For example, a putty knife works great as a spatula. There's been many times I've cooked up a nice omelette using an oil pan and a screwdriver. Why pay more for something you don't need when you have everything in your tool chest?

Space after —

Figure 11-4: Spacing in and around a paragraph.

Setting the line spacing

Changing the line spacing inserts extra space between *all* lines of text in a paragraph. Because Word adds the space *below* each line of text in the paragraph, the last line in the paragraph will also have a little extra space after it.

The Line Spacing command button displays a menu listing common line-spacing commands, as shown in Figure 11-5. Choose a new line-spacing value from that list to change the line spacing for the current paragraph or all paragraphs selected as a block.

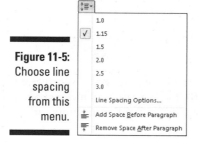

Figure 11-5: Choose line spacing from this menu.

✔ Word sets line spacing at 1.15 as its standard, or *default*. Supposedly, that extra .15 lines of text makes text more readable than using single spacing, or 1.0.

✔ In double spacing, or the line spacing value 2.0, one line of text appears with one blank line below it. Triple spacing, 3.0, makes one line of text appear with two blank lines below it.

✔ Ah! The keyboard shortcuts:

- To single-space, press Ctrl+1.

- To double-space, press Ctrl+2.

- To use 1½-spaced lines, press Ctrl+5.

✔ Yes, Ctrl+5 applies 1½-line spacing, not 5-line spacing. Use the 5 key on the typewriter area of the computer keyboard. Pressing the 5 key on the numeric keypad activates the Select All command.

✔ There's no such thing as having no line spacing. If you want to "remove" fancy line spacing, select some text and press Ctrl+1 for single spacing.

✔ When you want text to stack up one line atop another line, you use the *soft return*. See the section in Chapter 4 about soft and hard returns.

Setting specific line spacing options

To set the line spacing to a value other than the items shown in the previous section (refer to Figure 11-5), you summon the Paragraph dialog box, as described earlier in this chapter and shown in Figure 11-3.

In the Spacing area of the dialog box, the Line Spacing drop-down list is used to set various line-spacing values: Single, 1.5, and Double, just like the Line Spacing command button menu.

Additional options in the Line Spacing drop-down list require you to also use the At box. Values you set in the At box indicate line spacing as described in this list:

✔ **At least:** The line spacing is set to the specified value, which Word treats as a minimum value. Word can disobey that value and add more space whenever necessary to make room for larger type, different fonts, or graphics on the same line of text.

✔ **Exactly:** Word uses the specified line spacing and doesn't adjust the spacing to accommodate for larger text or graphics.

✔ **Multiple:** This option is used to enter line-spacing values other than those specified in the drop-down list. For example, to set the line spacing to 4, choose Multiple from the Line Spacing drop-down list and type **4** in the At box. Word's 1.15 line spacing value is set with the Multiple option.

You can specify values in the At box in increments of 0.1. So, when you want to tighten up text on a page, select all paragraphs on that page, choose Multiple from the Line Spacing drop-down list, and then type **0.9** in the At box. Or, to add more room subtly, type **1.2**.

Click the OK button to confirm your settings and close the Paragraph dialog box.

Making space between paragraphs

It's a silly thing to do: Press Enter twice to end a paragraph. People say that they need the extra space between the paragraphs, but what they don't realize is that Word can add that space for you, automatically. Here's how:

1. **Position the insertion pointer in the paragraph or paragraphs that you want more air around, or mark a block of paragraphs to affect them all.**

2. **Check the point size of your text.**

   It's listed on the Home tab, in the Font group.

3. **Click the Page Layout tab.**

4. **Use the After button in the Paragraph group to add space after the paragraph .**

   As you adjust the value, the paragraphs grow extra spacing.

For example, if your text size is 12, click the up arrow next to After until the value 12 appears in the box. This action adds 12 points, or one blank line, of space after each paragraph you type.

The space you add to the paragraph becomes part of its format, just like line spacing would, although the space afterward appears only *after* the paragraph's text. (You can see this space if you select the paragraph as a block.)

Most of the time, space is added following a paragraph, as just described. Word also lets you add space before a paragraph. For example, you can do this to further separate a document heading or subhead from the preceding paragraph. To add the space before, repeat the preceding steps and put a value in the Before box in Step 4.

- ✔ You can manually enter values in the After (or Before) box. But remember that the values are *points,* not inches or potrzebies.

- ✔ The spacing before or after a paragraph can also be set in the Paragraph dialog box.

- ✔ This trick is a great way to spread out a list of bullet points or numbered steps without affecting the line spacing within the bullet points or steps.

- ✔ Refer to Chapter 10 for more information points as they relate to text size.

✔ Adding space before or after a paragraph isn't the same as double-spacing the text inside the paragraph. In fact, adding space around a paragraph doesn't change the paragraph's line spacing.

Paragraph Indentation

Do you suffer from the shame of manual paragraph indenting? It's a hidden secret. Yes, even though computers enjoy doing tasks automatically, too many Word users still begin a paragraph of text by pressing the Tab key. It's ugly, but it's a topic that must be discussed.

Word can indent your paragraphs for you: left side, right side, both sides, or maybe just the first line. It can even outdent the first line, which is truly something to behold. This section discusses various paragraph-indenting and -outdenting options.

Indenting the first line of a paragraph

To have Word automatically indent the first line of every paragraph you type, heed these steps:

1. **Conjure up the Paragraph dialog box.**

   Refer to the section "Where the Paragraph Formatting Commands Lurk," earlier in this chapter, for proper conjuring incantations plus a bonus picture of what the Paragraph dialog box looks like (refer to Figure 11-3).

2. **In the Indentation area, locate the Special drop-down list.**

3. **Select First Line from the list.**

4. **Enter an amount in the By box (optional).**

   Unless you've messed with the settings, the box should automatically say 0.5", which means that Word automatically indents the first line of every paragraph a half-inch — one tab stop. Type another value if you want your indents to be more or less outrageous. (Items are measured here in inches, not in points.)

5. **Click OK.**

   The selected block, or the current paragraph (and the remaining paragraphs you type), all automatically has an indented first line.

To remove the first-line indent from a paragraph, repeat these steps and select (none) from the drop-down list in Step 3. Then click the OK button.

 Word's AutoCorrect feature can perform these steps for you, but it's tricky. First you must type the paragraph. Then go back to the start of the paragraph and press the Tab key. This action instantly fixes the paragraph indentation (if AutoCorrect is on), and you see the AutoCorrect icon on the screen. Here's the secret: Ignore the AutoCorrect icon and your paragraph indenting is fixed. *Ta-da!*

 You have two ways to separate paragraphs from each other in a document. The first is to add space between each paragraph, which is covered in the earlier section "Making space between paragraphs." The second way is to indent each paragraph's first line, as covered in this section. Choose one or the other — no need to use both.

Making a hanging indent (an outdent)

A *hanging indent* isn't in imminent peril, nor can it affect the outcome of an election. Instead, it's a paragraph in which the first line sticks out to the left and the rest of the paragraph is indented. It's a preferred way to present paragraph lists — like this:

Snore putty: It works every time. Just apply a little snore putty to your partner's mouth and nostrils. In just moments, that rattling din is gone and you're back to sleeping comfortably.

To create such a beast, position the insertion pointer in the paragraph you want to hang and indent. Press Ctrl+T, the Hanging Indent keyboard shortcut.

Because you probably won't remember Ctrl+T all the time (who could?), paragraphs can also be hanged and indented in the Paragraph dialog box. Follow the steps from the previous section, but in Step 3 choose Hanging from the drop-down list.

- As a bonus, every time you press Ctrl+T, your paragraph is indented by another half-inch.
- To undo a hanging indent, press Ctrl+Shift+T. That's the unhang key combination, and it puts your paragraph's neck back in shape.

Indenting a whole paragraph

Just as you can indent the first line of a paragraph, you can indent every line of a paragraph, by moving the paragraph's left margin over to the right a notch, just like Mr. Bunny: Hop, hop, hop. This technique is popular for typing block quotes or *nested* paragraphs.

 To indent a paragraph one tab stop from the left, click the Increase Indent command button in the Home tab's Paragraph group or press Ctrl+M.

 To unindent an indented paragraph, click the Decrease Indent command button in the Home tab's Paragraph group or press Ctrl+Shift+M.

Each time you use the Increase Indent command, the paragraph's left edge hops over one tab stop (typically, one half-inch). To undo this and shuffle the paragraph back to the left, use the Decrease Indent command.

When you want to get specific, you can set the left and right indents for a paragraph by using the Page Layout tab's Paragraph group. (Refer to Figure 11-2). The Left item sets the indentation for the paragraph's left edge. The Right item sets the indentation for the paragraph's right edge.

- ✔ Indenting a paragraph doesn't affect the paragraph's alignment.

- ✔ To indent both the left and right sides of a paragraph set both left and right indents to the same value.

- ✔ To undo any paragraph indenting, set both Left and Right indent values to zero.

- ✔ Although the Ctrl+M and Ctrl+Shift+M shortcuts aren't mnemonic, their only difference is a Shift key. So, after you get used to using them (hopefully, before the afterlife), they're easy to remember.

- ✔ Setting positive values for the paragraph's indent in the Page Layout tab's Paragraph group moves the paragraph's edges inward. Setting negative values moves the edges outward. When the values are set to zero, the paragraph's margins match the page's margin.

- ✔ You cannot decrease the indent beyond the left margin of the page.

- ✔ Refer to Chapter 13 for more information on the page margins.

- ✔ Use the Mirror Indents check box in the Paragraph dialog box to set the inside (toward the fold between the pages) and outside (toward the edges) margins so that an indented paragraph on one page mirrors the paragraph on the opposite page.

 ✔ Do not try to mix left and right indenting with a first-line indent or hanging indent while drowsy or while operating heavy equipment.

Who Died and Made This Thing Ruler?

Paragraph formatting can be confusing. Two places on the Ribbon are for paragraph formatting, or if you opt instead to use the Paragraph dialog box, your mind may go into shock from the abundance of options. A more graphical, and therefore more fun, way to manipulate a paragraph's indentation and margins is to use the Ruler.

 The Ruler may be hidden in your copy of Word. To show the Ruler, click the View Ruler button, found atop the vertical (right) scroll bar. Likewise, to hide the Ruler, click the button again.

The Ruler appears on the top of the writing part of the Word window, shown in Figure 11-6. In Print Layout view, a vertical ruler also shows up and runs down the left side of the window. (That ruler is just for show.)

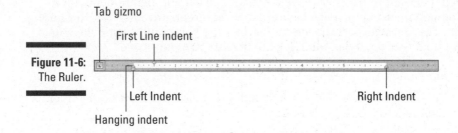

Figure 11-6:
The Ruler.

The dark gray part of the Ruler (outside ends) is beyond the page margins. The lighter gray part is inside the page margins, and the Ruler measures that space from the left, starting with zero inches.

On the Ruler, and illustrated in Figure 11-6, you find four gizmos that control paragraph indenting: one downward-pointing triangle, two upward-pointing triangles, and one block. Those gizmos reflect the current paragraph formatting, and they can be manipulated with the mouse to change the paragraph formatting. The next few paragraphs describe the settings they control:

 To adjust a paragraph's right margin, grab the Right Indent guy on the ruler and drag him to the right or left.

 To adjust the paragraph's left margin, grab the Left Indent thing on the Ruler and slide it to the left or right. Note that this gizmo moves both the Hanging Indent and First Line Indent guys together.

 The paragraph's first line can be set independently of the left margin by dragging the First Line Indent doojobbie to the left or right.

 The Hanging Indent thing controls all lines in the paragraph except for the first one. Normally, you don't mess with this gizmo: Use the Left Indent guy to set the paragraph's left margin. The exception is for creating a hanging indent, which is probably why this gizmo has such a clever name.

✔ The Ruler measures from the page's left margin, not from the left edge of the page.

✔ The page's left margin is set when you format a page of text. See Chapter 13.

✔ The Tab gizmo is used to set the various tab stops used in Word. This confusing and frustrating subject is covered in Chapter 12.

✔ The Ruler works fine for visually setting indents, but when you need to be precise, use the Paragraph dialog box.

Paragraph-formatting survival guide

This table contains all the paragraph-formatting commands you can summon by holding down the Ctrl key and pressing a letter or number. By no means should you memorize this list.

Format	Key Combination	Command Button
Center	Ctrl+E	≡
Fully justify	Ctrl+J	≣
Left-align (flush left)	Ctrl+L	≣
Right-align (flush right)	Ctrl+R	≣
Indent	Ctrl+M	
Unindent	Ctrl+Shift+M	⇥≣
Hanging indent	Ctrl+T	⇥≣
Unhanging indent	Ctrl+Shift+T	
Line spacing	Alt+H, K	
Single-space lines	Ctrl+1	↕≣▾
1.15 line spacing	Ctrl+0	
Double-space lines	Ctrl+2	
1½-space lines	Ctrl+5	

Chapter 12

Tab Formatting

. . . .

. . . .

The tab is one of the handiest and most overlooked and frustrating things in all of Word. By using tabs, you can quickly line up text, create lists, and format tables nice and neat. Yet most folks don't bother with tabs because, honestly, Word doesn't handle them in anything approaching a logical, friendly manner. Because of that frustration, and even though the tab is a part of paragraph formatting, I decided to create a special chapter just on the topic of using tabs in Word.

Once Upon a Tab

On my ancient Underwood typewriter, the Tab key is on the right side of the keyboard and is named Tabular Key. Elsewhere, I've seen it named Tabulator. In each case, the root word is *table*. The Tab key is used to help build tables or to organize information in a tabular way.

Pressing the Tab key in Word inserts a tab *character* into your document. That tab character works like a wide space character, where its size is determined by the tab stop. The *tab stop* is a predefined location marked across a page — say, every half-inch — although in Word you can set tab stops at any interval.

It's the tab stop that makes the Tab key work: Press the Tab key, and the insertion pointer hops over to the next tab stop. That way, you can line up text on multiple lines with tabs and tab stops, keeping things nice and even — definitely much nicer than trying to fudge and line up text with the spacebar.

 Tabs can be set in Word by using the Tabs dialog box or, better, by using the Ruler, shown in Figure 12-1. To make the Ruler visible, click the View Ruler button, which is found roosting atop the vertical scroll bar (and shown in the margin).

Tab gizmo

Figure 12-1: Important tab things on the Ruler.

Left tab   Center tab   Right tab

Tab stops appear as tiny black symbols clinging on the Ruler , as shown in Figure 12-1. Three tab stops are set in the figure: a left tab stop at the half-inch mark, a center tab stop at the 3-inch mark, and a right tab stop at the 5½-inch mark.

You manipulate tab stops on the Ruler by using the mouse. That's the easy part. The difficult part is that Word has *five* different types of tab stops:

 The *left tab* is the traditional type of tab stop.

 The *center tab* centers text, mostly for titles or headers.

 The *right tab* right-justifies text.

 The *decimal tab* aligns numbers by their decimal parts.

 The bar tab isn't a tab stop, but is, rather, a decorative ornament.

Setting a tab involves two steps:

1. **Ensure that the Tab gizmo on the left end of the Ruler displays the type of tab stop you want.**

   Clicking the Tab gizmo displays a different tab type. (The Tab gizmo also displays some paragraph-indent symbols, covered in Chapter 11.)

2. **Click the Ruler at the exact spot where you want the tab stop set.**

For example, to set a left tab stop, you choose the left tab from the Tab gizmo and then click the Ruler where you want that tab stop positioned. Click the

3-inch mark, and the plump L of the left tab stop settles down at that position nicely.

Later sections in this chapter discuss each of the five different types of tab stops, when and how to set them, as well as how to set tabs in the Tabs dialog box.

- ✔ You use Backspace or Delete to remove a tab character, just as you delete any character in a document.

- ✔ Format tabs for a single line of text or for only the first line of a paragraph. For anything more complex, use Word's Table command. See Chapter 19.

- ✔ Anytime you press the spacebar more than once, you *need* a tab. Believe me, your documents will look prettier and you'll be happier after you understand and use tabs rather than spaces.

- ✔ Tabs are paragraph-level settings. Tab settings affect only the paragraph that the toothpick cursor is blinking in. To set tabs for several paragraphs, you must first select the paragraphs as a block. Refer to Chapter 6 for more blocky stuff.

- ✔ When you're selecting several paragraphs, you may spot a light gray, or *phantom,* tab stop on the Ruler. The phantom indicates a tab stop that's set in one paragraph but not in all. To apply the tab stop to all selected paragraphs, click the phantom tab stop once. Otherwise, you can remove the tab stop by following the instructions found in this chapter's later section "Tab Stop, Be Gone!"

- ✔ Tab characters can often confuse you because, like spaces, they don't show up on the screen. But you can see them, if you like. To direct Word to display the tab character, which looks like a tiny arrow, as shown in the margin, choose Options from the File tab's menu. Click Display from the left side of the Word Options dialog box. On the right side of the window, put a check mark by the Tab Characters option. Click OK.

- ✔ The diet beverage Tab was named for people who like to keep a tab on how much they consume.

The Standard Left Tab Stop

The left tab stop is the traditional type of tab stop. When you press the Tab key, the insertion pointer advances to the left tab stop, where you can continue to type text. This works best for typing lists, organizing information in single-line paragraphs, or indenting the first line of a multiline paragraph. This section provides some examples.

Creating a basic tabbed list

A common use for the tab stop is to create a simple two-column list, as shown in Figure 12-2.

Film	Android
Metropolis	Maria
The Day the Earth Stood Still	Gort
Forbidden Planet	Robbie the Robot
King Kong Escapes	Mechani-Kong
THX-1138	The fuzz
Logan's Run	Box
Alien	Ash
Aliens	Bishop

Figure 12-2:
Two-column
list.

The following steps describe how to set up this type of list:

1. **On a new line, press Tab.**

2. **Type the item for the first column.**

   This item should be short — two or three words, max.

3. **Press Tab.**

4. **Type the item for the second column.**

   Again, make it short.

5. **Press Enter to end that line and start a new line.**

   Yes, your list looks horrible! Don't worry. Just get the data typed first and then format it.

6. **Repeat Steps 1 through 5 for each item in the list.**

   After the list is finished, you set the tab stops visually by using the Ruler.

7. **Summon the Ruler, if necessary.**

   Click the View Ruler button to display the Ruler, if it's hidden.

8. **Select all lines of text that you want to organize into a two-column tabbed list.**

   Refer to Chapter 6 for more information on marking blocks of text.

9. **Click the Tab gizmo until the Left Tab icon appears.**

   If the icon already shows up in the Tab gizmo, you're set.

You can see what a Left Tab icon looks like right here in the margin.

10. Click the mouse on the Ruler at the number 1, the 1-inch position.

This step sets a left tab stop at one inch. You see how the text you selected falls into place immediately.

11. Click the mouse to set a second tab stop at the 3-inch mark.

The list looks nice and even, in two columns (refer to Figure 12-2).

12. Adjust the tab stops, if necessary.

Slide the tab stops left or right on the Ruler as needed to help clean up your list. As you slide the tab stops, notice how a dashed vertical line extends through your text. That line shows you where text lines up.

These steps can also be used to create a three- or even four-column list. The idea is to keep the text on one line and separated by single tabs. Then use the tab stops on the Ruler to line up the columns and make them look pretty.

✔ You need only one tab between items in a column list. That's because:

It's the *tab stop,* not the tab character, that lines up your text. As with using two spaces in a row, you never need two tabs in a row.

✔ You type the text first and then select the text and set the tab stops last.

✔ You can adjust tab stops for the entire block of text by using the mouse and the Ruler.

✔ For a tabbed list to work, each paragraph must be a line by itself and the items in each column should be only a word or two long. Any longer and you need to use Word's Table command, as covered in Chapter 19.

Creating a two-tab paragraph thing

Tabs can also be used to form an item list where the paragraph text remains in the rightmost column. Figure 12-3 shows how the two-tab paragraph thing works. It combines both paragraph- and tab-formatting skills.

Follow these steps to create a similar list:

1. On a new line, type the item for the first column.

The shorter, the better.

2. Press Tab.

Figure 12-3:
A tab-tab-paragraph format for text.

Participant	Dish	Judge's Description
Edna Cuttle	Yeast pudding	I think Edna simply took some instant pudding mix and added yeast. It looked like pudding and smelled interesting, but tasted like old bread. I believe I could feel the yeast breeding on my tongue.
Lois Bronston	Cod Jello	Jello is good. Jello is fun. I like jello, despite its reputation as a kid's dessert. Still, what the heck is fish doing in jello? Further, I don't believe that Lois even cooked the fish.
Olive Petunia	Bacon Fudge	I figured, why not? I mean, there are weirder things I've eaten. Still, I expected the fudge to be wrapped in bacon. But no. The bacon was minced into the fudge. It was a weird taste, and one I don't want to try again.

3. Type the second column's text and press Tab.

This step is optional; you can create a simpler tab-paragraph list, which looks just like the one shown in Figure 12-3, but without the Dish column (and spaced accordingly).

4. Type the paragraph text.

Unlike with the first two items, you're free to type more text here. That's because this final paragraph column will wrap (refer to Figure 12-3).

5. Press Enter to end the line and start a new line.

Don't let the ugly text format fool you at this point. The text beautifies itself when you add the tab stops.

6. Repeat Steps 1 through 5 for all items in the tab-paragraph list.

When you're done, you can set the tab stops. You need the Ruler for Step 7.

7. Bid the Ruler appear, if need be.

Click the View Ruler button to show a hidden Ruler.

8. Select all the lines of text you want to organize into a tab-tab-paragraph list.

Chapter 6 discusses block-selection techniques.

9. Slide the Hanging Indent triangle to the 3-inch position on the Ruler.

The paragraph appears.

10. Ensure that the left tab is chosen on the Tab gizmo.

The margin shows the Left Tab symbol.

11. Click the mouse to set a tab stop at 1.5 inches.

The second column snaps into place.

12. Adjust the tab stop and hanging indent triangle as necessary.

With the text still selected, you can slide the tab stop and the Hanging Indent things on the Ruler to the left or right to adjust the look of your tab-tab-paragraph. Whatever looks best works best.

You can vary these rules to have a tab-paragraph or even a triple-tab-paragraph. The more tabs you have, the tighter the paragraph gets, so be careful. (The notes from the preceding section also apply to this technique.)

The Center Tab Stop

The *center tab* is a unique critter, and it has a special purpose: Text placed at a center tab is centered on a line. Unlike centering a paragraph, only text placed at the center tab stop is centered. This feature is ideal for centering something in a header or footer, which is about the only time you use the center tab stop.

Figure 12-4 shows an example of a center tab. The text on the left is at the start of the paragraph, which is left-justified. But the text typed after the tab is centered on the line.

Figure 12-4:
A center tab
in action.

A Trip To Uranus   Chapter 9: Exploring the curious crevasse

Here's how to make that happen:

1. **Start a new paragraph, one containing text that you want to center.**

   Center tabs are found in one-line paragraphs.

2. **Set a center tab.**

   If necessary, show the Ruler: Click the View Ruler button. Click the Tab gizmo until a center tab appears (refer to Figure 12-4). Click the mouse on the light gray part of the Ruler to set the tab. In Figure 12-4, the center tab is set at the center of the page, at the 3-inch position.

3. **Type some text to start the line (optional).**

   The text you type should be short; it appears only at the start of the line.

4. **Press the Tab key.**

   The insertion pointer hops over to the center tab stop.

5. **Type the text to center.**

   As you type, the text is centered on the line. Don't type too much; remember that the center tab is a single-line thing.

6. **Press Enter to end the line of text.**

Obviously, if you just want to center text on a line, centering the entire paragraph is a better choice; see Chapter 11. Otherwise, this technique finds itself used mostly in page headers and footers, which are covered in Chapter 14. Look there for an additional example.

- ✔ You can also add a right tab stop to the line, to have text lined up left, center, and right, which happens a lot in headers and footers and is shown earlier, in Figure 12-1.

- ✔ Center tabs are best used on a single line of text, usually by themselves. There's no reason to do them any other way.

The Right Tab Stop

A right tab seems useless until you've seen one in action. You use it to right-justify text at a tab stop, allowing a single line of text to contain both right- and left-justified text. You've probably seen, but not recognized, examples of a right tab all over the place, so I give you Figures 12-5 and 12-6 to gawk at in the following section.

- ✔ As with the other unusual tab stops, right tab stops work best on a single line of text.

- ✔ The following two sections describe how to set up right tab stops as shown in Figures 12-5 and 12-6. In both cases, you use the Ruler; to show the Ruler in Word, click the View Ruler button, found on top of the vertical scroll bar.

Making a right-stop, left-stop list

To create a centered, two-column list with a right tab stop and a left tab stop, as shown in Figure 12-5, obey these steps:

1. **Start out on a blank line, the line you want to format.**

2. **Choose the right tab stop from the Tab gizmo.**

   Keep clicking the Tab gizmo with the mouse until the right tab stop appears.

Figure 12-5:
Right tab
stops are
used to
center-align
this list.

Dorothy	Taylor Swift
Scarecrow	Ashton Kutcher
Tin Man	Jude Law
Cowardly Lion	Seth Rogan
Wizard	Lewis Black
Wicked Witch of the West	Madonna

3. **Click the mouse at the 3-inch position on the Ruler.**

4. **Choose the left tab stop from the Tab gizmo.**

   Click, click, click until you see the left tab stop.

5. **Click the mouse at the 3⅛-inch position on the Ruler.**

   Use Figure 12-5 as your guide. Don't fret — you can change the tab stop positions when you're just about done.

6. **Press the Tab key.**

   The insertion pointer hops over to the 3-inch stop, the right tab stop.

7. **Type your text.**

   The text is right-justified at the right tab stop.

8. **Press the Tab key.**

9. **Type your text.**

   The text is left-justified (normal).

10. **Press Enter to end the line of text.**

11. **Repeat Steps 6 through 10 for each line in the list.**

As long as you limit the text to one line, the list should look great (refer to Figure 12-5).

To make adjustments, select the list as a block (see Chapter 6) and use the mouse to adjust the tab stops on the Ruler. As you move the tab stops, a dashed line extends through your text, showing you where the text lines up. Or, to be more precise, you can use the Tabs dialog box as covered later in this chapter.

Building a two-column right stop list

Another type of right tab stop list is shown in Figure 12-6. This type is commonly found in dramatic programs but works just as well for a variety of purposes. Here's how to concoct such a thing:

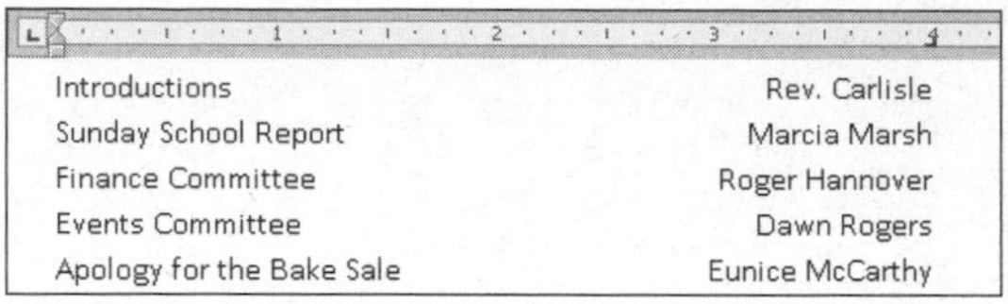

Figure 12-6:
Right tab
stops right-
align the
second
column of
this list.

Introductions	Rev. Carlisle
Sunday School Report	Marcia Marsh
Finance Committee	Roger Hannover
Events Committee	Dawn Rogers
Apology for the Bake Sale	Eunice McCarthy

1. **Start out with a blank line of text.**

2. **Ensure that the Tab gizmo on the Ruler shows the right tab stop.**

   Refer to Figure 12-6.

3. **Click the mouse at the 4-inch position on the Ruler.**

   The position is just a guess at this point. Later, you can adjust the right tab stop setting to a more visually appealing one.

4. **Type the left column text.**

   The text is left-justified, like normal.

5. **Press the Tab key.**

   The insertion pointer hops to the right tab stop.

6. **Type the right column text.**

   The text you type is right-justified, pushing to the left as you type.

7. **Press Enter to end the line of text.**

8. **Repeat Steps 4 through 7 for each line in the list.**

Afterward, you can mark the text as a block and then use the mouse to drag the right tab stop back and forth to whatever looks more visually appealing.

✔ You can drag the left indent toward the center of the page to offset the list from the left margin.

✔ Also refer to the section "Setting leader tabs," later in this chapter, for information about adding a dotted leader to the right tab stop.

The Decimal Tab

The decimal tab is used to line up columns of numbers. Although you can use a right tab to do this job, the decimal tab is a better choice. Rather than right-align text, as the right tab does (see the previous section), the decimal tab aligns numbers by their decimal portion — the period in the number, shown in Figure 12-7.

Luggage Check	$20.00
Extra Luggage (per piece)	$10.00
Onboard meal	$8.00
Onboard snack	$5.00
Beer	$7.00
Wine	$7.00
Soda	$2.00
Unlimited use of the bathroom	Free!

Figure 12-7:
Lining up
numbers
with the
decimal tab.

Here's how to work with such a beast:

1. **Start a blank line of text.**

2. **Choose the Decimal tab stop from the Tab gizmo on the Ruler.**

   The Decimal tab stop icon is shown in the margin.

3. **Set the tab stop on the Ruler by clicking the mouse at the 3-inch position.**

4. **Type the left column text.**

5. **Press the Tab key.**

6. **Type the numerical amount.**

   The number is right-justified until you press the period key. After that, the rest of the number is left-justified. The effect is lined up that the value is at the decimal tab stop by the period in the number.

7. **End that line of text by pressing Enter.**

8. **Repeat Steps 4 through 7 for each line in the list.**

When you type something without a period in it (refer to Figure 12-7), it's shown right-justified.

You can adjust your text by selecting all lines as a block and then using the mouse to move the decimal tab stop on the Ruler.

The Bar Tab

Aside from being a most excellent pun, the bar tab isn't a true tab stop in Word. Instead, consider it a text decoration. Setting a bar tab merely inserts a vertical line into a line of text, as shown in Figure 12-8. Using this feature is much better than using the pipe (|) character on the keyboard for drawing a vertical line in your document.

Cat	Kingdom	Animal
	Phylum	Chordata
	Class	Mammalia
	Order	Carnivora
	Family	Felidae
	Genus	Felis
	Name	Morton Boop

Figure 12-8:
The mysteri-
ous bar tab.

The setup to create the three-column text shown in the figure is similar to the one presented earlier in this chapter for a two-column list (see the earlier section "The tabbed list"), though Figure 12-8 shows a three-column list with the first column at the start of a line.

You set a bar tab the same way you set any other type of tab. But, rather than insert a tab, you insert a black vertical line in the text. The line always appears, even when no text or tab is used on a line, as you can see in the last row of text (empty) in Figure 12-8.

In Figure 12-8, observe that a left tab stop is set immediately after the bar tab to help organize text on a line. This is normally how bar tabs are used, although, for all practical purposes, it's just easier in Word to surrender here and use the Table function instead; see Chapter 19.

The Tabs Dialog Box

If setting tabs on the Ruler is the right-brain approach, using the Tabs dialog box is the left-brain method of setting tab stops in Word. The Tabs dialog box, shown in Figure 12-9, gives you more precision over using the Ruler by itself.

Getting to the Tabs dialog box is a journey, the type of journey that ends with an "All I got was this stupid Tabs dialog box T-shirt." The simplest way to beckon forth the Tabs dialog box is to double-click the mouse on a tab in the middle of the Ruler (on the light gray part). Of course, that technique also *sets* a tab stop, which can be frustrating.

The other way to open the Tabs dialog box is to summon the Paragraph dialog box: Click the Dialog Box Launcher button in the lower right corner of the Paragraph group, on the Home tab. When the Paragraph dialog box is visible, click the Tabs button in the lower left corner to bring forth the Tabs dialog box.

Figure 12-9:
The Tabs
dialog box.

Setting a tab in the Tabs dialog box

When you need for your tab stops to be precise and the Ruler is proving unruly, follow these steps to set tabs in the Tab dialog box:

1. **Enter the exact tab stop position in the Tab Stop Position box.**

   For example, type **1.1875** to set a tab at exactly that spot.

2. **Choose the type of tab stop from the Alignment area.**

   The standard tab stop is named Left. Other types of tab stops are covered elsewhere in this chapter.

3. **Click the Set button.**

   The Set button — not the OK button — creates the tab stop. After you click Set, the tab stop is placed on the list below the Tab Stop Position dialog box. (You may notice that numbers are rounded to the nearest hundredth; Word interprets 1.1875 as 1.19, for example.)

4. **Continue setting tabs.**

   Repeat Steps 1 through 3 for as many tabs as you need to set.

5. **Click OK.**

The tabs you set affect the current paragraph or a selected group of paragraphs. If the Ruler is visible, you can see the tabs and adjust them by using the mouse.

You must click the Set button to set a tab! I don't know how many times I click OK, thinking that the tab stop is set when it isn't.

Setting leader tabs

You can do only one task in Word in the Tabs dialog box that you cannot do with the Ruler: Set a leader tab.

What is a leader tab?

A *leader tab* produces a row of dots, underlining (in a fashion) the tab character. Three styles are available:

Fearless dot leader tabs...180

Zipper line leader tabs _ 180

U-boat underline leader tabs _____180

You can apply a leader tab to any tab stop in Word other than the bar tab. To do so, refer to other sections in this chapter that tell you how to set the various types of tab stops—specifically, the right tab stop. To add the dot leader to the tabbed list you've created, follow these steps:

1. **Select the text as a block.**

   Refer to Chapter 6 for block-marking directions.

2. **Bring forth the Tabs dialog box.**

3. **Select the tab stop from the Tab Stop Position list.**

   For example, in Figure 12-6, the right tab stop shows up in the Tab Stop Position list as 4". Click to select that item in the list.

4. **In the Leader area, choose the leader style.**

   None means "no leader," and it's selected already. Choose one of the other three options.

5. **Click the Set button.**

   Don't click OK before you set the tab stop to add the leader. This step is the one you'll screw up most often.

6. **Click OK.**

   After clicking the Set button, you can click OK to close the Tabs dialog box and gawk at your text.

The leader tab that uses the underline character is also the best way to create fill-in-the-blanks forms. Use the Tabs dialog box to set a left tab stop at the far right margin (usually, 6.0 inches). Choose an underline leader for that tab.

Click Set and then OK. Back in your document, type the prompt for the fill-in-the-blanks line, such as

```
Your name:
```

Rather than type a zillion underlines, just press the Tab key. Instantly, a line extends from the colon to the right margin.

Tab Stop, Be Gone!

Removing a tab stop is as easy as dragging the Tab Stop icon from the Ruler: Point and click at the tab stop and drag the mouse downward, and the tab stop is gone.

The Tabs dialog box can also be used to remove tab stops. It's especially good for those times when you may have several tab stops close together and plucking one out with the mouse would be tiresome. In the Tabs dialog box, choose the tab stop position in the Tab Stop Position list and then click the Clear button. Poof! It's gone!

Clicking the Clear All button in the Tabs dialog box removes all tabs from the Ruler in one drastic sweep.

To delete a Tab character, of course, simply back up over it with the Backspace key.

Chapter 13

Page Formatting

*B*ack in the old days, page formatting meant fitting your document on a sheet of paper. You could choose from two paper sizes, letter and legal, and you could print normal or sideways. That was in the old days.

Today, you don't just print a document, you *publish* it. You can put the thing on paper, or you can distribute your document to the world electronically. Because the final destination need not be paper, a document's page size becomes nontraditional. You can use Word's page formatting tools to set the size of the paper or the direction the text flows and use other fun features such as page numbers, all covered in this chapter.

Describe That Page

Page formatting starts with the size of the page, which is normally the size of the paper you're printing on. As far as Word is concerned, page and paper are similar concepts, though in theory you can set the page size to anything, which is covered in this section.

Setting page size

When Word starts out, it assumes that your document is destined to be printed on a sheet of paper and that the paper will be the standard size for your region, such as 8½-by-11 inches in the United States and the A4 size just about everywhere else. As the computer user, you have every right to disagree with Word and choose a different page size for your document, and you're not limited to the standard paper sizes, either.

To set the page size, click the Page Layout tab and use the Size button in the Page Setup group. Clicking the Size button displays the page Size menu, shown in Figure 13-1. Choose a page size from the list.

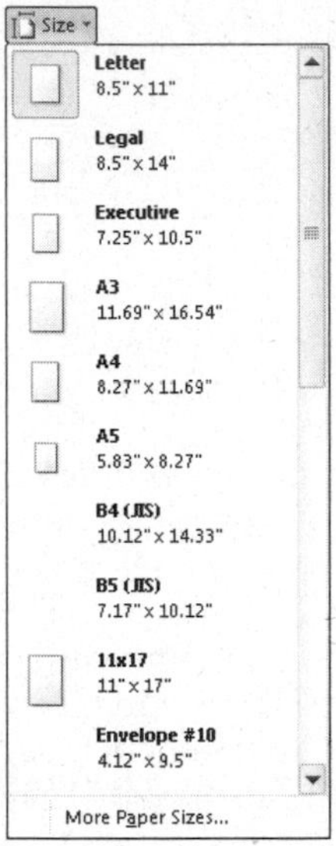

Figure 13-1:
The Size
menu.

For example, if you want to print on that tall, legal-size paper, choose Legal from the list. Your entire document is then updated to reflect the new page size.

✔ To select a size not shown on the menu, choose the More Paper Sizes command, found at the bottom of the Size menu. You can then manually set the page size by using the Paper tab in the Page Setup dialog box. See the later section "Using the Page Setup dialog box," for more information.

✔ Page-size changes are reflected in the entire document, from first page to last — unless you divide your documents into sections, that is. Then you can use different page sizes within each section. Refer to Chapter 14 for information on sections.

- ✔ If you plan to print on a nonstandard page size, you need to find that specific paper size, possibly at an office supply store, plus have a printer that can swallow that specific paper size.

- ✔ A typical sheet of paper, at least in the United States, measures 8½ inches across by 11 inches tall. Most of the rest of the world uses the A4 paper-size standard, which is slightly longer and a tad narrower.

Setting orientation (landscape or portrait)

Word assumes that you want your document's text to print from left to right on a page that's taller than it is wide. That's what it considers *normal*. It's also called *portrait* mode because the page orientation is vertical, like a portrait.

Word can also be told to print longways, or in *landscape* mode. To perform this trick, you choose Landscape from the Orientation command in the Page Layout tab's Page Setup group, shown in Figure 13-2.

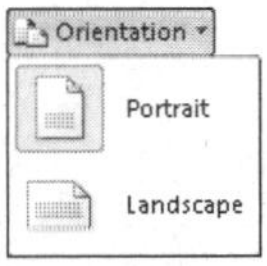

Figure 13-2:
Setting page
orientation.

Choosing Orientation⇨Landscape directs Word to shift the paper orientation for every page in your document. This doesn't mean that the text is sideways any more than it means that the text prints wide on a page (though I suppose you could look at it as printing sideways).

To change the pages back, choose Orientation⇨Portrait.

- ✔ Changing between Portrait and Landscape modes may require you to adjust the document's margins; see the next section.

- ✔ Make the decision to have your document in landscape mode before you do any extensive formatting. That mode affects your paragraphs and other "lower-level" formatting, so you should have it done first, before you start composing text.

- ✔ Scientists and other people in white lab coats who study such things have determined that human reading speed slows drastically when people must scan a long line of text, which happens when you use Landscape mode. Reserve Landscape mode for printing lists and tables and items for which normal paper is too narrow.

✔ Consider using multiple columns in Landscape mode. See Chapter 20.

✔ Also see the section "Using the Page Setup dialog box," later in this chapter, for more page-orientation settings and options.

Configuring the page margins

Every page has *margins*. They provide the air around your document — that inch or so of breathing space that sets off the text from the rest of the page. As with other things in Word, these margins can be adjusted, fooled, cajoled, or otherwise obsessed with.

Word automatically sets page margins at 1 inch from every edge of the page. Most English teachers and book editors want margins of this size because these people love to scribble in margins. (They even write that way on blank paper.) In Word, you can adjust the margins to suit any fussy professional.

To change the margins, you use the Margins button, found in the Page Setup group on the Page Layout tab. Clicking the Margins button displays a menu full of common margin options, as shown in Figure 13-3.

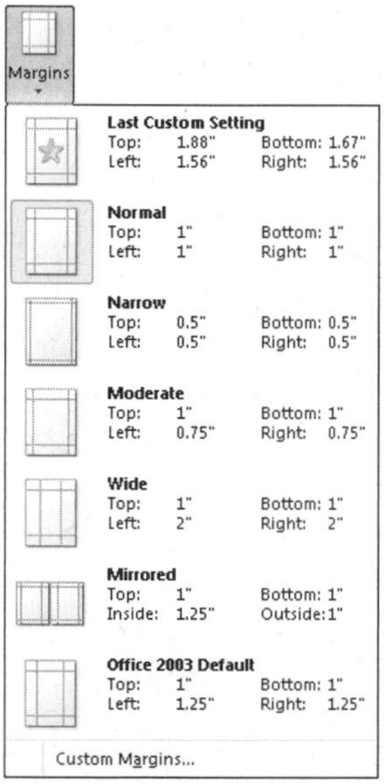

Figure 13-3: The Margins menu.

Specific margins can be set by clicking the Custom Margins button at the bottom of the Margins menu. Doing so displays the Margins tab in the Page Setup dialog box, where specific margin information can be entered, including information on printing more than one page on a sheet of paper. Refer to the next section for more information.

✔ Margins on a page are covered in this chapter. To set the indents for a single paragraph, you use a paragraph-formatting command. See Chapter 11.

✔ The stars on the Margin menu's icons represent popular or recent margin choices you've made.

✔ Keep in mind that most laser printers cannot print on the outside half-inch of a piece of paper — top, bottom, left, or right. This space is an *absolute* margin; although you can tell Word to set a margin of 0 inches right and 0 inches left, text still doesn't print there. Instead, choose a minimum of 0.5 inches for the left and right margins.

✔ Likewise, many ink printers have a taller top or bottom margin requirement. If you attempt to print outside that area, a dialog box appears, informing you of your offense.

Using the Page Setup dialog box

As with many features in Word, when you want more control over page formatting, you must flee from the Ribbon interface and use an old-fashioned dialog box. In this case, it's the Page Setup dialog box, shown in Figure 13-4.

Figure 13-4:
The Margins tab in the Page Setup dialog box.

To summon the Page Setup dialog box, click the Dialog Box Launcher in the lower right corner of the Page Setup group on the Page Layout tab. Or, you can use the keyboard shortcut: Alt+P, S, P.

The Page Setup dialog box sports three tabs: Margins for setting margins, Paper for selecting the page size, and Layout for dealing with other page-formatting issues.

Click the OK button to confirm your changes and close the Page Setup dialog box.

✔ To print on three-hole paper, use the Margins tab in the Page Setup dialog box to set the gutter margin to about half an inch. That moves the entire margin "frame" one half-inch from where the three holes are punched. You can set the Gutter Position to Left option, unless the holes are punched on the top of the page, in which case you set the Gutter Position to Top option.

✔ Changes made to a page's format — size, orientation, and margins — normally affect an entire document. By using the Apply To drop-down list in the Page Setup dialog box, however, you can determine which portion of a document will be affected by the margin change. You have three options:

   • **Whole Document** changes the margins for your whole document, from bonnet to boot.

   • **This Point Forward** makes the new margins take place from the insertion pointer's position onward.

   • **This Section** means applies the margins only to the current section. (See Chapter 14 for more information on sections.)

Dangerous treading in the Multiple Pages area of the Page Setup dialog box

Nestled on the Margins tab of the Page Setup dialog box is the Pages area (refer to Figure 13-4). The Multiple Pages drop-down list tells Word how to use the paper on which your document is printed. Surprisingly, you have more than one way to print a document on a page. The following definitions help, as does the little preview page at the bottom of the Page Setup dialog box:

Normal means one page per sheet of paper. You can't get more normal than that.

Mirror Margins is used when your printer is smart enough to print on both sides of a sheet of paper. That way, every other page is flip-flopped so that your margins always line up. For example, the gutter may be on the left side of one page, but on the right for the page's back side.

2 Pages per Sheet splits the paper right down the center and forces Word to print two "pages" per sheet of paper. Note that this option works best when used in landscape mode.

Book Fold is Word's attempt to create a multiple-page booklet by printing the proper pages on both sides of a sheet of paper. This option works best if you have a printer capable of printing on both sides of a sheet of paper. The Sheets Per Booklet option that appears helps tell Word how long your booklet is.

Despite these options, Word is a poor bookbinding program. If you're into any type of publishing, consider getting a desktop publishing program, such as Adobe InDesign or Microsoft Publisher, which are far better equipped to deal with this topic.

Page Numbering

I'm still puzzled by people who manually number their pages when they use a computer and a word processor. Such a thing is silly beyond belief. That's because

Your word processor numbers your pages for you!

Memorize it. Live it. Be it.

Adding an automatic page number

Not only can Word automatically number your pages, but it also lets you place the page number just about anywhere on the page and in a variety of fun and interesting formats.

Start your page numbering odyssey thus:

1. **Click the Insert tab.**
2. **In the Header & Footer area, click the Page Number command button.**

   A menu drops down, listing various page-numbering options. The first three are locations: Top of Page, Bottom of Page, and Page Margins, or the sides of the page.

3. **Choose where to place the page numbers.**

   I want my page numbers on the bottom of the page, so I regularly choose the Bottom of Page option.

4. **Pluck a page-numbering style from the scrolling list.**

   You can see oodles of samples, so don't cut yourself short by not scrolling through the menu. You can even choose those famous *page X of Y* formats.

Dutifully, Word numbers each page in your document, starting with 1 for the first page, up to however many pages long the thing grows. Plus, if you delete a page, Word renumbers everything for you. Insert a page? Hey! Word renumbers everything for you again, automatically. As long as you insert the page number by following the preceding set of steps, Word handles everything.

✔ The page numbers are placed into the document's header or footer, so you don't see them on the screen unless you're using Word in Print Layout view. Even when you work in Draft view, the page numbers are still there.

✔ Headers and footers are parts of a page that you can format with all sorts of interesting elements, including your own page number style or even page numbers on both the top *and* bottom of the page. Refer to Chapter 14 for details.

✔ To change the page number format, simply choose a new one from the Page Number menu.

✔ Page numbers can be removed just as easily: See the section "Removing page numbers," later in this chapter.

✔ See Chapter 23 for information on inserting a page number into your document's text as opposed to in a header or footer.

Starting off with a different page number

You and I know that the first page of a document is page 1, but Word doesn't care. It lets you start numbering your document at whichever page number you want. If you want to start numbering your document at page 42, you can do so, if you follow these instructions:

1. **Click the Insert tab.**

2. **In the Header & Footer area, choose Page Number⇨Format Page Numbers.**

   The Page Number Format dialog box materializes, as shown in Figure 13-5.

3. **Click the Start At radio button and type the beginning page number in the box.**

4. **Click OK to close the Page Number Format dialog box.**

Word starts numbering your document at the specified page number. So, if you enter 47 in Step 3, the first page of your document is now page 47, the next page is 48, and so on.

When you want the page number to jump in the middle of your document from, say, page 5 to page 16 or (more likely) from page *iv* to page 1, you use sections to divide the document. You can start page numbering over again, and at any number or in a new section. See Chapter 14 for more information on sections.

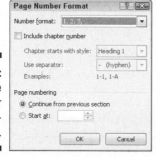

Numbering with roman numerals

When the urge hits you to regress a few centuries and use roman numerals to tally a document's pages, Word is happy to oblige. Summon the Page Number Format dialog box (refer to Figure 13-5) by following Steps 1 and 2 in the preceding section. Simply choose the style you want from the Number Format drop-down list.

Removing page numbers

To strip out page numbers you've inserted into your document, choose the Remove Page Numbers command from the Page Number menu (in the Header & Footer group on the Insert tab).

The Remove Page Numbers command rids your document of only those page numbers you've inserted by using the Page Number menu. If you've manually added a page number in a header or footer, you must manually delete it. See Chapter 14.

New Pages from Nowhere

As you type your document, Word keeps adding new, blank pages for you to write on. These pages are appended to the end of the document, so even if you're typing in the midst of a chapter, the extra pages keep appearing so that no text is lost and nothing falls off the edge. That's all normal and good.

For those times when you need to stick a blank page in the middle of a document, Word provides two interesting commands. This section explains them.

Starting on a new page

To start typing on a new page in your document, you insert a manual page break, or *hard page break.* The simplest way to do this is to press the Ctrl+Enter key combination. Word then begins a new page On That Very Spot. All text before the insertion pointer is on the previous page, and all text afterward is on a new page.

You can also insert a hard page break by choosing the Page Break command from the Pages group on the Insert tab.

In Print Layout view, a hard page break looks like any other page break. The only way to know the difference is to switch to Draft view and use the Show/Hide command (found in the Home tab and shown in the margin). In Draft view, the words *Page Break* appear before the break in your document. That's your clue that you have a hard page break.

Keep these points in mind when you're dealing with hard page breaks:

✔ Never, never, never start a new page by repeatedly pressing the Enter key until a new page pops up. That just leads to trouble later as you edit your document.

✔ Pressing Ctrl+Enter inserts a hard page-break *character* in your document. That character stays there, always creating a hard page break no matter how much you edit the text on previous pages.

✔ You can delete a hard page break by pressing either the Backspace or Delete key. If you do this accidentally, just press Ctrl+Z to undelete.

✔ If you set hard page breaks, switch to Full Screen Reading view to preview your document before you print it. Sometimes, the process of editing moves text around, making the hard page breaks unnecessary and awkward. Refer to Chapter 9 for more information on Full Screen Reading view.

✔ You can also insert a hard page break by choosing Breaks⇨Page from the Page Setup group. Remember that this command is on the Page Layout tab, not on the Insert tab.

✔ Don't fall into the trap of using hard page breaks to adjust your page numbering. You can use the power of the computer to alter page numbers without having to mess with page formatting. See the earlier section "Starting off with a different page number."

Inserting a whole, blank page

To shove a fresh, blank sheet of paper into the middle of a document, you can use the Blank Page command button, found in the Insert tab's Pages group. That command inserts _two_ hard page breaks into a document, which creates a blank sheet of paper.

I don't recommend using this command unless you truly need a blank page in the midst of a document (you plan never to write on that page). Putting graphics on the page is fine. Adding a table, or any other one-page element, to the blank page is also fine. But because the blank page is inserted by using two hard page breaks, writing on it leads to formatting woes down the line.

Page Froufrou

Page formatting happens above your text, below your text, to the sides of your text, and even _behind_ your text. This section demonstrates the things you can format on a page that appear behind your words.

Coloring pages

To color your document's pages, use the Page Color command button from the Page Layout tab's Page Background group. Clicking that button displays a menu full of colors, some based on the document theme and some based on standard colors, or you can choose your own color by choosing the More Colors menu command. _Gradients,_ or multiple colors, can be chosen by using the Fill Effects menu command.

As you move the mouse over the various colors on the Page Color menu, your document's page color is updated to reflect that new color (but only in Page Layout view). The text color may change as well (for example, from black to white) to remain visible.

The color you choose is produced by your printer, but you must direct the printer to print the page color by following these steps:

1. **Click the File tab.**

2. **Choose Options from the File tab menu.**

3. **Choose Display from the left side of the Word Options window.**

4. **In the Printing Options area, put a check mark by the item labeled Print Background Colors and Images.**

5. **Click OK.**

   You can now print the background color.

The color, because it's generated by Word and isn't part of the paper you're printing on, doesn't cover the entire printed page. That's because your printer cannot mechanically access the outside edge of a page, so a white border (or whatever other color the paper is) appears around your colored page. At this point, you need to ask yourself whether it's easier to use colored paper rather than expensive printer ink or toner.

> ✔ To remove page coloring, choose the No Color command from the Page Color menu.
> ✔ See Chapter 10 for information on coloring text.

Adding a watermark

When finer papers are held up to the light, they show a *watermark,* an image embedded into the paper. The image is impressive but faint. Word lets you fake a watermark by inserting faint text or graphics behind every page in your document. Here's how:

1. **Click the Page Layout tab.**

2. **In the Page Background group, click the Watermark button.**

   A menu plops down with a host of predefined watermarks that you can safely duck behind the text on your document's pages.

3. **Choose a watermark from the long, long list.**

   The watermark is applied to every page in your document.

Sadly, you have few options for customizing the watermark. You can choose the More Watermarks command from the Watermark menu, which displays the Printed Watermark dialog box. In there, you can choose between a picture or text watermark. The picture item is handy because you can choose any graphical image that's available on your computer (such as a company logo) to use as a watermark. The text item, however, lets you choose only predefined bits of text.

To rid your document's pages of the watermark, choose the Remove Watermark command from the Watermark menu.

If the watermark doesn't show up in the printed document, you may need to enable the Print Background Text and Images setting. Refer to the steps in the preceding section.

Chapter 14

Document Formatting

1 don't do much document formatting on my shopping lists or my kids' chore charts; it's not necessary. For the important stuff — the *real* documents — it's useful to employ some of Word's fancy document-formatting tricks. I'm talking about big-picture stuff that includes the handy-yet-weird concept of sections as well as headers and footers. The formatting information in this chapter might not be stuff you use all the time, but it's there for when you need to make documents look *extra* spiffy.

The Oft Misunderstood Yet Useful Concept of Sections

Most of the Word page-formatting commands affect every page in a document: The settings for margins, page orientation, paper size, and other types of formatting apply themselves not to a single page but rather to every dang doodle page, from 1 to *N*, where *N* is the mathematical variable best expressed as "I don't know how huge this value could be."

Sometimes, however, you need a document that isn't formatted the same way page after page. For example, you may want to number pages 1–4 in Roman numerals and then start over on page 5 with page 1 in human numerals. Or, you may want the first page of a document to be an unnumbered cover page.

Or, you may need to display a table on page 14 in landscape orientation. All these tricks are possible when you understand the section concept.

Understanding sections

A *section* is a part of a document that contains its own page formatting. For example, all documents have one section. That's the way they're born. All the page-formatting commands affect all the pages in the document the same way because the document has only one section. That's expected. It's a given. But it doesn't always have to be that way.

Figure 14-1 shows how a document can use two sections. The first section is four pages long and uses Roman numeral page numbers. The second section starts on page 5, where the page number format is restored to normal but starting at page number 1.

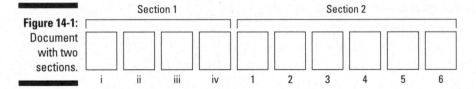

Figure 14-1: Document with two sections.

The document illustrated in Figure 14-2 has four sections. The first is the cover page, followed by a regular document format. Section 3, however, contains one page in landscape format. That's followed by Section 4, which reverts to the regular format.

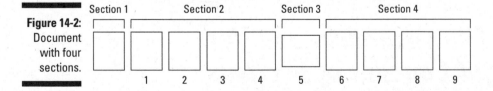

Figure 14-2: Document with four sections.

It if weren't for sections, you couldn't change the page format or the format for a document's headers or footers; everything would be the same. So a section isn't necessary in every document, but when you need one, it's truly a blessing.

- ✔ A *section* is basically a chunk of your document where page formatting is different from or unique to the rest of your document.

- ✔ Text and paragraph formatting, as well as any styles you may create, don't give a hoot about sections. Sections affect only page formatting. See Chapter 13 for more information on page formatting.

Creating a section

Breaking up your document isn't hard to do. Word has wisely placed all its breaking commands on the Breaks menu: Click the Page Layout tab and then click the Breaks command button, found in the Page Setup group. The menu is shown in Figure 14-3. Page-breaking commands are at the top of the menu; section breaks are at the bottom.

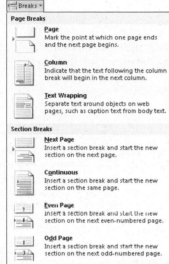

Figure 14-3:
Ways to
break text
or an entire
document.

The simplest way to create a new section is to choose Next Page from the Breaks menu. This command creates a page break, by starting a new page as a new section in your document.

In Print Layout view, the section break appears just like any other page break. To determine whether a page break is a real page break or something else, you must switch to Draft view and use the Show/Hide command: click the Show/Hide command button on the Home tab or press Ctrl+Shift+8.

In Draft view, the section break appears with the text `Section Break (Next Page)` in the middle of a double row of dots.

After the section is created, you can then modify the page layout and format for each of the sections, a topic that's covered in the next section.

> ✔ Use the Continuous section break to mix formatting styles within a page. For example, if you have columns of text sharing a page with regular text, the Continuous section break is the ideal way to separate the individual formats. See Chapter 20 for more information on columns.

✔ You can use the Even Page and Odd Page options to start the next section on the next even or odd page — ideal for those futile times when you try to use Word to bind a book or pamphlet.

✔ Column and Text Wrapping breaks have nothing to do with sections. Text Wrapping breaks work like soft returns (see Chapter 2), except that they're designed to be used on text that wraps around a figure or table. See Chapter 20 for information on column breaks.

Using a section

To apply a specific page format to one section only, use the dialog box associated with the format, such as the Page Setup dialog box. In the dialog box, look for the Apply To drop-down list. To apply the format to the current section, choose This Section. That way, the format controls only the pages in the current section.

To determine which section you're in, right-click the status bar (at the bottom of Word's window). A pop-up Status Bar Configuration menu appears. Near the top, you see the item named Section, and on the right you see the current section number. To see that information always displayed on the status bar, choose Section from the menu; otherwise, press the Esc key to make the pop-up menu go away.

Deleting a section break

A section break is just like a character in your document. To delete the break, you can use the Backspace or Delete keys. For example: Position the insertion pointer just before the section break and then press the Delete key. This technique works best in Draft view with the Show/Hide command working to display the section breaks.

✔ The Show/Hide command's keyboard shortcut is Ctrl+Shift+8.

✔ Deleting a section removes any formatting, including headers and footers, that were unique to that section.

✔ If you accidentally delete a section break, you lose any special formatting you applied to the section. In this case, press the Undo shortcut, Ctrl+Z, before you do anything else.

Add a Cover Page (Sneaky and Quick)

I'd guess that the most popular use of section breaks is to thwack down a title or cover page to a document. Typically, you don't want page numbers or header or footer information on the title page, so making that page its own section is ideal. But conniving Word to create a single page section and then fussing with headers and footers isn't anyone's idea of a fun time. Therefore, it pays to use Word's Cover Page menu. Here's how it works:

1. **Click the Insert tab.**

2. **In the Pages group, click the Cover Page button.**

   A fat, fun menu full of various cover-page layouts appears.

3. **Choose a cover-page layout that titillates you.**

   That cover page is immediately inserted as the first page in your document. Then Word displays it onscreen for further editing.

4. **Click the bracketed text on the cover page.**

5. **Type the required replacement text.**

   For example, click [Type the document title]. Then type your document's real title. The text you type replaces the bracketed text.

6. **Repeat Steps 4 and 5 until the cover page looks the way you like it.**

You can change a cover page at any time by choosing a new one from the Cover Page menu, although I recommend removing the old one first: To remove a cover page you've inserted, choose the Remove Current Cover Page command from the Cover Page menu. It helps to have the insertion pointer on the cover page to delete it.

✔ The Cover Page menu doesn't create a new section in your document. If you're using headers and footers, they appear on the inserted cover page. To avoid this situation, position the insertion pointer at the top of page 2 (after the cover page), and from the Page Layout tab, choose Break⇨Continuous. You can then modify the header and footer as described elsewhere in this chapter.

✔ As you learn more about Word, you can even modify or add elements to the cover page after it's inserted. Refer to Chapter 22 for more information about Word's drawing commands.

✔ Leaving the bracketed text on your title page is tacky. Your boss doesn't want to see a report that has [Company Name] on it rather than your company's real name.

Headers and Footers

Documents can have headers and headings, footers and footnotes. You can easily confuse things — until you read these handy bullets and peruse this section.

- A *header* is text that appears at the top of every page. It's contained in a special, roped-off part of the page where you can place special text.

- A *heading* is a text style used to break up a long document, to introduce new concepts and help organize the text. See Chapter 15 for more information on headings.

- A *footer* is text that appears at the bottom of every page. Like the header, it has its own, special area and contains special text.

- A *footnote* is a tiny bit of text that appears at the bottom of a page, usually a reference for some bit of text on that page. See Chapter 21.

- Headers and footers contain elements such as your name and the document name and the date, page number, title, and phone number. ("Hurry! Buy now! Operators are standing by!")

- Headers can also be called *eyebrows*. Weird, huh?

- Footers can include page numbers, a chapter or document title, and soft, cushiony insoles.

The following sections refer to both headers and footers. Even when the information appears to be about only the header, it also applies to footers.

Adding a header or footer

You can use a header. You can use a footer. You can use them both. You can use neither. Either way, the technique is the same:

1. **Click the Insert tab.**

2. **From the Header & Footer group, choose the Header button.**

   A list of preformatted headers is displayed.

3. **Choose the format you want from the list.**

   The header is added to your document, saved as part of the page format.

   If Word is in Draft view, it immediately switches to Print Layout view so that you can edit the header. (Headers and footers don't appear in Draft view.)

Notice the new tab on the screen? When you're editing a header, the Header & Footer Tools Design tab appears. Refer to the following section for details.

4. **Click any bracketed text.**

5. **Type the required replacement text.**

   For example, replace [Type text] with the title of your document.

6. **Repeat Steps 4 and 5 for all bracketed text in the header.**

7. **When you're done, click the Close Header and Footer command button in the Close group on the far right side of the Ribbon.**

In Print Layout view, you can see the header or footer displayed in ghostly gray text. In Draft view, you can't see a header or footer, even though it's still there. (You can also use Full Screen Reading view, as covered in Chapter 9, to see the header or footer.)

✔ You can also exit from editing a header by double-clicking the mouse in the main part of your document

✔ You don't have to go to page 1 to insert a page number in the header. Word is smart enough to put the proper number on the proper page, no matter where you're editing the header in your document.

✔ Headers and footers are geared to sections in your document. Therefore, as long as you're in the same (or only) section, you can edit the header or footer for that section.

✔ The Header and Footer command buttons are found on the Insert tab, not on the Page Layout tab.

Editing a header or footer

Face it: Word's preset designs for the header are dull. Splashy, but dull. And, chances are good that they don't contain all the information you want or need. That's no problem. You can edit the header using what Word created as a starting point, or you can just quickly whip up your own header. It's easy. Here's how:

1. **Click the Insert tab.**

2. **In the Header & Footer group, choose Header⇨Edit Header.**

   When you edit the header, Word tosses you into a special mode of operation. The header appears on the screen as part of the page in Print

Layout view. Plus, the Header & Footer Tools Design tab appears with groups customized for creating and editing headers.

3. **Use the Go to Header or Go to Footer command button to switch between the header and footer for editing.**

4. **Edit or modify the header.**

   Items in the header are edited just like anything else in Word. You can add or edit text and format that text by using any of Word's text- and paragraph-formatting commands, including tabs. (See Chapters 10, 11, and 12.)

   You can modify any graphics in the header, although I recommend that you read Chapter 22 before doing so.

   Word preformats headers with center and right tabs at the center and far right side of the page. You can then press the Tab key and type some text to have the text automatically centered at the bottom (or top) of the header or footer.

5. **Use the command buttons on the Design tab's Insert group for special items.**

   Here are some of the more useful special items you can insert into a header (the inserted items appear wherever the insertion pointer is located):

   - **Page number:** Choose Quick Parts⇨Page Numbers and choose a page number format from the list. The page number text then appears in the header. If you want to center the page number, press the Tab key and then insert the page number.

   - **Date & Time:** Clicking the Date & Time button displays a Date and Time dialog box, which lists various date, time, and combination formats. Choose one and then click the OK button to insert that date or time text into the header.

   - **Graphics:** Use the Picture button to browse for graphical images on your PC's hard drive, which you can insert into the header. Or use the ClipArt button. Be sure to brush up on graphics in Word by reading Chapter 22 first.

   - **Fields:** The most versatile thing you can insert into a header or footer is a field; choose Quick Parts⇨Field from the Insert group. Fields, however, require extra explanation. Refer to Chapter 23 for details.

6. **Click the Close Header and Footer command button when you're done.**

   You're back in your document.

The header is the same on every page in your document. Word is happy to oblige, however, whenever you want a different header, such as for the first page or alternating pages or for different sections in a document. The last few sections in this chapter explain the details.

✔ In Print Layout view, you can quickly edit any header or footer by double-clicking its ghostly gray image.

✔ If you need a header only for a page number, I highly recommend using the batch of page-numbering tricks I cover in Chapter 13 as an easier alternative to working with headers directly.

Making odd and even headers or footers

This book is formatted with odd and even headers: The header on the odd (left) pages contains the page number and then the part number and title. On the (right) even pages, the header shows the chapter number and title and then the page number. You can pull off this type of trick in your document as well.

To force Word to accept odd and even headers, obey these steps:

1. **Click the Insert tab.**

2. **From the Header & Footer group, choose Header⇨Edit Header.**

   The Header & Footer Tools Design tab is displayed on the screen.

3. **Click to put a check in the box by Different Odd & Even Pages, found in the Options group.**

   This step tells Word that you want two sets of headers: one for odd pages and one for even pages. Notice how the tag identifying the header changes:

   The tag tells you which header you're editing; in this case, it's the Odd Page header.

4. **Create the header for the odd pages.**

   Refer to the preceding section for notes on making a header or footer. Remember that the footer can contain any formatted text you would otherwise stick into a Word document.

5. **Click the Next button, found in the Navigation group.**

   Word displays the even page's header, allowing you to create or edit its contents. The Header tag changes to reflect which header you're editing:

   By the way, you click the Next button to move from the odd header to the even header. You must click the Previous button to return to the odd header from the even header.

6. **Click the Go To Footer button to edit the footer's odd and even pages.**

   Edit the footer's contents and click the Next button to ensure that you work on both the odd and even footers (as you do in Steps 4 and 5 for the header).

7. **Click the Close Header and Footer button when you're done.**

Removing the odd/even header option is as simple as deselecting the Different Odd & Even Pages option in the Options group (the opposite of Step 3). When you do that, the even-page header and footer are deleted, leaving only the odd header and footer.

Removing the header and footer from the first page

Most people don't want the header or footer on the first page, which is usually the title page or a cover page. Suppressing the header for that page is easy. Just follow these steps:

1. **Click the Insert tab.**

2. **From the Header & Footer group, choose Header⇨Edit Header.**

3. **In the Options group, select Different First Page.**

   You see the Header tag change to First Page header, and the Footer tag change likewise. That's your visual clue that the first page of the document sports a different header from the one in the rest of the document.

You can still edit the First Page header, if you like. It's merely different, not necessarily empty.

Working with headers and footers in document sections

Just as Superman is limited in his powers by the crippling force of kryptonite, the mighty header is limited in its scope and power by the limiting force of the document section. A header, or footer, can exist within only one section. Creating a new section creates a new set of headers and footers.

Word flags each set of headers and footers in the tag just below or above the header or footer area, such as this:

Footer -Section 2-

This tag helps you determine which section's header or footer you're editing.

To switch to the next section's header, click the Next button.

To switch to the previous section's header, click the Previous button.

 A source of frustration with multiple sections exists when you use the Link to Previous option. What this option does is set one section's header to match the previous section. That way, you can keep the same header in multiple sections. For example, sometimes you merely want to change the page orientation, not the header, in the middle of a document. At other times, the Link to Previous button may be source of frustration because it causes changes made in one section to be either replaced in another section or ignored.

As a hint, when the Link to Previous option is selected, the header is tagged on the left side with the following:

That's a big clue to why you may be unable to edit a header, when such a thing causes you frustration.

Same as Previous

✔ A header is a section-long element. By placing multiple sections in your document, you can have multiple headers. Refer to the first part of this chapter for information on sections.

✔ You use multiple sections to change headers throughout a document or to suppress the header on a single page and then "pick it up" again after that page.

✔ To suppress the header on the first page of a document, follow the instructions in this chapter's earlier section "Removing the header and footer from the first page."

✔ Changing a header in one section doesn't affect any other section in the document — unless you're using the Link to Previous option.

✔ When you have selected the Different First Page option (as you do in the earlier section "Removing the header and footer from the first page"), note that each section has its own first-page header and footer, which are different from (and separate to) the other headers in that section.

✔ The Different Odd & Even Pages option affects all sections of a document.

Removing a header or footer

The simplest way to remove a document header is to use the Header⇨Remove Header command. Here's how it's done:

1. **Open the page where the header exists.**

   Use Print Layout view for this step so that you can see the ghostly image of the header at the top of the page.

2. **Click the Insert tab.**

3. **From the Header & Footer group, choose Header⇨Remove Header.**

   The header is gone.

This trick removes only the header for the current section. To remove headers in other sections, you must repeat these steps when the insertion pointer is in that section.

To remove a footer, choose Footer⇨Remove Footer in Step 3.

Another way to remove a header is to delete all text in a header: Press Ctrl+A to select all the text when editing the header, and then press the Delete key. *Poof!* The header is gone.

I recommend removing the header on any pages in your document that change orientation. That's because the header prints on the "wrong" edge of the page, which is inconsistent with the rest of the document. Because the page (or pages) with a different orientation is in its own section anyway, simply delete the header for that section. Then the reoriented pages can continue with headers and footers throughout the rest of the document.

Chapter 15

Word Formatting Styles

1 assume that some people never format their documents. That's okay. Boring, but okay. Other people format every detail of every document, using just about all the formatting commands available in Word. It's those folks for whom I write this chapter. That's because Word employs something called *styles*. You can use preset styles to instantly format your prose. Or, if you fancy creating text formatting, you can make your own styles. It's easy, and it's a powerful way to instantly change the look of your entire document.

The Big Style Overview

Styles are a traditional ingredient of the word processing stew, designed to save you formatting toil. The idea is to save time. So when you change your mind and decide that you want all figure captions in your document to be left-aligned rather than centered, you make only one change and it's done. That's the beauty of styles.

✔ A style is nothing more than a clutch of text and paragraph formats. You give the style a name, and then you use it to format your text. Or, you can format your text first and then make a style to match.

✔ In addition to the formatting information, styles have names. The names try to give you a clue to how to use the style, such as Heading 1 for the document's first heading, or Caption, which is for figure and table captions.

✔ All text in Word has a style. As configured, Word uses the Normal style to format text. Unless you specify otherwise, Word uses the Normal style — typically, the Calibri font, 11 points, left-aligned paragraphs, line spacing at 1.15, and no indenting, with 10 points of air after each paragraph.

✔ Styles are part of the document template. See Chapter 16 for more information.

✔ Using styles is optional. They do, however, make formatting your documents easier.

Understanding style types

Word sports five different types of styles, each customized to format a different document element in Word:

✔ **Paragraph:** The paragraph style contains both paragraph and text formatting attributes: indents, tabs, font, text size, — you name it. It's the most common type of style.

✔ **Character:** The character style formats only characters, not paragraphs. All character formatting mentioned in Chapter 10 can be stuffed into a character style.

✔ **Linked:** The linked style is a combination style that can be applied to both paragraphs and individual characters. The difference depends on which text is selected when you apply the style.

✔ **Table:** The table style is applied to tables, to add lines and shading to the table cells' contents. Refer to Chapter 19 for more information on tables in Word.

✔ **List:** The list style is customized for presenting lists of information. The styles can include bullets, numbers, indentation, and other formats typical for the parts of a document that present lists of information. See Chapter 21 for info on lists.

These style types come into play when you create your own style as well as when you're perusing styles to apply to your text. For example, if you want to create a new look for tables in your document, you make a Table style. Or, when you want a style to affect only text and not paragraphs, you create a Character style.

Finding the styles in Word

You find styles located on the Home tab, in the aptly named Styles group, shown in Figure 15-1. Most obvious there is the Quick Style Gallery, which can be expanded into a full menu of style choices.

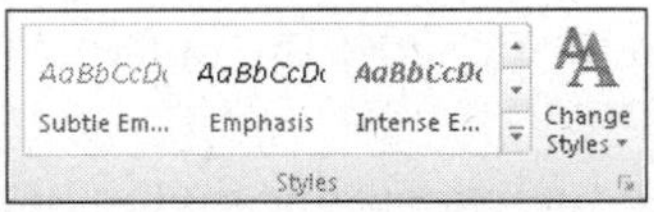

Figure 15-1:
Where
Word styles
lurk.

The Change Styles button displays a menu for choosing document styles as well as themes, which are the focus of Chapter 16.

Finally, the dialog box launcher, in the lower right corner of the Styles group, is used to quickly display a task pane full of styles, as shown in Figure 15-2. To dismiss the Styles task pane, click the X (close) button in its upper right corner.

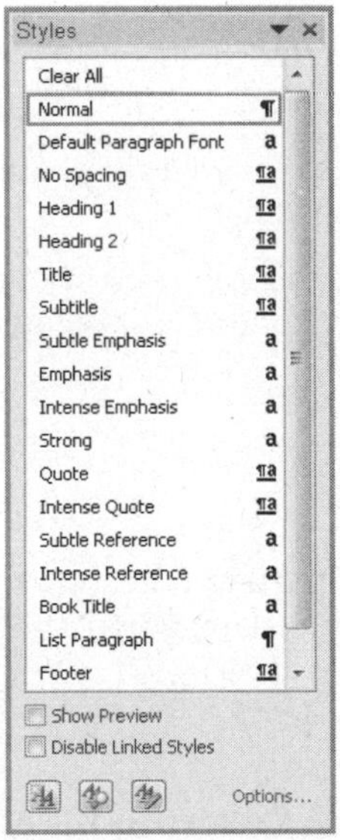

Figure 15-2:
Styles task
pane.

To preview the styles in the Styles task pane, put a check in the box by the Show Preview option, found at the bottom of the task pane. You can also see more information about a style by simply hovering the mouse pointer over the style's name in the Style task pane.

The Styles task pane lists only "recommended" styles. To see the whole slew of styles available in Word, follow these steps:

1. **Summon the Styles task pane.**

2. **Click the Options link in the lower right corner of the Styles task pane.**

3. **In the Styles Pane Options dialog box, choose the option All Styles from the Select Styles to Show drop-down list.**

   Or, if you want to keep the list shorter, choose the option In Use or In Current Document.

4. **Click OK.**

If you chose the All Styles option, the Styles task pane is updated to list every dang doodle style available in Word. It has quite a few of them.

- ✔ Word's predefined styles are specified in the Quick Style Gallery, though you can customize the list to replace Word's styles with your own. See the section "Customizing the Quick Style Gallery," later in this chapter.

- ✔ In addition to listing style names, the Quick Style Gallery gives you a teensy hint of how the style looks.

- ✔ The Styles task pane lists more styles than the Quick Style Gallery, including styles you've created.

- ✔ A more abbreviated version of the Styles task pane is available: Press Ctrl+Shift+S to call forth the Apply Styles task pane.

- ✔ The keyboard shortcut for the Styles task pane is Ctrl+Shift+Alt+S. It helps to be quite dexterous with your left hand to conjure up that shortcut.

Using a style

Applying a style to your text works just like formatting. The major difference is that rather than apply a single format, the style slaps down multiple formats on your text. It works like this:

1. **Select the text you want to format.**

2. **Choose a style, from either the Quick Style Gallery or the Styles task pane.**

   Refer to the preceding section for information on both the Quick Style Gallery or Styles task pane.

After you choose a style, your document's text is reformatted to reflect that style. That style is *applied* to the selected text.

- ✔ As you hover the mouse over each Quick Style, text in your document is updated to reflect the style's appearance — a boon to help you make that difficult choice. (This trick may not work in all documents.)

- ✔ Styles can be applied by using a keyboard shortcut. For example, the Normal style shortcut key is Ctrl+Shift+N. Not all styles have keyboard shortcuts, however.

- ✔ You can also choose a new style and then just start typing; the new style affects the new text you type.

Understanding heading styles

A special style in Word is the Heading style. Word has several of them, starting with Heading 1 and progressing through however many Heading styles your document needs.

Heading styles are designed for organization: Heading 1 is for your document's main headings, Heading 2 is for subheadings under Heading 1 styles, and down the line through Heading 3, Heading 4, and so on.

Using Heading styles is about more than just document formatting. Not only do they help keep your document visually organized, but they also take advantage of other Word features.

For example, the Heading styles appear when you use the vertical scroll bar to skim a document. They appear in the Navigation pane when you search for text. They can also be used when creating a table of contents. And, they're used in Word's Outline mode. These examples are noted throughout this book.

- ✔ Heading 1 is similar to the A-level heading found in other word processors and desktop publishing programs. Heading 2 is the B-level heading, and so on.

- ✔ Headings should be only one line long.

- ✔ You can break up headings: Press Shift+Enter to create a soft return in the middle of a long heading.

- ✔ When you're done typing a heading formatted with Heading 1 or Heading 2 or another heading level, press the Enter key. Automatically, the following paragraph is formatted using the Normal style. Normal is the "follow me" style used for all Word heading styles. Refer to the sidebar "The follow-me style," later in this chapter, to find out how it works.

✔ The Title style isn't a heading style.

✔ You can create your own Heading styles. The secret is to set an outline level for the heading style in the Paragraph formatting dialog box. See the section "Make Your Own Styles," later in this chapter, for the details.

Determining which style you're using

Discovering which style is applied to your text is often difficult. Sometimes, the style is highlighted in the Quick Style Gallery. The current style is highlighted in the Home tab's Styles group, although that group doesn't list all styles, but that list can be a long one. The Home tab's Font group displays the text (Heading) or (Body) when you've selected Heading- or Normal-formatted text. But that just isn't good enough.

No, when you want to know what's truly going on with styles, use the Style Inspector, shown in Figure 15-3. Activate the inspector by clicking the Style Inspector button, such as the one found at the bottom of the Styles task pane (refer to Figure 15-2).

Figure 15-3: Style Inspector.

Close the Style Inspector task pane by clicking the X in its upper right corner.

To *really* see the details of how your text is formatted, click the Reveal Formatting button in the Style Inspector. Clicking that button summons the gruesome Reveal Formatting task pane, which shows the specifics of which formats are applied to any text. It's nerdy but accurate. Click the X button in the task pane's upper right corner to hide the thing.

The keyboard shortcut for the Reveal Formatting command is Shift+F1.

Switching to another style set

One reason that you would want to use the Emphasis style rather than apply italics directly to your text is that Word comes with a bunch of style sets. You can universally change the look of your document by simply choosing a new style set.

To select a new style set, from the Home tab's Styles group, click the Change Styles button. From the menu that's displayed, choose Style Set and then move the mouse over the various menu items. As each menu item is highlighted, your document's formatting is updated with new styles (if you used Quick Styles to format your document). Choose a style you find pleasing.

✔ The Default style set is the one you probably used originally, unless you specifically chose a style set to use.

✔ Also refer to the topic of document themes, covered in Chapter 16.

Unapplying a style

Word doesn't remove styles as much as it replaces a style with Normal. So you don't truly unapply a style as much as you reapply the Normal style to text. Because this task seems to be something that people want, Word has the Clear Formatting command. You can find it lurking in the Font group on the Home tab.

To peel away stubborn style stains, select the text you want to cleanse and choose the Clear Formatting command button from the Font group on the Home tab. Whatever text you have selected is stripped of formatting by that command.

✔ The keyboard shortcut for the Clear Formatting command is Ctrl+spacebar. When you think about it, the spacebar produces the "clear" character, so it makes sense, and making sense of computers will always be novel.

✔ The Style Inspector is a great place to remove specific formatting from text without affecting other formatting. Refer to the earlier section "Determining which style you're using" for information; use the Clear Formatting buttons in the Style Inspector to selectively peel off formatting.

Make Your Own Styles

Considering all the restaurants out there in the world, one wonders why anyone would be so foolhardy as to cook their own meals. I suppose that the reason, aside from home-cooked food being better and cheaper than restaurant food, is that some people truly prefer to do things themselves. They're fussy. They're exacting. The same statement holds true for using styles in Word: Some people like to create their own styles.

You can make your own styles in two ways: Create the style in a document and then base a new style on your already formatted text. Or, build a style from scratch by using Word's version of a formatting style salad bar. The following two sections cover these methods.

Creating a style based on text you've already formatted

The easiest way to make up a new style is to use all your formatting skills and power to format a single paragraph just the way you like. Then create the style based on that formatted paragraph. Here's how:

1. **Type and format a paragraph of text.**

   Choose the paragraph formatting and also any text formatting, such as size and font.

2. **Mark your paragraph as a block.**

   See Chapter 6 to find out how to mark a block of text.

3. **Press Ctrl+Shift+Alt+S to summon the Styles task pane.**

4. **Click the New Style button.**

   Look in the lower left corner of the Styles task pane for this button.

   The Create New Style from Formatting dialog box appears, as shown in Figure 15-4. It's the place where new styles are born.

5. **In the Name box, type a short and descriptive name for your style.**

6. **Ensure that Paragraph is chosen from the Style Type drop-down list.**

7. **Click the OK button to create your style.**

   The style is added to Word's repertoire of styles for your document.

The style you created now applies to the paragraph you typed (on which the style is based), and you can apply the style to other paragraphs.

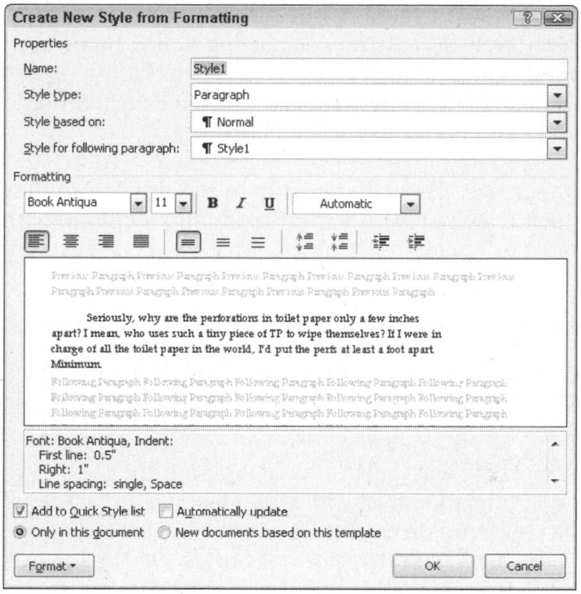

Figure 15-4:
The Create
New
Style from
Formatting
dialog box.

And now, the shortcut!

The fastest way to create a new paragraph style based on text you've typed and formatted is to follow Steps 1 and 2 in the preceding set of steps and then, from the Quick Style Gallery, choose the command Save Selection As New Quick Style. Doing so displays a tiny dialog box in which you merely have to type the name of your style. Click the OK button and you're done. Cinchy.

The follow-me style

When I write a new chapter in a book, I start with my own Chapter Title style. The next style I use is my Intro Paragraph style. Intro Paragraph is followed by TextBody, which is followed by TextBody, TextBody, TextBody, and so on. There's no point in my having to apply those styles because I can tell Word to change styles automatically.

In the Create New Style from Formatting dialog box (refer to Figure 15-4), locate the Style for Following Paragraph drop-down list. The style shown on that list tells Word which style to

switch to when you press the Enter key to end a paragraph. Normally, it's the same style, which makes sense for most of your work. But in situations where you *know* that the style will switch, you can demand that Word do the switching for you. You can edit the Chapter Title style so that the Intro Paragraph style is selected from the Style for Following Paragraph drop-down list. That way, pressing the Enter key after typing the chapter title switches the style to Intro Paragraph. Very nice.

Even though there's a quick way to create a style, don't be too quick to discard using the Create New Style from Formatting dialog box (refer to Figure 15-4). That method gives you much more control, including options to make changes to the font you created as well as other tricks explained in this chapter — stuff you can't do by using the shortcut.

- ✔ The styles you create are available only to the document in which they're created. They're saved with the document, along with your text.

- ✔ If you create scads of styles that you love and you want to use them for several documents, create a *template*. Chapter 16 covers this procedure, in the section about making a new template from scratch.

- ✔ You may have to tweak some settings in your style. If so, you use the Style and Formatting task pane. See the section "Modifying a style," later in this chapter.

- ✔ A quick way to create a style is to base it on another, existing style. Choose that existing style from the Style Based On drop-down list in the Create New Style from Formatting dialog box (refer to Figure 15-4). Use the dialog box controls and the Format button (in the lower left corner) to subtly modify the style. Give the style a new name and — ta-da! — you have a new style.

Creating a style from scratch

Using the Create New Style from Formatting dialog box (refer to Figure 15-4), you can create any one of the five Word style types. The key is to choose the type from the Style Type drop-down list. When you do, the contents of the dialog box change to reflect whatever options are available for that style type.

For example, when you choose Character from the Style Type drop-down list, only character-formatting commands and settings are available in the Create New Style from Formatting dialog box.

- ✔ See the "Understanding style types" section, earlier in this chapter, for more information on Word's five different style types.

- ✔ Character styles don't affect paragraph formatting. Selecting a character style changes only the font, style, size, underlining, bold, and so on.

Modifying a style

Styles change. Who knows? Maybe blow-dried hair and wide lapels will creep back into vogue someday.

Just as fashion styles change, you may need to change styles in your document. Nothing is wrong with that. In fact, by changing a style, you demonstrate the power of Word: Changing a style once causes all text formatted with that style to be updated with the change in your document. That beats the pants off making that change manually.

To modify a style, heed these steps:

1. **Summon the Styles task pane.**

   Click the dialog box launcher in the lower right corner of the Styles group (on the Home tab) or press Ctrl+Shift+Alt+S.

2. **Point the mouse at the style you want to change.**

   A menu button appears on the right end of the style's entry.

3. **Click the menu button to display the style's menu.**

4. **Choose Modify.**

   A Modify Style dialog box appears, although it's the same Create New Style from Formatting dialog box (refer to Figure 15-4). This time, however, the settings you make now *change* the style rather than create a new style.

5. **Change the formatting for your style.**

   You're free to use any Word formatting option to change your style. You can even add new formatting options or a shortcut key (covered in the next section).

6. **Click OK when you're done.**

Close the task pane if you're done with it.

Giving your style a shortcut key

Style shortcut keys make formatting even better because pressing Alt+Shift+T to apply the TextBody style is often faster than messing with the Quick Style Gallery or the various task panes.

To give your style a shortcut key, follow these steps:

1. **Work through Steps 1 through 4 from the previous section.**

   Your goal is to display the Modify Style dialog box for your soon-to-be shortcut-key-blessed style.

2. **Click the Format button.**

   It dwells in the lower left corner of the dialog box.

3. **Choose Shortcut Key from the menu.**

   The cryptic Customize Keyboard dialog box appears.

4. **Press your shortcut key combination.**

   Notice that the key combination you press appears as text in the Press New Shortcut Key box. (See the middle right side of the dialog box.) If you make a mistake, press the Backspace key to erase it and choose another key combination.

   Most of the good shortcut key combinations have already been put to work in Word. For example, Word uses Ctrl+B as the Bold character-formatting shortcut key. My advice is to use Ctrl+Alt and then a letter key for your style's shortcut. Most of the Ctrl+Alt key combinations are unassigned in Word.

5. **Confirm that the key combination you've chosen isn't already in use.**

   Refer to the text found below the Current Keys box. The text there explains which Word command uses the key combination you've pressed. When you see [unassigned], however, it means that your key combination is good to go.

   Press the Backspace key when the key combination you've chosen is already in use. Try again.

6. **Click the Assign button.**

7. **Click the Close button.**

   The Customize Keyboard dialog box skulks away.

8. **Click the OK button.**

   You can also close the Style task pane, if you're done with it.

Congratulations! You now have a usable shortcut key for your style. Try it out: Position the insertion pointer in a block of text and press the key. Ta-da! Your style is applied instantly.

Customizing the Quick Style Gallery

You're not stuck with the styles assigned to the Quick Style Gallery. You're free to add or remove any styles you like.

To remove a style from the Quick Style Gallery, right-click the style and choose the command Remove from Quick Style Gallery from the shortcut menu that appears.

To add a style to the Quick Style Gallery, follow these steps:

1. **Summon the Styles task pane.**

   Click the dialog box launcher in the lower right corner of the Styles group on the Home tab, or press the ungainly Ctrl+Shift+Alt+S key combination.

2. **Right-click the style you want to add.**

3. **Choose the command Add to Quick Style Gallery.**

You can continue to add styles to the Quick Style Gallery or close the Styles task pane.

If the style you want to add doesn't show up, ensure that all styles are being shown in the Styles task pane's list. See the section "Finding the styles in Word," earlier in this chapter, and ensure that All Styles is displayed in the Styles task pane.

Deleting a style

You can delete any style you create. It's easy: Display the Styles task pane (press Ctrl+Shift+Alt+S), right-click the style's name in the list, and choose Delete from its menu. You're asked whether you're sure you want to delete the style. Choose Yes.

You cannot delete the Normal or Heading or any other standard Word style.

Chapter 16

Fun with Themes and Template Formatting

. . . .

. . . .

Some folks toil countless and trivial hours to put monumental effort into their word processing labors. If you're one of them, you probably get upset at the individuals who seem to sport some sort of inborn talent for formatting their documents. Their stuff looks great. It makes you seethe with anger, but that's only because you don't know their secret: themes and templates.

The topic is looking good. The method is to use Word's themes and templates to help you format and prepare a document all at one time. This chapter shows you how it's done. With your newfound knowledge, you too can join the ranks of those who seem to effortlessly toss together a document.

The Theme of Things

Themes apply decorative styles to your document, such as fonts and colors, which gives your prose a professionally formatted look and appeal. It's like having a professional graphics designer assist you but without having to suffer through her lamentable complaints about how her boyfriend doesn't pay any attention to her.

A theme consists of three elements:

Colors: A set of colors is chosen to format the text foreground and background, any graphics or design elements in the theme, plus hyperlinks.

Fonts: Two fonts are chosen as part of the theme — one for the heading styles and a second for the body text.

Graphical effects: These effects are applied to any graphics or design elements in your document. The effects can include 3D, shading, gradation, drop shadows, and other design subtleties.

Each of these elements is organized into a theme, given a name, and placed on the Page Layout tab's Themes menu for easy application in your document.

Refer to the next section for information on applying a theme.

- ✔ A theme's fonts, colors, and design effects are created by a professionally licensed graphics designer so that they look good and work well together.

- ✔ A theme doesn't overrule styles chosen for a document. Instead, it accents those styles. The theme may add color information, choose different fonts, or present various graphical elements. Beyond that, it doesn't change any styles applied to the text.

- ✔ The graphical effects of a theme are only applied to any graphics in your document; the theme doesn't insert graphics into your text. See Chapter 22 for information on graphics in Word.

- ✔ You can use the various Themes menu commands to search for even more themes.

- ✔ Choosing a theme affects your entire document all at once. To affect individual paragraphs or bits of text, apply a style or format manually. Refer to Chapter 15.

- ✔ Themes work only with Word 2010 and Word 2007 documents. To apply a theme to an older Word document, you must *convert* the document's format. Refer to Chapter 24 for more on converting old Word documents.

Applying a document theme

You choose a theme from the Page Layout tab, in the Themes group. Built-in themes are listed on the Themes button's menu along with any custom themes you've created. Figure 16-1 illustrates the Themes menu.

- ✔ Each of the built-in themes controls all three major theme elements, changing your document's contents accordingly.

- ✔ Pointing the mouse at a theme previews your document, by showing how it would look if you went ahead and applied that theme.

✔ Because a document can use only one theme at a time, choosing a new theme replaces the current theme.

✔ To remove a theme from your document, choose the Office theme or the menu command Reset to Theme from Template (refer to Figure 16-1).

✔ If you would rather change only one part of a theme, such as a document's fonts, use the Colors, Fonts, or Effects command button in the Themes group.

✔ Themes affect only Word 2010 and Word 2007 documents saved in the .docx format. You cannot apply themes to an older Word document unless you convert that document to the newer format. See Chapter 24.

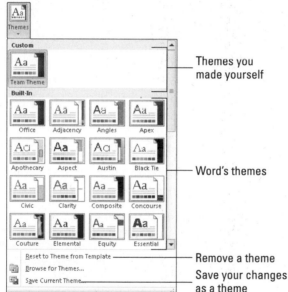

Figure 16-1: The Themes menu.

Themes you made yourself

Word's themes

Remove a theme

Save your changes as a theme

Modifying or creating a theme

You can't create your own themes from scratch, but you can modify existing themes to make your own, custom theme. You start by modifying existing theme colors and fonts:

To create a custom color theme, choose Colors⇨Create New Theme Colors. Use the Create New Theme Colors dialog box to pick and choose which colors apply to text or various graphical elements in your document.

To create a custom font theme, choose Fonts⇨Create New Theme Fonts. Use the Create New Theme Fonts dialog box to select your fonts — one for the headings and another for the body text.

In each case, give the new theme a name and save it. You can then choose that theme from the Custom area of either the Colors or Fonts menu.

When you're using a set of theme colors, fonts, and graphics styles — even if you didn't create them yourself but, rather, merely used them to organize your document — you can collect the various elements as a theme: Choose Save Current Theme from the Theme menu and use the dialog box to give your theme a proper descriptive name and save it. The theme you create then appears in the Custom area of the Themes menu (refer to Figure 16-1).

To remove a custom theme, right-click it on the Themes menu and choose the Delete command. Click the Yes button to remove the theme.

Create Instant Documents by Using Templates

A template is a special type of Word documents. It can contain styles, formatting, and perhaps a header or footer — and even some text. You create a template just like you create a document except that you save it in a unique way. That's because you never really use the template itself, but, rather, a copy. By using that copy, you can create an entirely new document; the template merely helps you get started by doing some of the routine tasks for you.

Document templates help to save time and prevent you from having to repeat your efforts. I use one template for sending faxes, one for writing letters, and one for writing plays, for example. This book has its own *Dummies* template that contains all the text styles the publisher's production department uses to produce the book. Whenever I need to start a new chapter, I use the *Dummies* template so that the paragraph, heading, caption, and other styles match the ones my publisher uses, which keeps them happy. I hope.

It's worth your time to create a template for all the common document types you use regularly. The following sections describe how.

- All documents in Word are based on a template. When you don't specify a template, Word uses the Normal document template, NORMAL.DOTM.

- Word uses three filename extensions for its document templates: DOT was the template filename extension for older versions of Word. In Word 2007, DOTX and DOTM are used. DOTX refers to a template that doesn't employ macros; the DOTM indicates a template that uses macros. (This book doesn't cover macros; I wish it did, but the book just doesn't have any more room.)

Starting a new document by using a template

Word comes with a host of templates already created, as well as any templates you whip up yourself. To see them, you must venture to the File tab's New menu, shown in Figure 16-2. Common templates are shown at the top of the window, with online templates listed at the bottom.

Your templates are
found here.

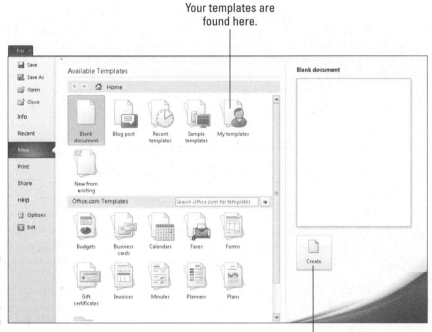

That big Create button

If you see a template in the list, choose it and then click the Create button, as shown in the figure.

Most of the time, you'll probably choose the My Templates item, shown in the figure. Doing so displays the New dialog box, which lists icons representing all the templates you've created. Choose an icon for the template you want to use and then click the OK button in the New dialog box. Instantly, Word loads up that template and starts a new document for you.

The new document contains the styles and formats and perhaps even some text that's ready for you to use or edit. At that point, you work with the document just like any other document in Word, though a lot of the formatting and typing has been done for you.

✔ Even though the template has saved you some time, you still need to save your work! Use the Save command and give your document a proper name as soon as possible!

✔ Editing the document doesn't change the template. To change or modify a template, see the section "Modifying a template" later in this chapter.

✔ If you don't see your custom template in the New dialog box, Word probably goofed up when it saved your template. Instead, look in the Documents or My Documents folder for the Word template file; double-click to open that icon, which starts a new document using the template. Yes, this route is a crummy workaround, but Word often forgets to put your templates in the proper file location.

Creating a template based on a document you already have

Rome wasn't built in a day, but building your own document template can take even less time. That's because you can easily create a template based on a document you've already slaved over. So when the formatting and styles and all that junk have already been created, making a template is a snap — and doesn't require a large army or navy nor any ambitious politicians.

To make a template based on a document you've already created, follow these steps:

1. **Find or create the document, one that has styles or formats or text you plan to use repeatedly.**

2. **Strip out any text that doesn't need to be in every document.**

   For example, my play-writing template has all my play-writing styles in it, but the text includes only placeholders — just to get me started.

   The template should contain only the styles you need for that document, plus any text that's common to all documents.

3. **Choose the Save As command from the File tab menu.**

   The Save As dialog box appears. It's the same Save As dialog box that Word uses for saving everything. Refer to Chapter 8 if you need a refresher.

4. **Type a name for the template.**

   Type the name in the File Name box. Be descriptive.

You don't need to name the template using the word *template*.

5. **From the Save As Type drop-down list, choose `Word Template` (`*.dotx`).**

Ah-ha! This is the secret. The document must be saved in a document template format. That's what makes a template superior over a typical, boring Word document.

6. **Click the Save button.**

Your efforts are saved to disk as a document template, nestled in the proper place where Word keeps all its document templates.

7. **Close the template.**

Choose the Close command from the File tab menu, just as you would close any other document in Word.

The reason for closing it is that any changes you make from now on are made to the template. If you want to use the template to start a new document, you choose that template from the New window as described earlier in this chapter.

Refer to the later section "Modifying a template " for information on updating or changing a template.

Making a new template from scratch

After you become well versed in creating Word styles, and after you fully understand the template concept, you can begin creating Word templates from scratch. It's easy, but only when you *truly* know what you want.

The basic trick is to build the styles you need and then add any text you may want. Then use the Save As dialog box to save the document as a template.

The biggest drawback to this approach is that your template probably isn't complete. As you start creating new documents based on the template, you find that you need to modify existing styles as well as add new ones. That just means more template editing, which is covered in the next section.

Modifying a template

Changing or editing a document template is identical to changing or editing any document. You simply create a new document by using the existing template. Make your changes, and then use the Save As command to either overwrite the existing template or save the document as a new template, by following Steps 3 and 4 in the earlier section "Creating a template based on a document you already have."

Yes, you can edit a document template in other ways. You can open the template itself in Word, but the steps involved are rather convoluted because you have to have some computer-savvy skills just to find where Word hides the template files. No, you're much better to start with the template as though you're creating a new document and then simply save the document again as a template.

Changing a template has a widespread impact. When you update or modify a template, you're basically changing all documents that use the template. Be mindful of your changes!

Attaching a template to a document

Documents have templates like people have last names. Mostly, the documents are born with their templates. You either choose the template when the document is first created, as covered earlier in this chapter, or just create a new document, in which case the NORMAL.DOTM template is used. You can change it by assigning or attaching a new template to a document. Here's how:

1. **Open the document that needs a new template attached.**

2. **From the File tab menu, choose the Options command.**

3. **Choose Add-Ins from the left side of the Word Options dialog box.**

4. **On the right side of the window, near the bottom, choose Templates from the Manage drop-down list.**

5. **Click the Go button.**

   The Templates and Add-ins dialog box appears. You should see which template is attached to the document, such as Normal. Whichever template name appears there is whichever template is attached to the document.

6. **Click the Attach button.**

   Word displays the Attach Template dialog box, which looks and works like the Open dialog box.

7. **Select the template you want to attach.**

8. **Click the Open button.**

   The template is now attached, but you may need to do one more thing back in the Templates and Add-ins dialog box.

9. **Select Automatically Update Document Styles (Optional).**

   Updating styles means that your document's current styles are changed to reflect those of the new template, which is probably what you want. If not, skip this step.

10. **Click OK.**

The styles (plus custom toolbars and macros) stored in that template are now available to your document, and the document is now attached to the template.

Note that attaching a template doesn't merge any text or graphics stored in that template. Only the styles (plus custom toolbar and macros) are merged into your document.

You can also follow these steps to unattach a template. Do that by selecting NORMAL.DOTM as the template to attach.

Borrowing an existing document as a template

A quick-and-dirty way to create a template is to basically steal an existing document, using it as a template. All text from the document is sucked into the new document, plus any styles or other template-y things found in the original document. Basically, this is the easiest and sneakiest way to make one document share information from your already created efforts.

To use an existing document as a template, follow these steps:

1. **Click the File tab.**

2. **Choose the New command.**

3. **Choose New from Existing item.**

Choosing this option displays the New from Existing Document dialog box, which is essentially an Open dialog box, the kind you're familiar with through songs and tales told by our tribal elders.

4. **Pluck out a Word document to use as a template.**

5. **Click the Open button.**

It looks as though Word just opened the document you selected, but a quick glance at the title bar shows you that a new, blank document has been created instead. All styles and any text from the document you chose (Step 4) appear in the new document. At this point, you can edit your new document, saving it as you go.

Chapter 17

Sundry Formatting

Say hello to the formatting leftovers, the items that are related to formatting but that may not fit into another chapter in this part of the book or, as is my feeling, were added to the Word formatting mix in a weird or hodgepodge manner. In this chapter, you find a plethora of formatting tricks and tidbits. It's random stuff, various and sundry. Welcome to the Word formatting buffet dessert bar!

Weird and Fun Text Attributes

There is a fuzzy button. It's found on the Home tab's Font group. It looks like a big *A*, and it's one of those menu button items that dot the ribbon like ticks on the back of an Alabama hound dog. Regardless, what it does is let you apply some interesting and nonstandard effects to text in your document.

To apply the text effects, simply choose one from the Text Effects button menu. The effect you choose is applied to any new text you type or any selected text in the document.

You can specifically apply an effect or change a color by choosing the specific item from the Text Effects menu, shown in Figure 17-1. Or, if you want to get fancy, you can use the Format Text Effects dialog box. To get there, follow these steps:

Figure 17-1:
Text Effects
menu.

1. **Click the dialog box launcher, found in the lower right corner of the Font group on the Home tab.**

   Or, you can press Ctrl+D to quickly summon the Font dialog box.

2. **Click the Text Effects button in the Font dialog box.**

   The button is dimmed when your document has been saved using an older Word format.

3. **Choose the custom text effects by manipulating the various gizmos in the Format Text Effects dialog box.**

   Wonderful and detailed controls are available in the Format Text Effects dialog box, but, sadly, no preview window.

4. **Click the Close button to dismiss the Format Text Effects dialog box.**

5. **Click the OK button to close the Font dialog box.**

The font effects you select affect any selected text in the document or any text you type from that point onward.

- ✔ Font effects are best used for document headings and other decorative text.

- ✔ The text effects covered in this section are in addition to the standard font-formatting text attributes, such as bold, italics, and outline. See Chapter 10.

- ✔ The Word 2010 text effects can be applied only to Word 2010 DOCX documents, not to documents created by or compatible with older versions of Word.

Automatic Formatting

Part of Word's AutoCorrect function (covered in Chapter 7) is a feature named AutoFormat. Whereas AutoCorrect is used to fix primarily typos and common spelling boo-boos, AutoFormat is used to fix formatting fumbles. This section demonstrates AutoFormat's prowess.

Enjoying automagical text

AutoFormat controls some minor text formatting as you type. The best way to demonstrate this concept is to have a Word document on the screen and then type the examples in the following sections. Note that these are only a few of the things AutoFormat can do.

When you find any of these tricks upsetting, see the later section "Disabling the @#$%&! AutoFormat." You can also refer to that section to find out how to enable some of the tricks that don't work as expected.

Smart quotes

The quote characters on the keyboard are tick marks: " and '. AutoFormat converts them into more stylish open and closed curly quotes. Type hither:

```
She said, "Yes, I'm being honest. I really do love
you. And I'm sorry that I shot you in the elbow."
```

Both the single and double quotes are properly used and converted.

Real fractions

You can format a fraction by typing the first value in superscript, the slash mark, and then the second value in subscript. Or, you can let AutoFormat do it for you. Here's an example:

I spend twice the time doing ½ the work.

The characters 1/2 are converted into the single character ½. This trick works for some, but not all, common fractions. When it doesn't work, use the superscript/subscript trick described in Chapter 31, in the section about building your own fractions.

Hyperlinks

Word can underline *and* activate hyperlinks typed in your document, such as

```
I've been to www.hell.com and back.
```

The Web site www.hell.com is automatically underlined, painted blue, and turned into an active Web page link for you.

Ordinals

You're guessing wrong if you think that *ordinals* are a baseball team or a group of religious leaders. They're numbers that end in the letters *st, nd,* or *rd,* as this line demonstrates:

```
There were two of us in the race; I came in 1st
and Barbara came in 3rd.
```

Word automatically superscripts ordinal numbers, making them look oh-so-spiffy.

Em dashes

An *em dash* is the official typesetting term for a long dash, longer than the hyphen (or its evil twin, the en dash). Most people type two hyphens to emulate the *em dash.* Word fixes that problem:

```
A red one is a slug bug--not a punch buggy.
```

As you type the–(dash-dash), AutoFormat replaces it with the official em dash character.

✔ The keyboard shortcut for typing an em dash is Ctrl+Alt+minus sign, where the minus sign is the minus key on the numeric keypad.

✔ The keyboard shortcut for typing an en dash is Ctrl+minus sign.

✔ The en dash is approximately the width of the letter *N.* Likewise, the em dash is the width of the letter *M.*

Paragraph formatting tricks

At the paragraph level, AutoFormat helps you quickly handle some otherwise irksome formatting issues. Some folks like this feature, some don't. The following sections provide a few examples of what AutoFormat is capable of.

If you find any of these AutoFormat tricks annoying, refer to the later section "Disabling the @#$%&! AutoFormat" for information on shutting the dumb thing off!

Numbered lists

Any time you start a paragraph with a number, Word assumes (through AutoFormat) that you need all your paragraphs numbered. Here's the proof:

```
Things to do today:
1. Get new treads for the tank.
```

 Immediately after typing 1., you probably saw the infamous AutoFormat lightning bolt icon and noticed your text being reformatted. Darn, this thing is quick! That's AutoFormat guessing that you're about to type a list. Go ahead and finish typing the line; after you press Enter, you see the next line begin with the number 2.

Keep typing until your list ends or you get angry, whichever comes first. To end the list, press the Enter key again. That erases the final number and restores the paragraph formatting to Normal.

- ✔ This trick also works for letters (and Roman numerals). Just start something with a letter and a period, and Word picks up on the next line by suggesting the next letter in the alphabet and another period.

- ✔ Bulleted lists can also be created in this way: Start a line by typing an asterisk (*) and a space to see what happens.

- ✔ See Chapter 21 for more information on creating numbered or bulleted lists.

- ✔ I tell you earlier in this book not to press the Enter key twice to end a paragraph. That statement still holds true: When you press Enter twice to end an AutoFormat list, Word sticks only one Enter "character" into the text.

Borders (lines)

A line above or below a paragraph in Word is a *border*. Most folks call them lines, but they're borders. Here's how to whip out a few borders by using AutoFormat:

```
---
```

Typing three hyphens and pressing the Enter key causes Word to instantly transmute the three little hyphens into a solid line that touches the left and right paragraph margins.

- ✔ To create a double line, type three equal signs and press Enter.

- ✔ To create a bold line, type three underlines and press Enter.

- ✔ Refer to Chapter 18 for more information on borders and boxes around your text.

Undoing an AutoFormat

You have two quick ways to undo AutoFormatting. The first, obviously, is to press Ctrl+Z on the keyboard, which is the Undo command. That's easy.

You can also use the lightning bolt icon to undo AutoFormatting. Clicking the icon displays a drop-down menu (see Figure 17-2) that you use to control the AutoFormat options as you type. Three options are usually available: undo what has been done, disable what has been done so that it never happens again, and, last, open the Control AutoFormat Options dialog box, which is covered in the next section. Choose wisely.

Figure 17-2: AutoFormat options.

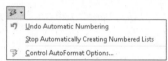

> Undo Automatic Numbering
> Stop Automatically Creating Numbered Lists
> Control AutoFormat Options...

Disabling the @#$%&! AutoFormat

Formatting is subjective. Sometimes you want AutoFormat to help you out, and sometimes AutoFormat makes you angry enough to want to hurl the computer out a convenient window. Either way, AutoFormat is controlled by a special dialog box buried deep within Word's bosom. Here's the treacherous trail leading to that location:

1. **Choose the Options command from the File tab's menu.**

   The Word Options window steps front and center.

2. **Select Proofing from the left side of the window.**

3. **Click the button labeled AutoCorrect Options.**

4. **Click the AutoFormat As You Type tab in the AutoCorrect dialog box.**

   This part of the dialog box, shown in Figure 17-3, is where all the AutoFormat options dwell. Turning an option off or on is as easy as removing or adding a check mark.

5. **Set the options as you like.**

   I don't mind certain options, but I detest the Apply As You Type options, so I unchecked them all.

6. **Click the AutoFormat tab.**

   Gadzooks! More options.

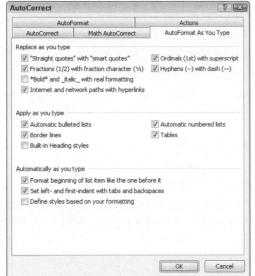

Figure 17-3:
AutoFormat
As You Type
settings.

7. **Set the options on the AutoFormat tab.**

   Repeat your choices here; I don't know why some things are listed twice in the dialog box. Silly Microsoft.

8. **Click OK to confirm your choices and then close the Word Options window.**

Center a Page, Top to Bottom

Nothing makes a document title nice and crisp like having it sit squat in the center of a page. The title is centered left to right, which you can do by selecting Center alignment for the title's paragraph. But how about centering the title top to bottom? Word can do that too:

1. **Move the insertion pointer to the start of your document.**

   The Ctrl+Home key combination moves you there instantly.

2. **Type and format your document's title.**

   It can be on a single line or on several lines.

   To center the title, select it and press Ctrl+E, the Center keyboard short-cut. Apply any additional font or paragraph formatting as necessary.

Avoid the temptation to press the Enter key to add space above or below the title. The title sits by itself at the top of the page, but that problem is fixed in a jiffy.

3. **Insert a section break after the title's last line: On the Page Layout tab, choose Breaks⇨Next Page from the Page Setup area.**

   The section break ensures that only the first page of your document is centered top to bottom. Review Chapter 14 for more information on document sections.

4. **Ensure that the insertion pointer is once again on the document's first page.**

   You need to be on the page you want to format.

5. **Summon the Page Setup dialog box: Click the Page Layout tab and choose the dialog box launcher from the lower right corner of the Page Setup area.**

   The Page Setup dialog box appears.

6. **Click the Layout tab.**

7. **Select Center from the Vertical Alignment drop-down list.**

   You can find this item in the bottom half of the dialog box.

8. **Confirm that the Apply To drop-down list shows This Section.**

9. **Click OK.**

Your changes are easy to see when you use Print Layout view. The first page of the document will be centered, top to bottom.

Steal This Format!

It's not a whisk broom and you'd have to be old to think it's a shaving brush. No, it's a paint brush. Not only that, but it's a special paint brush — one that steals text and paragraph formatting, by borrowing it from one place in your document and splashing it down in another. It's the Format Painter, and here's how it's used:

1. **Force the insertion pointer into the middle of the text that has the formatting you want to copy.**

   The insertion pointer must be in the midst of the word, not to the left or right of it. (The pointer doesn't have to be exactly in the middle — just "in the word.") If it's not, this trick doesn't work.

2. **On the Home tab, click the Format Painter command button in the Clipboard group.**

   The cursor changes to a paint brush/I-beam pointer, as depicted in the margin. This special cursor is used to highlight and then reformat text in your document.

3. **Hunt for the text you want to change.**

4. **Highlight the text.**

   Drag the mouse over the text you want to change — to "paint" it. (You must use the mouse here.)

Voilà! The text is changed.

✔ The Format Painter works with only character and paragraph formatting, not with page formatting.

✔ To change the formatting of multiple bits of text, double-click the Format Painter. That way, the Format Painter cursor stays active, ready to paint lots of text. Press the Esc key to cancel your Dutch Boy frenzy.

✔ If you tire of the mouse, you can use the Ctrl+Shift+C key combination to copy the character format from a highlighted block to another location in your document. Use the Ctrl+Shift+V key combination to paste the character format elsewhere. Just highlight the text in your document and press Ctrl+Shift+V to paste in the font formatting.

✔ You can sorta kinda remember to use Ctrl+Shift+C to copy character formatting and use Ctrl+Shift+V to paste because Ctrl+C and Ctrl+V are the copy-and-paste shortcut keys. Sorta kinda.

✔ Don't confuse the Format Painter with the highlighting tool, found in the Font group. See Chapter 26.

Part IV
Spruce Up a Dull Document

The 5th Wave   By Rich Tennant

©RICHTENNANT

AIRPORT SECURITY

"They won't let me through security until I remove the bullets from my Word document."

In this part . . .

Somewhere in the history of computer software, someone decided that if you could put it on a page, it was a chore that must be handled by a word processor. I'm not talking about thumb smudges, sneeze drops, or flecks of kung pao shrimp. I'm referring to anything you can imagine that can be printed in a document. Call them the fancy things that spruce up your documents, perhaps not relevant to the chore of processing words but still part of Word itself and, therefore, covered in this part of the book.

Chapter 18

Lines and Colors

ext can be dull. Even after the most creative formatting is applied, text is just text. To add another dimension, the mind first goes to the basics: lines and color. Lines can be joined to form boxes and be filled with color. Word handles the job quite well so that you can forget about using the hyphen key and the weird | character to create lines and boxes, and please stop using a highlighter pen after you print to add color. Just read this chapter and you'll be on your way to creating borders, boxes, and background colors with ease.

The Basics of Lines and Colors

Lines and colors in Word are handled by two command buttons found in the Home tab's Paragraph group. That's the easy part. The hard part is remembering that a line is known as a *border* in Word. Furthermore, background colors are known as *shading*. Keep those two concepts in your head and you're well on your way to drawing all sorts of lines in, on, around, above, and over your text, as well as coloring the background of that text.

✔ A line is a *border* in Word.

✔ An exception to the line-is-a-border concept is the Horizontal Line, a special border that's applied between paragraphs. See the later section "Drawing a fat, thick line."

> ✔ Word's Shading (background color) command affects the text background. Text color is applied by using the Font Color command, which is covered in Chapter 10.
>
> ✔ Not all lines in Word are borders. A thin border on the left margin of a line of text can be a sign that something was changed on that line. Refer to Chapter 26 for more information on revision marking.

Using the Border command button

Word places its basic text decoration doodlings on the Border command button menu, which is found in the Home tab's Paragraph group. Clicking that button immediately applies the indicated border to your text, or removes the borders, as is the case with the No Border button, shown in the margin.

The Border command button can also be used to display a menu full of border choices, as shown in Figure 18-1. Choosing a border from the menu not only applies that border to your text but also changes the Border command button to reflect the new border style.

Figure 18-1:
The Border
menu.

You can use only one border style at a time from the Border menu. Choosing another style replaces the first style. If you want a combination of borders, you must use the Borders and Shading dialog box, as described in the next section. That dialog box also allows you to change the line style, color, and thickness of the border.

Summoning the Borders and Shading dialog box

For true control over borders, you summon the Borders and Shading dialog box, shown in Figure 18-2. Choosing the Borders and Shading command from the bottom of the Border menu (refer to Figure 18-1) does the job.

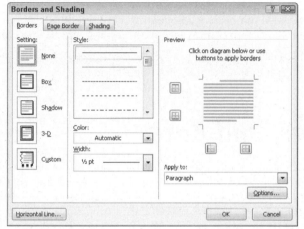

Figure 18-2:
The Borders and Shading dialog box.

Unlike on the Border menu, several options are available in the Borders and Shading dialog box for setting borders. Most notably, you can set the border line style, thickness, and color.

You can also use the Borders and Shading dialog box to create a page border and apply background color (shading). Later sections in this chapter discuss the details.

Click the OK button to apply your border settings and close the dialog box, or press Cancel to give up and quit.

Using the Shading command button

Background color is applied to your text by using the Shading button. As with the Borders command button, the background color shown on the button is applied to selected text or to new text you type. You can choose a new color from the menu that's displayed when you click the Shading command button's down-arrow thing, as shown in Figure 18-3.

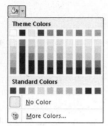

Figure 18-3:
Shading
(background
color) menu.

✔ The basic palette of colors is chosen by the current document theme.
See Chapter 16 for more information on themes and theme colors.

✔ You can also set background grayscale colors and patterns by using the
Shading tab in the Borders and Shading dialog box.

Lines, Borders, and Boxes

Here a line. There a line. Everywhere a line-line. This section describes various ways to apply lines, borders, and boxes to your text. This section refers to the Border menu and the Borders and Shading dialog box, as described earlier in this chapter.

Putting a line above a heading

A common use of lines in Word is to apply a line to a heading in your document. It's a form of text decoration, plus it helps to break up the document. Here's how it's done:

1. **Place the insertion pointer in a heading or paragraph.**

2. **From the Borders command button, choose the Top Border command.**

If you want to change the border thickness, color, or style (dashed or dotted), you summon the Borders and Shading dialog box. Use the Color and Width menus to apply color and thickness.

Boxing text or paragraphs

To stick a box around any spate of words or paragraphs, summon the Borders and Shading dialog box (refer to Figure 18-2) and choose a box style from the Setting column: Box, Shadow, or 3-D. Click OK.

To ensure that the border is applied to text (words) and not to the entire paragraph, select the text first and then choose Text from the Apply To drop-down list in the Borders and Shading dialog box.

Word lets you create graphical pull quotes by putting text in graphical boxes. Refer to Chapter 23 for more information on text boxes and pull quotes.

Boxing a title

Someday when you're tasked with creating an organizational newsletter, you can surprise all your friends and others who were smart enough to avoid that task by coming up with a fancy title, similar to the newsletter heading in Figure 18-4. It looks complex and such, but it's nothing more than the crafty application of borders plus some deft text, paragraph, and tab stop skills.

Figure 18-4:
Top and bottom borders.

> Vol. XXIII, Issue 13   November 2010
>
> # Zamboni Professional
>
> Frank's Favorite Patterns   *You* are the show!
> Your Second Business: Shaved Ice   Hockey Players: Don't get me started!

The key to creating such a heading is to type the text first and then use the Borders and Shading dialog box to add different border styles above and below the paragraphs.

Use the Preview window in the Borders and Shading dialog box to set the line style. Click the mouse in the Preview window to add or remove lines above or below or to either side of the text.

Making rules

A common trick in page design is to apply a line above or below text. The line is a *rule,* and it helps to break up the text, highlight a specific paragraph, or create a *block quote, callout,* or *pull quote.* Here's how:

1. **Click the mouse to place the insertion pointer into a given paragraph of text.**

   Yes, it works best if you've already written that paragraph. Remember my admonition: Write first, format later.

2. **Summon the Borders and Shading dialog box.**

3. **Choose a line style, thickness, and color, if needed.**

4. **Click the Top button.**

5. **Click the Bottom button.**

6. **Click OK.**

You may also want to adjust the paragraph margins inward so that your text further stands out on the page. Refer to Chapter 11 for more information.

If you press Enter to end the paragraph, you carry the border formatting with the insertion pointer to the following paragraph. See the section "Removing borders," later in this chapter, to find out how to prevent that situation.

Drawing a fat, thick line

Sometimes you need one of those fat, thick lines to break up your text. I dunno *why,* but the *how* is to choose the Horizontal Line command from the Border menu. Word inserts a thin, inky stroke running from the left to right margins on a line all by itself.

✔ Unlike a border, the horizontal line isn't attached to a paragraph, so it doesn't repeat for every new paragraph you type.

✔ To adjust the horizontal line, click to select it with the mouse. Six "handles" appear (top and bottom and the four corners) around the selected image. You can drag those handles with the mouse to set the line's width or thickness.

✔ Double-clicking the horizontal line displays a Format Horizontal Line dialog box, where further adjustments can be made and color added.

✔ To remove the horizontal line, click once to select it and then press either the Delete or Backspace key.

Putting a border around a page of text

Borders are popular for pages as well as for paragraphs, although this application can often be frustrating because the border may not print completely. I've studied the issue and found the problem. My solution to the putting-a-border-around-a-page-of-text puzzle is presented in these steps:

1. **Put the insertion pointer on the page you want to border.**

   For example, you might put it on the first page in your document.

2. **Summon the Borders and Shading dialog box.**

3. **Click the Page Border tab.**

   Whoa! The Page Border tab looks *exactly* like the Borders tab (refer to Figure 18-2). It's such a coincidence.

4. **Choose the border you want: Use a preset box or pick a line style, color, and width.**

   You can select a funky art pattern from the Art drop-down list.

5. **Choose which pages you want bordered from the Apply To drop-down list.**

   You can select Whole Document to put borders on every page. To select the first page, choose the This Section–First Page Only item. Other options let you choose other pages and groups, as shown in the drop-down list.

   And now, the secret:

6. **Click the Options button.**

   The Border and Shading Options dialog box appears.

7. **From the Measure From drop-down list, choose the Text option.**

   The Edge of Page option just doesn't work with most printers. Text does.

8. **Click OK.**

9. **Click OK to close the Borders and Shading dialog box.**

To add more "air" between your text and the border, use the Border Shading Options dialog box (from Step 6) and *increase* the values in the Margin area.

Refer to Chapter 14 for more information on creating a section break in your document. By using sections, you can greatly control which pages in a document have borders and which do not.

To remove the page border, choose None under Settings (refer to Step 4) and then click OK.

Removing borders

When you don't listen to my advice and you format a paragraph before you type its contents, notice that the borders stick with the paragraph like discarded gum under your shoe. To peel annoying borders from a paragraph, you choose the No Border style.

From the Border menu, choose No Border.

In the Borders and Shading dialog box, double-click the None button and then click OK.

You can also use the Borders and Shading dialog box to selectively remove borders from text. Use the Preview window and click a specific border to remove it; refer to Figure 18-2.

Background Colors and Shading

Word lets you splash a dash of color behind any text as well as inside any borders you create. It's all done by simply using the Shading command button, found in the Paragraph group, or, for more complexity, by using the Shading tab in the Borders and Shading dialog box.

The key to applying a background color is to first mark the text, such as a document title, as a block. (See Chapter 6 for block-marking instructions.) Then choose a color from the Shading command button's menu (refer to Figure 18-3). Or, if the colors don't suit you, choose the command More Colors from the menu and conjure up your own, custom color.

To apply a gray background, you summon the Shading tab in the Borders and Shading dialog box. Choose the gray scale percentage from the Style menu in the Patterns area. You can also choose a pattern from that menu, though I recommend against patterns because they aren't well suited for shading text.

✔ You can best apply background color to a page by using the Page Color command, described in Chapter 13.

✔ To create white text on a black background, select the text and apply white as the text foreground color (refer to Chapter 10). Then, from the Shading command button, choose black as the background color.

✔ Remove a background color by choosing No Color as the color.

Chapter 19

Able Tables

*W*ord processing is a linear task. Characters flow into words, which flow into sentences, which form paragraphs. You start reading here and end up there. It's basic stuff. That is, until the information you're trying to organize is best presented in a grid.

Rather than rely on linear words, you need rows and columns to work information into a grid. Word accommodates you, providing ample tools for placing text (and even graphics) into a grid. In Word parlance, the grid is known as a *table*. Yes, that's correct: Word lets you make tables. It's surprisingly easy, far more easy than assembling that build-it-yourself furniture that comes from Scandinavia.

Suddenly There's a Table in Your Document

My guess is that Word's ability to create tables came about because organizing information into rows and columns by using the Tab key was causing too many migraines. Yes, it's true: Making a table in Word is easier than succumbing to internal cranial pressure. This section explores the various table-creation methods.

Before you venture into Table Creation Land, I recommend that you peruse these points:

- ✔ Any time you need information in a grid, or in columns and rows, you're better off creating a table in Word than fussing with tabs and tab stops.
- ✔ Rows in a table appear left to right across the screen.
- ✔ Columns in a table go up and down.
- ✔ Each "cubbyhole" in a table is a *cell*.
- ✔ Cells can have their own margins, text, and paragraph formats. You can even stick graphics into cells.
- ✔ Unlike working with tabs, Word tables can be resized and rearranged to fit your data. Try doing that with tabs!
- ✔ Print Layout view works best with tables. The sections in this chapter assume that you're using Print Layout view, not Draft view.

Working with tables in Word

There are two ways to create a table in your document: Draw a table from scratch and then fill it in, or write your text first and then magically convert that text into a table. Unlike at other times where it works best to first write your prose and then format it, I highly recommend that you create the table first and then fill it with text.

A table is an element you insert into your document, so Word's Table commands are found on the Ribbon's Insert tab, in the aptly-named Tables group. Only one button is in that group, and it's the menu shown in Figure 19-1. The following sections describe how to use the menu.

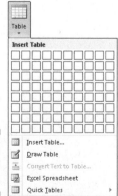

Figure 19-1:
The Table menu.

After creating a table in Word, or any time the insertion pointer dwells in a table's midst, you'll find two new tabs on the Ribbon: Design and Layout. They both appear beneath the label Table Tools. Using these tabs is covered in the section "Table Formatting," later in this chapter.

After filling the table, you can format it using the various table-formatting tricks and techniques covered in the latter half of this chapter.

✔ Word lets you easily add or remove rows or columns to or from a table. Don't worry about getting the table dimensions wrong when you first create it.

✔ When you've already typed the table's data, or maybe the data you want to put into a table is now formatted with tabs, refer to the section "Converting text into a table," later in this chapter.

✔ I recommend starting the table on a blank line by itself. Furthermore, type a second blank line *after* the line you put the table on. That makes it easier to continue typing text after the table is created.

Creating an instant table

Word comes with an assortment of predefined, formatted tables. Plopping one down in your document is as easy as using the Quick Tables submenu, chosen from the Table menu on the Insert tab (refer to Figure 19-1). It's a useful way to instantly make a calendar.

After inserting a Quick Table, all you need to do is add or edit the existing text. You can even use the Table Tools Design tab to instantly reformat the table. Or, just succumb to the desire to manually format your table, as described elsewhere in this chapter.

Making a table "this" big

When you have a good idea of a table's dimensions, the easiest way to plop down that table in your document is to use the grid found at the top of the Table menu. (Refer to Figure 19-1.) Drag the mouse through the grid to create in your document a table that has the same number of rows and columns as you select in the grid.

For example, Figure 19-2 shows a 4-column-by-3-row table being created by dragging the mouse. As you drag the mouse on the menu, the table's grid appears in your document.

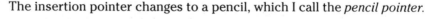

Figure 19-2:
Creating a
4-by-3 table.

> ✔ Don't fret over guessing the correct number of rows and columns: You can add or remove rows or columns at any time in Word.
>
> ✔ The table is created at the same width as your document's paragraph margins. When you add more columns, each column gets smaller.
>
> ✔ Column width can be adjusted, as described elsewhere in this chapter.
>
> ✔ If you prefer a more right-brain approach to creating a table, choose the Insert Table command from the Table menu. Use the Insert Table dialog box to manually enter the number of rows and columns you need. Click the OK button to plop down your table.

Drawing a table

Feeling artistic? For a more freeform approach to table creation, you can use a special drawing mode to create a table in your document. Obey these steps:

1. **From the Table menu on the Insert tab, choose Draw Table.**

   The insertion pointer changes to a pencil, which I call the *pencil pointer*.

2. **Drag the mouse to "draw" the table's outline in your document.**

   Start in the upper left corner of where you envision your table and drag to the lower right corner, which tells Word where to insert your table. You see an outline of the table as you drag down and to the right, as shown in Figure 19-3.

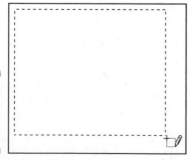

Figure 19-3:
Drawing a
table in a
document.

Don't worry about making the table the right size; you can resize it later.

3. Use the pencil pointer to draw rows and columns.

As long as the mouse pointer looks like a pencil, you can use it to draw the rows and columns in your table.

To draw a row, drag the pencil pointer from the left side to the right side of the table.

To draw a column, drag the pencil pointer from the top to the bottom of the table, as shown in Figure 19-4.

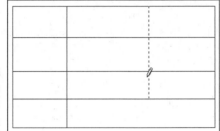

Figure 19-4:
Drawing a
column.

You can split columns or rows into more cells by simply dragging the pencil pointer inside a cell and not across the entire table.

Don't worry if you have too many or too few rows or columns. You can add or delete them later, as you see fit. And, don't worry about uneven spacing; you can rearrange your rows and columns later.

4. Click the Draw Table button or press the Esc key when you're done creating the table's columns and rows.

The mouse pointer returns to normal. You can begin putting text in the table.

You can draw more lines in a table by simply clicking the Draw Table button in the Design tab's Draw Borders group. The table you modify need not be created by the Draw Table command, either; any table can be modified by using that tool.

Text in Tables

Text pours into a table on a cell-by-cell basis. Each cell can have its own paragraph format and its own set of tabs. Groups of cells, rows, and columns, and the entire table, can be selected and formatted at one time, if you like. All the standard text and paragraph formats apply to cells in a table just as they do to regular text.

- Avoid paragraph indents and first-line indents for text in a cell. Such formatting in a cell isn't necessary and can be a pain to manipulate.
- Show the Ruler when you work with formatting a table — it's a boon. Use the View Ruler button, as explained in Chapter 2.

Putting text into a table

To populate a table with text, simply type. All the text you type fits into a single cell. Cells grow taller to accommodate long bits of text. Certain keys perform special functions within the table:

- **Tab:** To move to the next cell, press the Tab key. You move from cell to cell, from left to right. Pressing Tab in a table's last (rightmost) column moves you down to the next row.
- **Shift+Tab:** To move backward to the previous cell, press Shift+Tab.
- **Arrow keys:** The up, down, left, and right keys also move you around within the table, but they still move within any text in a cell. Therefore, using the arrow keys to move from cell to cell is rather inefficient.
- **Enter:** The Enter key adds a new paragraph to a cell.
- **Shift+Enter:** The Shift+Enter key combination can break up long lines of text in a cell with a soft return.
- **Ctrl+Tab:** To use tabs or indentation within a cell, press Ctrl+Tab rather than Tab.

By the way, pressing the Tab key in the table's last, lower right cell automatically adds another row to the table.

Selecting text in a table

Selecting text in a table can get funky. Here are my suggestions:

- Triple-click the mouse in a cell to select all text in that cell.
- You can select a single cell by positioning the mouse in the cell's lower left corner. The mouse pointer changes to a northeastward-pointing arrow, as shown in the margin. Click to select the cell.
- Move the mouse into the left margin and click to select a row of cells.
- Move the mouse above a column and click to select that column. When the mouse is in the "sweet spot," the pointer changes to a downward-pointing arrow (shown in the margin).

✔ Selecting stuff in a table can also be accomplished from the Table group on the Layout tab. Use the Select menu to select the entire table, a row, a column, or a single cell.

✔ Clicking the table's "handle" selects the entire table. The handle is visible whenever the mouse points at the table or when the insertion pointer is placed inside the table.

Converting text into a table

If you started working on your document before you discovered the Table command, you probably have lists set up using tabbed text. If so, you can easily convert that text into a bona fide table by following these simple steps:

1. **Select the text you want to convert into a table.**

   It helps if the text is arranged into columns, with each column separated by a tab character. If not, things get screwy but still workable.

2. **From the Insert tab, choose Table⇨Convert Text to Table.**

   Ensure that Tabs is selected in the Convert Text to Table dialog box.

3. **Click OK.**

   A table is born.

You probably need to make adjustments, reset column widths, and so on and so forth. These tasks may be a pain, but they're better than retyping all that text.

✔ You can confirm that your text-to-table transition is set up properly by consulting the Number of Columns item in the Convert Text to Table dialog box (refer to Step 2). If the number of columns seems correct, the conversion most likely is a good one. When the number of columns is off, you have a rogue tab somewhere in your text.

✔ The Convert Text to Table item is available only when text is selected.

Turning a table back into plain text

To boost your text from the confines of a table's cruel and cold cells, obey these steps:

1. **Click the mouse inside the table you want to convert.**

2. **Click the Table Tools Layout tab.**

3. **From the Table group, choose Select⇨Select Table.**

4. **From the Data group, choose Convert to Text.**

   The Convert to Text dialog box appears.

5. **Click OK.**

   Bye-bye, table. Hello, ugly text.

As with converting text to a table, some clean-up is involved. Mostly, it's resetting the tabs (or removing them) — nothing complex or bothersome.

When a table's cells contain longer expanses of text, consider choosing Paragraph Marks from the Convert to Text dialog box (before Step 5). The text then looks less ugly after the conversion.

Table Formatting

You just can't leave a table alone — they cry out "Mess with me!" You may need to add or remove a row or column, adjust the width or height of a table element, or add fancy features such as color and lines. It's all possible using the Table Tools tabs after the table has been created.

✔ The Table Tools tabs show up only when a table is being edited or selected.

✔ The best time to format and mess with a table is after you finish putting text into the table.

Manipulating a table with the mouse

For quick-and-dirty table manipulation, you can use the mouse. Here are some tips:

✔ Positioning the mouse on a vertical line in the table's grid changes the mouse pointer to the thing shown in the margin. You can adjust the line left or right and resize the surrounding cells.

✔ You can also adjust cell width by using the Ruler, by pointing the mouse at the Move Table Column button that appears above each table cell gridline.

✔ Pointing the mouse at a horizontal line changes the mouse pointer to the one shown in the margin. At that time, you can use the mouse to adjust the line up or down and change the row height of surrounding cells.

Adjusting the table

It's the Table Tools Layout tab that harbors many of the command buttons and items that let you manipulate and adjust a table. Start your table design journey by placing the insertion pointer somewhere within the table itself. Then you can peruse this section for some popular things to do with the table by using the Table Tools Layout tab.

Deleting cells, columns, or rows

The key to deleting all or part of a table is to first position the insertion pointer in the part of the table you want to remove. Then choose the table element to remove from the Delete button's menu.

When you choose the Delete Cells command, you see a dialog box asking what to do with the other cells in the row or column: move them up or to the left. Yes, deleting a cell may make your table asymmetrical.

Inserting columns or rows

You can expand a table by adding rows or columns, and the rows or columns can be added inside the table or appended to any of the table's four sides. Four commands in the Rows & Columns group make this task possible: Insert Above, Insert Below, Insert Left, and Insert Right. The row or column that's added is relative to where the insertion pointer is within the table.

Adjusting row and column size

Gizmos in the Cell Size group let you fine-tune the table's row height or column width. Adjustments that are made affect the row or column containing the insertion pointer.

 The Distribute Rows and Distribute Columns command buttons, found in the Cell Size group, help clean up uneven column or row spacing in a table. With the insertion pointer anywhere in the table, click either or both buttons to even things out.

Aligning text

Text within a cell can be aligned just like a paragraph: left, center, or right. Additionally, the text can be aligned vertically: top, middle, or bottom. Combine these options and you have an explanation for the nine orientation buttons in the Alignment group.

Reorienting text

 The Text Direction button in the Alignment group changes the way text reads in a cell or group of selected cells. Normally, text is oriented from left to right. By clicking the Text Direction button once, you change the text direction to top-to-bottom. Click the button again and direction is changed to bottom-to-top. Clicking a third time restores the text to its normal direction.

Sadly, you cannot create upside-down text with the Text Direction button.

Designing a table

The Table Tools Design tab is used to help you quickly (or slowly) format your table. The tab shows up whenever the insertion pointer lies somewhere in a table's realm. This section covers some common table design tricks and tips you can pull using the Table Tools Design tab.

Using Quick Styles

The Table Styles group can quickly apply formatting to any table. Choose a style or click the menu button to see a whole smattering of styles. You can use the settings in the Table Style Options group to determine how the table styles shape up. Choose an option to apply that type of formatting to the table styles, such as Header Row to format a separate header row for the table.

The Quick Styles don't work when you have a table in a document created by or saved in an older version of Word.

Setting table line styles

The lines you see in a table's grid are the same borders you can apply to text with the Border command button, discussed in Chapter 18. The Border command button determines where the lines go; items on the left side of the Draw Borders group set the border line style, width, and color.

The border changes you make apply to whichever part of the table is selected. Refer to the section "Selecting text in a table," earlier in this chapter, for tips on selecting parts of a table.

Removing a table's lines

Occasionally, you may want a table without any lines. For example, I typically use a 1-column, 2-row table to insert a picture and its caption into my text. To remove the table's grid in that situation and others, select the table and choose No Border from the Borders menu.

Having no lines (borders) in a table makes working with the table more difficult. The solution is to show the table *gridlines,* which aren't printed. To do that, select the table and choose the Show Gridlines command from the Border menu.

Merging cells

 You can combine two or more cells in a table by simply erasing the line that separates them. To do so, click the Eraser command button found in the Draw Borders group. The mouse pointer changes to a bar of soap, but it's supposed to be an eraser (shown in the margin). Use that tool to erase lines in the table: Click a line and it's gone.

Click the Eraser button again when you're done merging.

✓ Erasing the line between cells merges the cells' contents, by combining the text.

✓ You cannot remove the outside lines of the table. Those lines hold the table together, and removing them would (theoretically) delete the table.

Splitting cells

 To turn one cell into two, you simply draw a line, horizontally or vertically, through the cell. Do so by clicking the Draw Table command button in the Draw Borders group. The mouse pointer changes to the pencil pointer, which you can use to draw new lines in the table.

Click the Draw Table button again to turn off this feature.

Deleting a table

To utterly remove the table from your document, click the mouse inside the table and then choose Delete⇨Table from the Rows & Columns group on the Layout tab. The table is blown to smithereens.

✓ Yes, deleting the table deletes its contents as well.

✓ If you'd rather merely convert the table's contents into plain text, refer to the section "Turning a table back into plain text," earlier in this chapter.

Chapter 20

Columns of Text

Here's a pop quiz: If someone asks about columns and you immediately think of something written in a magazine or newspaper, you're probably a writer. If you think Doric, Ionic, and Corinthian, you're probably a nerd. What you probably don't think of are text columns in Word. That's because placing columns across a page of text is a task that you probably don't believe a word processor can do. Man, are you wrong!

All about Columns

Here's a secret: All text you write in Word is already formatted in columns. Yep, although it's only one column of text per page, it still counts as a column.

Most folks don't think of their text in columns — that is, until you start talking about two or three columns of text per page. Such a thing is entirely possible in Word. The secret is the Columns command button, found in the Page Setup group on the Page Layout tab.

Clicking the Columns button displays a menu of handy column-formatting options, as shown in Figure 20-1. Splitting your text into columns is as easy as choosing a column format from that list.

Figure 20-1:
The
Columns
button
menu.

To be more specific with the number of columns or their layout, choose the More Columns command. You can then use the Columns dialog box to create and design multiple columns for your document.

✔ Word's paragraph formatting applies to columns. The column's left and right sides are equivalent to the paragraph margins.

✔ Rather than use the cursor-movement keys to move the insertion pointer between columns, use the mouse. Pointing and clicking in a column is easier than watching the insertion pointer fly all over the page.

✔ Choosing a column format from the Columns button menu affects your entire document, splitting it (or reducing it) into the number of columns specified — that is, unless you split your document into sections. In that case, the column type you chose affects only the current section. See Chapter 14 for more information on sections in Word.

✔ When you're working with columns and notice that Word starts acting slow and fussy, *save your work!*

✔ Although using columns for a short document seems to work well in Word, putting text into columns in a document of ten pages or more is better done in a desktop publishing program (DTP). See the nearby side-bar "For advanced formatting, nothing beats DTP."

✔ To best see columns in action, use Print Layout view. In fact, columns look downright weird in Draft view.

✔ Two columns are sufficient to impress anyone. More columns make your text skinnier and more difficult to read.

✔ To have only a portion of your document use columns, refer to the section "Mixing column formats," a little later in this chapter.

For advanced formatting, nothing beats DTP

I'll be honest up front: When you desire columns for whatever you're writing, what you need is *desktop publishing,* or *DTP,* software. Desktop publishing isn't about writing; it's about assembling text that you've already written with graphics and other design elements and then laying them out as a professional would. DTP is built for such a task. It can handle it.

Word's ability to march text into columns isn't its best feature. Columns work for smaller documents — say, one-sheet newsletters, trifold brochures, or fliers. Beyond that, I highly recommend using DTP software for your demanding documents. Both Adobe InDesign and Microsoft Publisher are good places to start, if you're interested in DTP software.

Making more than three columns

The Columns menu lists only 2-column formats, plus one 3-column format. For anything different, such as more than three columns, choose Columns⇨More Columns and use the Number of Columns box, shown in Figure 20-2.

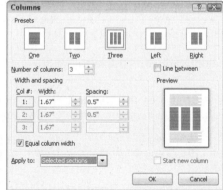

Figure 20-2: The Columns dialog box.

Set the number of columns you want by using the Number of Columns box. Use the Preview window to help determine how your page is formatted. Click the OK button to apply the column format to your document.

✔ The 3-column text format works nicely on paper in Landscape mode. This method is how most trifold brochures are created. Refer to Chapter 13 for information on Landscape mode.

✔ Maximum number of columns per page? That depends on the size of the page. Word's minimum column width is half an inch, so a typical sheet of paper can have up to 12 columns on it — not that such a layout would be appealing or anything.

Mixing column formats

Your whole document doesn't have to sport just one column format. You can split things up so that part of the document is in one column and another part is in two columns and then maybe another part goes back to just one column. The secret is to use the Columns dialog box. (Refer to Figure 20-2.)

When you're choosing a new column format, be sure to select the Apply To drop-down list. When you choose Whole Document, the format applies to the entire document. If you choose This Point Forward, the new columns start at the insertion pointer's location.

Choosing This Point Forward inserts a continuous section break into your document. So the real solution to mixing column formats is to read about sections in Chapter 14 and then divide your document into sections and apply the column formats accordingly.

Adjusting the columns in the Columns dialog box

There isn't much labor involved in formatting columns, other than setting their width and the space between them. This is done in the Columns dialog box. (Refer to Figure 20-2.) Here are some points to ponder:

- You can make specific column adjustments in the Width and Spacing area of the dialog box.

- If you want an attractive line between the columns of text, put a check mark in the Line Between box. You may not, however, find the line between columns attractive.

- Use the Preview window in the Columns dialog box to get an idea of what the heck you're doing.

- The space between columns is the *gutter*. Word sets the width of the gutter at 0.5" — half an inch. This amount of white space is pleasing to the eye without being too much of a good thing.

The End of the Column

You can end a column in one of several ways. For a newspaper column, the newspaper can go under. For a Doric, Ionic, and Corinthian column, your civilization can collapse. For a column of text in Word, however, there are a number of tricks to pull, none of which involves bankruptcy or revolution.

Giving up and going back to one column

The easiest way to undo a multicolumn document is to return it to a single column. It's cinchy: From the Columns button in the Page Layout tab, choose the item One. That restores your document back to single column mode, which is how Word naturally creates documents.

When a document is split into sections, or when you have multiple column formats sprinkled throughout a document, obey these steps:

1. **From the Page Setup area on the Page Layout tab, choose Columns⇨More Columns.**

   The Columns dialog box is displayed (refer to Figure 20-2).

2. **Choose One from the Presets area.**

3. **From the Apply To drop-down list, select Whole Document.**

4. **Click OK.**

As with other formatting elements in Word, you don't "remove" column formatting as much as you choose the standard column format, One. (Similarly, you don't remove right-justification for a paragraph — you restore left justification.)

Removing columns from a document doesn't remove any sections or section breaks. You must manually delete them, if you want. See Chapter 14 for more information on sections.

Ending multiple columns in the middle of a document

Say that you're using multiple columns in a document when suddenly, and for good reason, you decide to switch back to single column format. Here's how:

1. **Place the insertion pointer wherever you want your columns to stop.**

2. **Click the Page Layout tab.**

3. **From the Page Setup area, choose Columns⇨More Columns.**

4. **In the Columns dialog box, choose One from the Presets area.**

5. **From the Apply To drop-down list, select This Point Forward.**

6. **Click OK.**

   The columns stop and regular, 1-column text is restored.

When you work these steps, you place a continuous section break into your document. The multicolumn format is applied to the previous section, and the single ("One") column format is applied after the section break.

A continuous section break doesn't contain a page break; the new column format can pick up in the middle of a page.

Refer to Chapter 14 to bone up on section breaks.

Using a column break

When you want to continue using columns but want the text you're writing to start at the top of the next column, you need a *column break*. Figure 20-3 illustrates what I'm talking about.

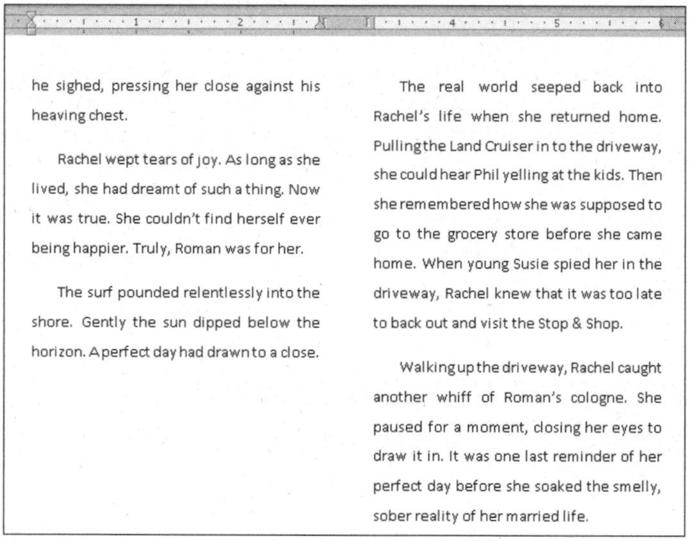

he sighed, pressing her close against his heaving chest.

Rachel wept tears of joy. As long as she lived, she had dreamt of such a thing. Now it was true. She couldn't find herself ever being happier. Truly, Roman was for her.

The surf pounded relentlessly into the shore. Gently the sun dipped below the horizon. A perfect day had drawn to a close.

The real world seeped back into Rachel's life when she returned home. Pulling the Land Cruiser in to the driveway, she could hear Phil yelling at the kids. Then she remembered how she was supposed to go to the grocery store before she came home. When young Susie spied her in the driveway, Rachel knew that it was too late to back out and visit the Stop & Shop.

Walking up the driveway, Rachel caught another whiff of Roman's cologne. She paused for a moment, closing her eyes to draw it in. It was one last reminder of her perfect day before she soaked the smelly, sober reality of her married life.

Figure 20-3:
How a
column
break
works.

To create such a thing, heed these steps:

1. **Place the insertion pointer where you want your text to start at the top of the next column.**

   For example, you might place it at the beginning of the word *close* in Figure 20-3.

2. **Click the Page Layout tab.**

3. **From the Page Setup group, choose Breaks⇨Column.**

   The text hops to the top of the next column.

Column breaks don't end columns; they merely split a column, ending text at a certain point on a page and starting the rest of the text at the top of the next column.

Use the Show/Hide command in the Home group (the paragraph mark button) to know where to exactly place the column break. You might want to insert the column break *after* a paragraph mark (¶) to have the columns line up at the top of the page.

Chapter 21

Lots of Lists

A variety of information can lurk in your documents — stuff that I refer to as *lists*. Here's my list of these lists: Lists of items noted with bullets (asterisks or dots) and lists of items that are numbered. You can also consider a table of contents as a list, a list of document headings. A list of keywords in your document is an index. And don't forget academic lists, such as footnotes and endnotes. All those lists are listed here in this chapter of lists.

Lists with Bullets and Numbers

Many documents contain lists of items, usually more than two. You have several ways to draw attention to those lists, to call them out from the rest of your text: You can try hanging indents, make the first few words **bold**, or take advantage of the Word bullets and line numbering features, covered in this section.

Making a bulleted list

In typesetting, a *bullet* is merely a graphical element, such as a ball or a dot, used to highlight items in a list. The word *bullet* comes from the French word *boulette* and has nothing to do with those things that come flinging from a firearm, like this:

✔ Bang!

✔ Bang!

✔ Bang!

 To apply bullets to your text, highlight the paragraphs you want to shoot and choose the Bullets command button, found in the Home tab's Paragraph group. Instantly, your text is not only formatted with bullets but is also indented and made all neat and tidy.

 ✔ You can choose a different bullet style by clicking the menu button next to the Bullets command. Choose your new bullet graphic from the list that appears or use the Define New Bullet command to dream up your own bullet style.

✔ Because the bullet is a paragraph format, it *sticks* to the paragraphs you type. To halt the bullets, click the Bullet command button again, and they're removed from the paragraph format.

✔ Bullets can also be applied by using Word's AutoFormat ability. See Chapter 17.

Numbering a list

 When a list contains items that are in a certain order or that need to be referenced elsewhere, you can apply numbers or letters or another type of sequential marking. To make it happen, select the paragraphs as a block and choose the Numbering command button from the Paragraph group on the Home tab.

When you click the button, each paragraph is numbered. You can use the Numbering command button's menu to choose another sequential format, such as letters or Roman numerals, or choose a specific numbering style. Or, when none of the predefined formats in the menu pleases you, choose Define New Number Format to create your own numbered list.

✔ List Numbering is a paragraph format. It sticks with every successive paragraph you type until you turn off numbering.

✔ To remove numbers, simply click the Numbering button again. This action removes numbering from the paragraph format.

 ✔ You can break and resume paragraph numbering, but it's tricky: Try to apply the numbering as you type paragraphs. Simply press the Backspace key to disable automatic paragraph numbering. To resume numbering, click the Numbering command button again, and the paragraph numbering should continue from where it left off before.

Creating a multilevel numbered list

 The Multilevel List button, found in the Paragraph group on the Home tab, is used to number a multileveled list, consisting of sublevels and indents, as shown in Figure 21-1. It's a tricky type of list to create, so pay attention!

North Diamond Mosquito Abatement Board By-Laws
1. Purpose.
   a. We exist to abate mosquitos.
2. Board composition.
   a. The board shall consist of seven (7) members.
      i. Two members shall be at large.
      ii. Five members shall be elected by district.
   b. Members shall be elected every year.
   c. The term of each member shall be 3 years.
   d. No mosquitoes are allowed to be members.
3. Duties

Figure 21-1: A multilevel list.

You can create a multilevel list from scratch, or you can apply the format to a selected block of text. The secret is to use the Tab and Shift+Tab keys at the start of the paragraph to shuffle the paragraphs higher and lower in the multi-level list hierarchy. It works like this:

✔ Press the Tab key at the start of a paragraph to indent that paragraph to a deeper level in the multilevel list format.

✔ Press the Shift+Tab key combination at the start of a paragraph to unindent a paragraph to a higher level in the multilevel list format.

✔ Press the Enter key twice to end the list.

✔ Also see Chapter 25 for more information about Word's Outline mode.

Numbering lines on a page

Though a list feature isn't involved, Word lets you slap down numbers for every line on a page, which is a feature that's popular with those in the legal profession as well as with folks who write radio scripts. It was also a feature that many former WordPerfect users demanded in Word. Here's how it goes:

1. **Click the Page Layout tab.**

2. **In the Page Setup group, click the Line Numbers command button to display its menu.**

3. **Choose a numbering format from the menu.**

Choosing the Line Numbering Options command from the menu displays the Page Setup dialog box. From there, click the Line Numbers button to summon the Line Numbers dialog box. Use that dialog box to create custom numbers and formatting for your document. For example, use the Line Numbers dialog box to start each page with a number other than 1 or to number lines by twos or threes.

Lists of Document Contents

Word sports a References tab that contains groups of commands you can use to build custom lists in your documents. This section covers the two most common list-making tricks: the table of contents and the index.

Creating a table of contents

One helpful example of how computers can save you time — and I'm not kidding — is to let Word create a table of contents (TOC) for your document. No, there's no need to manually type a TOC. As long as you use the built-in heading styles, Word can slap down a custom TOC in your document as easily as following these steps:

1. **Create a separate page for the TOC.**

   Word slaps down the table of contents wherever you place the insertion pointer, but I prefer to have the thing on its own page. Refer to Chapter 13 for information on creating new pages; a new, blank page near the start of your document is ideal for a TOC.

2. **Click the mouse to place the insertion pointer on the new, blank page.**

   The TOC is inserted at that point.

3. **Click the References tab.**

4. **In the Table of Contents group, click the Table of Contents button.**

   The Table of Contents menu appears.

5. **Choose an item from the menu based on what you want the table of contents to look like.**

   And there's your TOC.

You may have to scroll up to see the table of contents. You may also want to add a title above the TOC — something clever, such as *Table of Contents*.

✔ Cool people in publishing refer to a table of contents as a TOC, usually pronounced "tee-o-see" (or "tock").

✔ You can update a TOC if your document's contents change: Click the mouse in the TOC and choose the Update Table command from the top of the TOC list.

✔ When the steps in this section don't produce the effect you intended, it usually means that your document headings aren't formatted with the Heading styles.

✔ Word bases the TOC on text formatted with the Heading styles in your document. As long as you use Heading 1 for main heads, Heading 2 for subheads, and Heading 3 (and so on) for lower-level heads and titles, the TOC will be spot-on.

✔ Word's Table of Contents command also picks up your own document heading styles that are formatted with a specific outline level. See Chapter 15 for more information.

✔ The table of contents exists as a *field* in your document. When you click the field, the TOC is highlighted and a special tag appears on top. See Chapter 23 for more information about fields in Word documents.

Building an index

An *index* does the same thing as a table of contents, but with more detail and at the opposite end of the document. Also, the index is organized by topic or keyword as opposed to the organizational description a TOC offers.

Creating an index in Word is a two-part process. The first step is to identify the words or phrases in a document that need to be referenced in the index. The second part involves Word using those references to automatically build the index for you. The following sections explain the details.

✔ All indexing actions and commands take place under the realm of the References tab, in the Index group.

✔ Yes, you should write your document before you create the index.

Selecting text for the index

To flag a bit of text for inclusion in the index, follow these steps:

1. **Select the text you want to reference in the index.**

   The text can be a word or phrase or any old bit of text. Mark that text as a block.

2. **In the Index group on the References tab, click the Mark Entry button.**

   The Mark Index Entry dialog box appears. The text you selected in your document appears in the Main Entry box. (You can edit that text, if you want.)

3. **Type a subentry in the Mark Index Entry dialog box (optional).**

The subentry further clarifies the main entry. The subentry is especially useful when the main entry is a broad topic.

4. **Click *either* the Mark button or the Mark All button.**

The Mark button marks only this particular instance of the word for inclusion in the index. Use this button when you want to mark only instances that you think will most benefit the reader.

The Mark All button directs Word to seek out and flag all instances of the text in your document, to create an index entry for every single one. Use this option when you would rather leave it to your reader to decide what's relevant.

When you mark an index entry, Word activates the Show/Hide command, where characters such as spaces, paragraph marks, and tabs appear in your document. Don't let it freak you out. Step 7 tells you how to turn that thing off.

The Index code appears in the document looking something like this (the code is hidden when you turn off Show/Hide mode): {·XE·"pustule"·}

5. **Continue scrolling through your document and looking for stuff to put into the index.**

The Mark Index Entry dialog box stays open, allowing you to continue to create your index: Just select text in the document and then click the Mark Index Entry dialog box. The selected text appears in the Main Entry box. Click the Mark or Mark All button to continue building the index.

6. **Click the Close button when you're done.**

The Mark Index Entry dialog box disappears.

7. **Press Ctrl+Shift+8 to cancel the Show/Hide command.**

Use the 8 key on the keyboard, not on the numeric keypad.

Creating the index

After selecting, collecting, and marking all bits and pieces of text from your document for inclusion in the index, the next step is to create the index. Do this:

1. **Position the insertion pointer where you want the index to appear.**

If you want the index to start on a new page, create a new page in Word (see Chapter 13). I also recommend putting the index at the *end* of your document, which is what the reader expects.

2. **Choose the Insert Index button from the Index group on the References tab.**

The Index dialog box appears. Here are my recommendations:

- The Print Preview window is misleading. It shows how your index will look but doesn't use your actual index contents.

- Use the Formats drop-down list to select a style for your index. Just about any choice from that list is better than the From Template example.

- The Columns list tells Word how many columns wide to make the index. Note that two columns is the standard, though I usually switch to one column, which looks better on the page, especially for shorter documents.

- I prefer to use the Right Align Page Numbers option.

3. **Click the OK button to insert the index into your document.**

4. **Review the index.**

   Do this now, and do not edit any text. Just look.

5. **Press Ctrl+Z if you dislike the index layout, and start these steps over again.**

   If you think that the index is okay, you're done.

Obviously, the index needs to be updated when you go back and change your document. To update a document's index, click the mouse on the index. Then choose the Update Index command button from the Index group. Instantly, Word updates the index to reference any new page numbers and include new marked index entries.

- ✔ Feel free to add a heading for the index because Word doesn't do it for you.

- ✔ Word places the index into its own document section by using continuous section breaks. Refer to Chapter 14 for more information on sections.

Footnotes and Endnotes

The difference between a footnote and an endnote is that one appears on the same page as the reference and the other appears at the end of the document. Content-wise, a footnote contains bonus information, a clarification, or an aside, and an endnote is a reference or citation. That's just a guess.

In both cases, the footnote or endnote is flagged by a superscripted number or letter in the text[1]. And, both are created in the same manner, like this:

[1]See? It works!

1. **Click the mouse so that the insertion pointer is immediately to the right of the text that you want the footnote or endnote to reference.**

2. **Click the References tab.**

3. **From the Footnotes group, choose either the Insert Footnote or Insert Endnote command button.**

   A number is superscripted to the text.

   When Word is in Print Layout view, you're instantly whisked to the bottom of the page (footnote) or the end of the document (endnote), where you type the footnote or endnote.

   In Draft view, a special window near the bottom of the document opens, displaying footnotes or endnotes.

4. **Type the footnote or endnote.**

   There's no need to type the note's number; it's done for you automatically.

   Footnotes are automatically numbered starting with 1.

   Endnotes are automatically numbered starting with Roman numeral *i*.

5. **Click the Show Notes button, found in the Footnotes group on the References tab, to exit the footnote or endnote.**

   You return to the spot in your document where the insertion pointer blinks (from Step 1).

Here are some non-footnote endnote notes:

- ✔ The keyboard shortcut for inserting a footnote is Alt+Ctrl+F.

- ✔ The keyboard shortcut for inserting an endnote is Atl+Ctrl+D.

- ✔ The footnote and endnote numbers are updated automatically so that all footnotes and endnotes are sequential in your document.

- ✔ Use the Next Footnote button's menu to browse between footnote and endnote references in your document; the Next Footnote button is found in the Footnotes group in the References tab on the Ribbon.

- ✔ You can see a footnote or endnote's contents by pointing the mouse at the superscripted number in the document's text.

- ✔ Use the Show Notes button (Footnotes group, References tab) to help you examine footnotes or endnotes themselves.

- ✔ To quick-edit a footnote or endnote, double-click the footnote number on the page. Use the Show Notes button to return to your document.

- ✔ To delete a footnote, highlight the footnote's number in your document and press the Delete key. Word magically renumbers any remaining footnotes for you.

Chapter 22

Here Come the Graphics

*I*f you want any pictures in your document, you may think that you can just write a thousand words and that would suffice. But believe me, doing such a thing would be more effort than it's worth. That's because Word easily lets you slap down images and pictures and even draw and edit graphics right there amidst the plain old boring text in your document. This chapter explains how it works.

✔ Word prefers that you view your document in Print Layout mode when you're working with graphics.

✔ The more images you add in Word, the more sluggish it becomes. My advice: Write first. Add graphics last. Save often.

✔ Word lets you use graphics from any other graphics program you have in Windows. My advice is to use those other programs to create and refine an image, save the image using that program, and then put it into Word as described in this chapter.

Graphical Goobers in Your Text

When you feel the urge, when your text is just plain lonely, or when you want to push Word's abilities to the wall, you can stick a graphical goober into your document. This section highlights what you can do with graphics in Word.

✔ The different types of goobers are found on the Insert tab, in the Illustrations group.

✔ You can also copy any image from another program in Windows and paste that image into Word by using the Paste button found in the Clipboard group on the Home tab, or just press Ctrl+V.

✔ The easiest type of image to paste is one found on the Internet. Right-click the image on a Web page, all while dutifully remaining aware of various copyright laws around the world, and choose the Copy Image (or similar) command from the pop-up menu. Then you can paste the image into your document: Press Ctrl+V.

✔ Images are placed *inline* with your text, which means that they appear wherever the insertion pointer is blinking. You can, however, move the image around in your document; refer to the directions starting with the section "Images in and around Your Text," later in this chapter.

Plopping down a picture

The most common type of graphical goober you stick into your documents is a picture, an image file from your computer's mass storage system. Assuming that the image exists and you know where to find it on your computer, you can follow these steps to plop the image into your document.

1. **From the Insert tab's Illustrations group, click the Picture button.**

   The Insert Picture dialog box appears. It looks similar to the Open dialog box and works exactly the same. (Refer to Chapter 8 for details.) The difference is that you use the Insert Picture dialog box to hunt down graphical images.

2. **Use the dialog box controls to browse for the image you want.**

3. **Click to select the image.**

4. **Click the Insert button.**

   The image is slapped down into your document.

You may also notice that the image is *huge*. Don't fret! Working with graphics in Word involves more than just inserting pictures into a document. See the section "Image Editing," later in this chapter.

TIP

✔ After inserting a picture, the Picture Tools Format tab appears on the Ribbon. Later sections in this chapter explain how to use the tools found on that tab.

✔ Word recognizes and understands just about all popular graphics file formats.

✔ A cool thing to stick at the end of a letter is your signature. Use a desktop scanner to scan your John Hancock. Save your signature as an image file on your computer, and then follow the preceding steps to insert the signature in the proper place in your document.

Inserting clip art

Clip art is a collection of images, both line art and pictures, that you're free to use in your documents. Inserting a clip art image works much like inserting a graphics image (see the preceding section), except that the clip art is organized. You can search for an image by name or category. Here's how it goes:

1. **On the Insert tab, in the Illustrations group, click the Clip Art button.**

   The Clip Art task pane appears, as shown in Figure 22-1.

Figure 22-1:
The Clip Art task pane.

2. In the Search For box, type a description of what you want.

For example, a picture of a bikini babe may go well with your report on tide pools. Type **bikini** in the box.

3. Click the Go button.

The results are displayed in the task pane (refer to Figure 22-1). Peruse the results and note that you may have to scroll a bit to see all of them.

If you don't find what you want, go back to Step 2 and refine your search.

4. Click the image you want.

The image is plopped into your document.

5. Close the Clip Art task pane by clicking the X in its upper right corner.

Word sticks the clip art graphic into your text, just like it's a big character, right where the insertion pointer is blinking. At this point, you probably want to move the image, resize it, or do other things. Later sections in this chapter explain the details.

✔ After you insert a clip art image, you can use the Picture Tools Format tab on the Ribbon to adjust and modify the image. Various sections elsewhere in this chapter describe some tools you can use.

✔ Apparently, the clips are free to use; I don't see anything saying otherwise. But, then again . . .

✔ The problem with clip art is that it's inanely common. That means the image you choose will doubtless be used by someone else, which gives clip art an air of unoriginality.

✔ Clip art libraries exist that you can buy at the software store, such as those One Zillion Clip Art Pix collections that also come with fonts and other interesting toys. Because those images are stored on optical discs, you use the Picture command button to insert them into your documents. Refer to the preceding section.

Slapping down a shape

Word comes with a library of common shapes ready to insert into your document. Graphics professionals call the shapes *line art*. You can call them forth into your document by following these steps:

1. Choose a predefined shape from the Shapes button menu, found in the Illustrations group on the Insert tab.

The mouse pointer changes to a plus sign.

2. Drag the mouse in the document where you want the shape to appear.

Drag down, from the upper left corner of the shape to the lower right. The shape appears at the location where you draw it, as a size determined by how you drag the mouse.

The shape you insert floats over your text, hiding your document. To fix it, you need to use one of Word's text wrapping tools. See the section "Wrapping text around an image," later in this chapter. Other sections in this chapter tell you how to modify the shape, giving it color, effects, and a whole lotta *flair*.

✔ Editing the shape, including changing its colors and line thickness and performing other tricks, is accomplished by using the Drawing Tools Format tab on the Ribbon. Later sections in this chapter explain some things you can do.

✔ Some shapes require you to click the mouse two or three times to draw a line or create a curve.

✔ You can use the shape as a picture frame, combining Word's Shape and Picture commands. To do so, use the Drawing Tools Format tab. In the Shape Styles group, click the Shape Fill button and choose Picture from the menu. Use the Select Picture dialog box to hunt down an image to place into the shape.

Saving time with SmartArt

Clicking the SmartArt button in the Illustrations group on the Insert tab summons the Choose a SmartArt Graphic dialog box. You can use that dialog box to quickly arrange a layout of graphics in your document. After picking a layout, you type captions or choose images (or both) and you're done, fooling everyone who doesn't know about this trick.

Here are some suggestions for working with SmartArt:

✔ Click the mouse and type to replace the [Text] tags in the SmartArt.

✔ You can use the down-arrow key to hop between the various [Text] tags.

✔ The SmartArt Tools Design and Format tabs appear after you insert SmartArt or whenever you click in a SmartArt image to edit it.

✔ Use the Change Colors button to apply some life to the otherwise dreary SmartArt. The command button is in the Quick Styles group on the SmartArt Tools Design tab.

✔ Click outside the SmartArt graphic to resume editing your document.

✔ Use the Text Pane command button on the SmartArt Tools Design tab to summon a text pane for help in editing the artwork's text.

Choosing a chart

The Insert Chart button, found in the Insert tab's Illustrations group, allows Word and the Excel program to commingle, creating an Excel chart and plopping it into your document. It's *weird,* so I don't recommend using the Insert Chart button unless you're familiar with Excel *and* willing to experiment with computer-screen-altering drugs.

Briefly (because this command frightens even me), you click the Insert Chart button and then choose a type of chart from the Insert Chart dialog box. Click the OK button and instantly the screen changes; Word appears on the left and Excel on the right. Word's Ribbon changes as well, with the Chart Tools Design, Layout, and Format tabs appearing and clustering everything all to hell.

Use the Excel window (on the right) to input data for the chart. When you're done, close the Excel window. You return to Word, where you can further mess with the chart.

✔ You must have the Excel program installed on your PC for the Insert Chart button to work.

✔ To delete the chart, click to select it. You see a thick outline when the chart is selected. Press the Delete key on the keyboard.

Adding some WordArt

Perhaps the most overused graphic stuck into any Word document is WordArt. It's quite popular. If you haven't used it yourself, you've probably seen it in a thousand documents, fliers, and international treaties. Here's how it works:

1. **On the Insert tab, in the Text group, click the WordArt button to display the WordArt menu.**

2. **Choose a style from the gallery for your WordArt.**

   A WordArt graphic placeholder appears in your document.

3. **Type the (short and sweet) text you want WordArt-ified.**

Your bit of text appears as an image in your document, but it's just a graphic image, like any other graphic you can stick into your document. All the sections in this chapter that deal with editing graphics also apply to WordArt.

If you're editing a document saved in Compatibility mode or created by an older version of Word, WordArt is inserted differently: You see an Edit WordArt Text dialog box, where you type the text you want displayed using WordArt. Choose a font, size, and text style using the dialog box. Click OK to insert the WordArt image.

Taking a screenshot

When the image you need is on the computer screen, either in another program window or the other program window itself, you can use Word's Screenshot command to capture that image and stick it into your document.

To capture another program window, obey these steps:

1. **Set up the other program's window.**

   Switch to the program and position everything for picture-taking.

2. **Switch back to Word.**

3. **Click the Screenshot button, found in the Illustrations group on the Insert tab.**

   A stubby little menu appears. It lists any other program windows that are open and not minimized.

4. **Choose a program window to grab and paste into your document.**

   The image is slapped into your text just like any other picture.

If you need only a portion of another program's window, follow these steps:

1. **Follow Steps 1 through 3 just listed.**

2. **Choose the command Screen Clipping from the Screenshot button's menu.**

   You switch to the other program's window, though everything appears washed out. That's okay.

3. **Drag the mouse over the portion of the window you want to grab as an image.**

   Upon releasing the mouse, you return to your document and the image appears on the screen, ready for editing.

Once inside your document, you can edit, fix, and otherwise fool with the screenshot or partial image. Later sections in this chapter offer up a slew of things you can do.

Adding a caption

There are graphics you can use as text decorations, and then there are graphics you want to reference. To best reference an image, you should add a caption. The caption's text can identify the image with boring text ("Figure 1"), or it can explain what's in the image ("John touching the plant that he swore to us was not poison sumac").

To add a caption to an image, heed these steps:

1. **Click to select the graphic.**

2. **From the References tab's Captions group, click the Insert Caption button.**

   A caption frame is placed below the graphic, and the Captions dialog box appears.

3. **In the Caption text box, type the figure caption text.**

   You can remove any text that's already there, such as `Figure 1`.

4. **Choose a position for the caption from the Position drop-down list.**

   The caption position is relative to the figure.

5. **Click the OK button.**

   The caption is applied to the figure.

The caption itself is a special type of text box, which is like a graphic image but contains text. It's not grouped with the image, so if you move or resize the image, you have to move or resize the caption box as well.

✔ See Chapter 23 for more information on text boxes.

✔ You can change the caption at any time simply by clicking the mouse in the caption text box and typing a new caption.

✔ Captions are removed like any other graphic in your document; see the next section.

✔ An advantage to applying captions this way is that you can create a list of captions or figures for your document, summarizing them all along with their page references. To do so, use the Insert Table of Figures button, found on the References tab's Captions group.

Deleting an image or artwork

Getting rid of artwork in a document isn't the same as removing text. Graphics are special. The proper way to delete them is to click the image once to select it. Then press the Delete key.

Images in and around Your Text

You can place graphics into your document in three different ways:

- ✔ **Inline:** The graphic works like a large, single character sitting in the middle of your text. The graphic stays with the text, so you can press Enter to put it on a line by itself or press Tab to indent the image, for example.

- ✔ **Wrapped:** Text flows around the graphic, avoiding the image like all the girls at the high school dance avoid the guys from the chess club.

- ✔ **Floating:** The image appears behind your text as though it's part of the paper, or the image slaps down on top of your text like some bureaucratic tax stamp.

You're not stuck with these choices. You can modify any graphic in Word to be inline, wrapped, or floating. This section tells you how.

Wrapping text around an image

To control how an image and text interact, click the image to select it. When the image is selected, a Format tab appears, from which you can choose the Text Wrapping menu, found in the Arrange group. Here are my general thoughts on the wrapping options available on that menu:

- ✔ **In Line with Text:** The image is treated like text — specifically, like a large, single character. The image can have text before it or behind it, be in the middle of a paragraph of text, or be on a line by itself. The image stays with the text as you edit, and the line that the image is on grows extra vertical space to accommodate the image.

- ✔ **Square:** The image sits on the same plane as the text, but the text flows around the image in a square pattern, regardless of the image's shape.

- ✔ **Tight:** Text flows around the image and hugs its shape.

- ✔ **Through:** Text flows around the image as best it can, similar to the Tight option.

- ✔ **Top and Bottom:** Text stops at the top of the image and continues below the image.

- ✔ **Behind Text:** The image floats behind the text, looking almost like the image is part of the paper.

✔ **In Front of Text:** The image floats on top of your text, like a photograph dropped on the paper.

✔ **Edit Wrap Points:** You can specifically control how text wraps around an image. By adjusting tiny handles and dashed red lines, you can make text wrapping as tight or creative as you like. Of course, selecting the Tight option does pretty much the same thing.

✔ **More Layout Options:** This option summons the Advanced Layout dialog box, which provides custom controls for image position as well as wrapping options.

If you make the gutsy choice to edit the wrap points, here's a quick summary of the mouse commands used to manipulate the dashed red lines and handles that separate the image from the text:

✔ Use the mouse to move a handle.

✔ Ctrl+click a handle to delete it.

✔ Ctrl+click a red line to add a handle.

Moving an image hither and thither

You can lug around graphics in a document as easily as you move text. Consider the graphic as a *block* and simply drag it by using the mouse. Of course, how the graphic sits with your text, as covered in the preceding section, determines where and how you can move it. Basically, it works like this:

✔ Point the mouse in the center of the image to drag it around.

✔ Try not to point at one of the image's handles and drag. (Look ahead to Figure 22-2.) When you do, you end up resizing the image rather than moving it.

Choosing a specific position for the image

A handy way to place any graphic at a specific spot on the page is to use the Position command button, found in the Format tab's Arrange group. Clicking that button displays a menu full of options for locating an image to the left, right, center, top, or bottom or a combination of these.

✔ Before using the Position command button, zoom out so that your document's page fills the screen. Then you can see how choosing different options from the Position menu affects the page as you point the mouse at each one. See Chapter 29 for more information on zooming.

✔ To center an inline image, put the image on a line by itself (a paragraph) and then center that line by pressing Ctrl+E, the Center paragraph keyboard shortcut.

Unlinking an image from the surrounding text

Most images stay with the text they're near. When you edit text, the image shuffles up or down on the page to be near the original text it was placed in. When you want an image *not* to move with the text, follow these steps:

1. **Click to select the image.**

2. **From the Format tab, in the Arrange group, choose Text Wrapping⇨ More Layout Options.**

   The Advanced Layout dialog box appears.

3. **Choose the Position tab.**

4. **From the Horizontal area, choose Absolute Position.**

5. **Choose Page from the To the Right Of drop-down list.**

6. **From the Vertical area, choose Absolute Position.**

7. **Select Page from the Below drop-down list.**

8. **Click OK.**

This trick works best (but not exclusively) with objects placed behind your text. It makes the graphic or image appear to be part of the paper. (To further the effect, I recommend using very light colors or "washing out" a picture; see the later section "Changing an image's appearance.")

Image Editing

I hope you'll follow my earlier advice in this chapter and prepare your images before you slap them down in Word. That's because Word lets you work with graphics, even though it's not a graphics program. Still, Word offers some touch-up features for dealing with a document's illustrations. This section offers some suggestions.

When you're using a document theme, theme effects are automatically applied to any graphic inserted into your document. Refer to Chapter 16 for more information on themes.

Resizing an image

To change an image's size on the page, heed these steps:

1. **Click to select the image.**

   The image grows handles, as shown in Figure 22-2.

Rotation handle

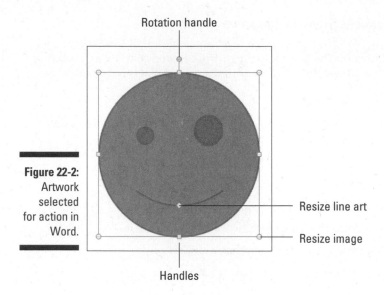

Figure 22-2:
Artwork
selected
for action in
Word.

Resize line art

Resize image

Handles

2. **Press and hold the Shift key.**

3. **Use the mouse to drag one of the image's four corner handles inward or outward to make the image proportionally smaller or larger.**

4. **Release the Shift key.**

Holding down the Shift key keeps the image proportional. Otherwise, you're changing the image's dimensions when you resize, which distorts the image. For example, grab the top handle and drag up or down to make the image taller or shorter.

You can use the buttons in the Format tab's Size area to nudge the image size vertically or horizontally or to type specific values for the image's size.

Cropping an image

In graphics lingo, *cropping* works like taking a pair of scissors to the image: You make the image smaller, but by doing so, you eliminate some content, just as an angry, sullen teen would use shears to remove his cheating-scumbag former girlfriend from a prom picture. Figure 22-3 shows an example.

To crop, click the image once to select it, and then click the Crop button in the Format tab's Size group. You're now in Cropping mode, which works much like resizing an image. Drag an image handle inward to crop, which slices off a side or two from the image.

Figure 22-3:
Cropping an
image.

I usually use the outside (left, right, top, or bottom) handles to crop. The corner handles never crop quite the way I want them to.

After you're done cropping, click the Crop command button again to turn off that mode.

Rotating an image

You have two handy ways to rotate an image, neither of which involves turning the computer's monitor or craning your neck to the point of chiropractic necessity.

The easy way to rotate an image is to use the Rotate menu found in the Format tab's Arrange group. From the menu, you can choose to rotate the image 90 degrees to the left or right or to flip the image horizontally or vertically.

To freely rotate an image, use the mouse to grab the rotation handle at the top of the image. (Refer to Figure 22-2.) Drag the mouse to twist the image to any angle.

Changing an image's appearance

Pictures can be manipulated by using the tools found in the Adjust group on the Picture Tools Format tab. Only a few tools are available, but the good news is that each tool's button shows a menu full of options previewing how the image will be affected. To make the change, simply choose an option from the appropriate button's menu.

For example, to wash out a picture you've placed behind your text, choose the color Washout from the Recolor part of the Color button's menu.

Undo an image appearance effect by choosing either the top or center item from the menu of one of the image adjustment buttons. You can also instantly undo an image adjustment by using the Undo command — Ctrl+Z on the keyboard.

Arranging multiple images

New images that you plunk down on a page appear one atop the other. You don't notice this arrangement unless two images overlap. When you're displeased with the overlapping, you can change the order of an image by using the Bring to Front and Send to Back buttons in the Format tab's Arrange group.

To help you keep multiple images lined up, use the Align button's menu. First select several images by holding down the Shift key as you click each one. Then choose an alignment option, such as Align Middle, from the Align button's menu to properly arrange images in a horizontal line.

To help you organize multiple images on a page, show the grid: Click the View tab; and then, from the Show/Hide group, select Gridlines. Instantly, the page turns into graph paper, to assist you in positioning your graphics and text.

Chapter 23

Even More Things
to Insert in Your Document

If inserting weird and wonderful things into your document weren't such a vital part of using Word, the program wouldn't sport an Insert tab on the Ribbon. Further, the Insert tab is the second tab over, right next to the pre-eminent Home tab. The Insert tab isn't over at the far right end, down there with the oddball Review and View tabs. Verily, inserting stuff into your document is a worthwhile endeavor.

Characters Fun and Funky

The computer's keyboard lets you type all 26 letters of the alphabet plus numbers 1 through 9 and 0, a smattering of symbols, and punctuation thingies. That's a lot to type, and some authors spend their entire lives weaving those characters into a tapestry of text heretofore unseen in literary history. As if that weren't enough, you can sprinkle even more characters into your document, spicing it up like garlic in a salad. Foreign language letters, symbols — all sorts of fun stuff is covered in this section.

Nonbreaking spaces and hyphens

Two unique characters in a document are the space and the dash, or hyphen. These characters are special because Word uses either of them to wrap a line of text: The space splits a line between two words, and the hyphen (using hyphenation) splits a line between two word chunks.

Sometimes, however, you don't want a line to be split by a space or a hyphen. For example, splitting a phone number is bad — you want the phone number to stay intact. There are also times when you need two words separated by a space to stick like glue. For those times, you need *unbreakable* characters.

- ✔ To prevent the hyphen character from breaking a line, press Ctrl+Shift+- (hyphen).
- ✔ To prevent the space character from breaking a line, press Ctrl+Shift+spacebar.

In either case, a nonbreaking character is inserted into the text. Word doesn't break a line of text when you use one of these special characters.

Typing characters such as Ü, Ç, and Ñ

You can be boring and type *deja vu* or be all fancy and type *déjà vu* or *café* or *résumé*. Your readers will think that you know your stuff, but what you really know is how to use Word's diacritical prefix keys.

Diacritical symbols appear over certain letters in foreign languages and in foreign words borrowed (stolen, really) into English. To create a diacritical when you're typing in Word, you press a special Control-key combination. The key combination you press somewhat represents the diacritical you need, such as Ctrl+' to produce a ' diacritical. The Ctrl-key combination is followed by the character that needs the new "hat," as shown in Table 23-1.

Table 23-1	Those Pesky Foreign-Language Characters
Prefix Key	*Characters Produced*
Ctrl+'	á é í ó ú ð
Ctrl+`	à è ì ò ù
Ctrl+,	ç
Ctrl+@	å
Ctrl+:	ä ë ï ö ü
Ctrl+^	â ê î ô û

Prefix Key	Characters Produced
Ctrl+~	ã õ ñ
Ctrl+/	ø

For example, to insert an é into your document, press Ctrl+' and then type the letter *E*. Uppercase *E* gives you É, and lowercase *e* gives you é. That makes sense because the ' (apostrophe) is essentially the character you're adding to the vowel.

Ctrl+' followed by a D equals Đ (or ð). That's the *eth* character.

Be sure to note the difference between the apostrophe (or *tick*) and back tick, or *accent grave.* The apostrophe (') is next to your keyboard's Enter key. The back tick (`) is below the Esc key.

For the Ctrl+@, Ctrl+:, Ctrl+^, and Ctrl+~ key combinations, you also need to press the Shift key, which is required anyway to produce the @, :, ^, or ~ symbols that are on your keyboard. Therefore, Ctrl+~ is really Ctrl+Shift+`. Keep that in mind.

Word's AutoCorrect feature has been trained to know some special characters. For example, when you're typing *café,* Word automatically sticks that whoopty-doop over the *e.*

Inserting special characters and symbols

The Symbol menu is nestled in the Symbol group on the Insert tab. Clicking the Symbol command button lists some popular or recently used symbols. Choosing a symbol from the menu inserts the special symbol directly into your text, just like you insert any other character.

Choosing More Symbols from the Symbol menu displays the Symbol dialog box, shown in Figure 23-1. Choose a decorative font, such as Wingdings, from the Font menu to see strange and unusual characters. To see the gamut of what's possible with normal text, choose (normal text) from the Font drop-down list. Use the Subset drop-down list to see even more symbols and such.

To stick a character into your document from the Symbol dialog box, select the symbol and click the Insert button.

You need to click the Cancel button when you're done using the Symbol dialog box.

✔ Click the Insert button once for each symbol you want to insert. When you're putting three Σ (sigma) symbols into your document, you must locate that symbol on the grid and then click the Insert button three times.

✔ Some symbols have shortcut keys. They appear at the bottom of the Symbol dialog box. For example, the shortcut for the degree symbol (°) is `Ctrl+@, spacebar` — press Ctrl+@ (actually, Ctrl+Shift+2) and then type a space. Doing so gives you the degree symbol.

✔ You can insert symbols by typing the symbol's code and then pressing the Alt+X key combination. For example, the code for Σ (sigma) is 2211: Type **2211** in your document and then press Alt+X. The number 2211 is magically transformed into the Σ character.

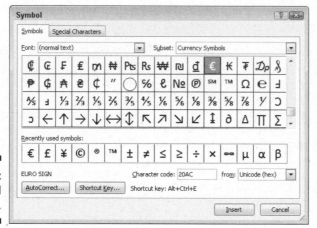

Figure 23-1:
The Symbol
dialog box.

Spice Up Your Document with a Text Box

A *text box* is a graphical element that contains — hold your breath, wait for it, wait — *text*. It can be used as a decorative element (as a *pull quote*) to highlight a passage of text on the page, or it can be just an information box or an aside, such as those that litter the pages of *USA Today*. Overall, the purpose of the text box is to prevent your document from becoming what graphic artists refer to as the dreaded Great Wall of Text.

Text boxes are easily shoved into a document by following these steps:

1. **Click the Insert tab.**

2. **In the Text group, choose Text Box⇨Draw Text Box.**

   The mouse pointer changes to a large plus sign.

3. **Drag the mouse pointer in your document to create the text box.**

   Drag from the upper-left corner down and to the right to create the box, similar to the way graphical shapes are drawn in a document, as discussed in Chapter 22.

4. **Type the text you need into the box.**

Click anywhere outside the box when you're done typing.

After a text box is on the screen, or whenever you click the mouse to select a text box, the Text Box Tools Format tab appears. It contains a lot of formatting and style commands for the text box. Most of them are similar, if not identical to, the formatting commands used on images and graphics in Word. Refer to Chapter 22 for details, hints, and tips.

✔ You can use all your basic text-writing and -formatting skills inside the box, just as you would type text outside the box. You can, for example, apply a bold font and center the text, which is common for creating text box *callouts*.

✔ You can turn text sideways inside the text box by using the Text Direction button. Look in the Text group on the Text Box Tools Format tab.

✔ To delete a text box, click it with the mouse and press the Delete button on the keyboard.

✔ You can make any shape into a text box by simply right-clicking the shape and choosing the command Add Text from the pop-up menu. See Chapter 22 for more information on shapes.

A Vast Depth of Fields

The phrase "carved in stone" refers to text that doesn't change. What you write in Word isn't carved in stone — well, unless you have a cool printer I've not heard of. Still, the text you forge with electrons is static. Assuming that the computer doesn't screw up (and that's a *big* assumption), your document remains the same unless you change it.

Word has a way to let you add *dynamic* (changing) elements to your document. You can insert *fields,* which are tidbits that can change, depending on a number of factors. The fields are updated as your document or its characteristics change. This section describes how you can use fields to put all sorts of useful, changeable information into your text.

Placing a field in a document

To take advantage of fields, you use the Field dialog box, shown in Figure 23-2. To summon this dialog box, click the Insert tab, and from the Text group, choose Quick Parts⇨Field.

Narrow down things
by choosing this category

Even more options!

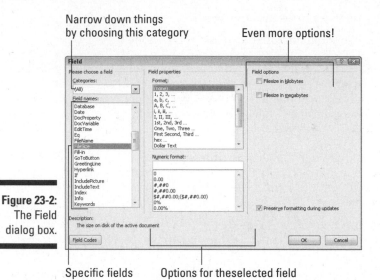

Figure 23-2:
The Field
dialog box.

Specific fields   Options for theselected field

The left side of the Field dialog box contains scrolling lists of categories in the Field Names list. These categories represent various changing items you can insert into your document. When you choose a category, the right side of the dialog box changes to show more detailed options.

Here's an example of how fields work:

1. **In Word, type** This document is **and type a space after the word** *is*.
2. **Choose Quick Parts⇔Field from the Insert tab's Text group.**
3. **In the Field dialog box, choose the FileSize item.**

   Additional options appear on the right side of the dialog box. For this example, however, you don't need to choose any of those options.

4. **Click the OK button.**

   The document's file size in bytes is inserted as text in your document. It's not really text, though: it's a field. The amount changes as your document is edited and saved.

5. **Type another space and then type** bytes in size **followed by a period.**

The text you end up with might look something like this:

```
This document is 58368 bytes in size.
```

The number of bytes you see reflects the size of your document.

Though fields look like regular text, they're not. For example, when you press Backspace to erase a field, the entire field becomes highlighted. It's your clue that you're about to erase a field, not regular text. Press Backspace again to erase the field (and its text).

- ✔ You cannot edit text in a field. You can only delete it: Do so by selecting the entire field as a block and then pressing the Delete key.

- ✔ To adjust a field, right-click the field and choose Edit Field from the pop-up menu. The Field dialog box is redisplayed, allowing you to make modifications to the field.

- ✔ To ensure that the field displays up-to-date information, right-click it and choose the Update Field command. For example, the FileSize field can be updated after you save your document, but the new value appears only when you use Update Field command.

- ✔ A document's table of contents and index are fields. See Chapter 21 for more information on Word's table of contents and index features.

- ✔ You can display the field's true, ugly self. Just as those mutants at the end of *Beneath the Planet of the Apes* removed their human masks, you can remove a field's mask by right-clicking it and choosing the Toggle Field Codes command. For example, the FileSize field looks like this:

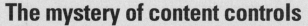

This document is { FILESIZE * MERGEFORMAT } bytes.

To restore the field to human-readable form, right-click it again and choose the Toggle Field Codes command. All praise be to the bomb.

The mystery of content controls

Word's fields aren't the only gizmos you can stick into a document that contains updating or dynamic text. Another gizmo is the content control. It's not really a field, though it can be inserted as though it's a field and can be updated. The primary difference is how a content control looks, which is something like this:

Content controls are usually inserted by Word commands, such as those that automatically create headers or footers or insert page numbers. You can also use the Quick Parts⇨Document Property command (found in the Insert tab's Text group) to insert a property control. The Equation menu, found in the Insert tab's Symbols group, also inserts content controls.

You can edit a content control's contents, if you like, and some controls are designed that way. But editing the text in other controls changes the thing to plain text, so be careful.

Time-sensitive content controls can be updated by pressing the F9 key.

Some Date content controls have a pick-the-date button, displaying a tiny calendar from which you can set the property's date.

Playing with fields

There are zillions of fields you can insert and use in Word. You might find, of the lot, only a smattering particularly useful. This section covers a few of my favorites. It assumes that the Field dialog box (refer to Figure 23-2) is open and ready for business as you start working the steps.

Also see the section "The Date and Time" for information on fields that display the current date and time and other variations.

Page numbers

My favorite fields are page number fields. For example, I may write in a document "Here you are on page 276, and you still have to refer to Chapter 23 to find out about hanging indents!" To ensure that the document accurately reflects the current page number, insert a current page number field:

1. **In the Field dialog box, select Numbering from the Categories drop-down list.**

2. **Select Page from the Field Names list.**

3. **In the Field Properties section of the Field dialog box, select a format for the page number.**

4. **Click OK.**

The current page number is plopped into your document. Of course, the page number could also land in a header or footer or anywhere else.

Total number of pages

To insert the total number of pages in your document, heed these directions:

1. **Select Document Information from the Categories drop-down list.**

2. **Select NumPages from the Field Names list.**

3. **Select a format.**

4. **Click OK.**

Word count

Getting paid by the word? Be sure to stick an automatic word count at the end of your document:

1. **From the Categories list, select Document Information.**

2. **Select NumWords from the Field Names list.**

3. **In the Field Properties section of the Field dialog box, select a format.**

4. **Click OK.**

Document filename

Many organizations place the document's filename into a document header or footer. Rather than guess, why not use a field that contains the document's exact name? Do this:

1. **From the Categories list, select Document Information.**

2. **Select FileName from the Field Names list.**

3. **In the field properties, choose the format (text case).**

4. **Optionally (though recommended), put a check mark by the option Add Path to Filename.**

5. **Click OK.**

The FileName field is updated even when you change the filename; the field always reflects the file's name. That's an advantage of using fields over typing static text.

The Date and Time

Here's a tip: With few exceptions, time travelers are the only ones who bother asking for the current year. Otherwise, you probably have people who want to know the current date and time, or maybe you just want to insert the date or time, or both, into your document. Word has many tricks for making it happen.

Sticking the current date or time into a document

Aside from looking at a calendar and typing a date, you can saunter the mouse on over to the Text group on the Insert tab. Clicking the Date and Time button in that group displays a dialog box from which you can choose how to insert the current date or time into your document. You can even click the Update Automatically option so that the date-and-time text is always current.

Typing date-and time keyboard shortcuts

To insert the current date into your text, press Alt+Shift+D. This command inserts a content control into your document — text that can be updated. See the sidebar "The mystery of content controls," earlier in this chapter.

To insert the current time into your text, press Alt+Shift+T. This command inserts a time field, which can be updated just like any other field.

Using the PrintDate field

One of the date fields I use most often is PrintDate. This field reflects the current date (and time, if you like) that a document is printed. Here's how it's done:

1. **Click the Insert tab.**

2. **In the Text group, choose Quick Parts⇨Field.**

   The Field dialog box appears.

3. **Select Date and Time from the Categories drop-down list.**

4. **Select PrintDate from the Field Names list.**

5. **In the Field Properties section of the Field dialog box, choose a date-and-time format.**

6. **Click OK.**

I like to put the PrintDate field into the header of important documents, which lets people know the date the thing was printed. PrintDate works well for that purpose; the other fields in the Date and Time category are updated only when you manually refresh them.

Part V
Even More Word

"Sure, at first it sounded great — an intuitive network adapter that helps people write memos by finishing their thoughts for them."

In this part . . .

Back in the 1940s, when I wrote the first edition of *Word For Dummies,* the program did a lot less. It was still a word processor, but most of its functions were basic — so basic that I was done writing the book after page 25 or so. I remember filling up the latter parts of the book with silly little stories and ribald limericks, just so that the publisher would believe that there was enough material for a 400-page book. Times have changed.

The Word program does so much that it's no longer my job to make up stuff, but rather to weed out what *not* to write about. After weighing the bulk of what's left in the program, I settled on six chapters that cover six useful and valuable topics in Word. I present them all in this part, the best of the Word leftovers.

Chapter 24

Multiple Documents, Windows, and File Formats

. . . .

In This Chapter

▶ Working with more than one document at a time

▶ Comparing documents side by side

▶ Seeing one document in two windows

▶ Splitting the screen

▶ Opening a non-Word document

▶ Saving a document in another format

▶ Updating older Word documents

. . . .

*W*ord is flexible. If Word were a person, I'm sure it could bend over and touch its toes, lick the end of its nose, and possibly even stick its own elbow into its ear — all at once. You never get to see that, of course (thankfully), but you can see how Word is flexible when it comes to playing with documents: Word can open and display multiple documents, work with a single document in multiple windows, and even toy with multiple document formats. It's all covered in this single chapter.

Multiple Document Mania

O the things Word can do with documents! You need not limit your word processor usage to toiling with a single document in a single window. Oh, no! You can open multiple documents, you can work on the lot, you can even split a document in a window or open a single document in two or more windows. It's not impossible. It's not insane. And it's covered in this section.

Opening several documents at once

It's not a question of whether Word can work on more than one document at a time. No, it's a question of how you open those documents. Let me count the ways:

- **Just keep using the Open command to open documents.** (See Chapter 8.) No official limit exists on the number of documents Word can have open, though I would avoid having too many open (more than ten or so), because they slow down your computer.

- **In the Open dialog box, select multiple documents to open.** Press and hold the Ctrl key as you click to select documents. Click the Open button and all the documents open, each in its own window.

- **From any folder window, select multiple Word document icons.** Lasso them with the mouse, or Ctrl+click to select multiple documents. Press the Enter key to open the lot.

- See the next section for information on how to handle multiple document windows in Word.

Switching between multiple documents

Each document dwells in its own Word program window. One way to switch between them is to use the Switch Windows menu on the View tab. The menu lists as many as nine open documents in Word: To switch to another document, choose it from the menu.

When more than nine documents are open at a time, the last item on the Switch Windows menu is the More Windows command. Choosing that item displays the Activate dialog box, which lists *all* open document windows. Select a document from the window and click OK to switch to it.

- A quick way to switch from one document window to another is to press the Alt+Tab key combination.

- Each window also has its own button on the Windows taskbar. To switch between windows in Word, choose the document name from a button on the taskbar.

- The names on the taskbar buttons are the names you gave your documents after saving them for the first time. When you see *Document* displayed, it means that you haven't yet saved your stuff. *Do so now!* Refer to Chapter 8.

Viewing more than one document at a time

To see two or more documents displayed on the screen at the same time, click the View tab and choose the Arrange All button. Immediately, Word organizes all its windows, by placing them on the screen like the pieces of a jigsaw puzzle.

- ✔ Using the Arrange All command is fine for a few documents, but for too many, you end up with a useless mess.

- ✔ Because Word doesn't arrange minimized windows, one way to keep multiple windows open yet arrange only two is to minimize the windows you don't want arranged. Then click the Arrange All button.

- ✔ Yes, the Ribbon disappears when the document window gets too small.

- ✔ Although you can see more than one document at a time, you can *work* on only one at a time. The document with the highlighted title bar is the one "on top."

- ✔ After the windows are arranged, you can manipulate their sizes and change their positions by using the mouse. This is a Windows thing, not a Word thing.

- ✔ Clicking a window's Maximize button restores the document to its normal, full-screen view.

Comparing two documents side by side

A quick and handy way to review two documents is to arrange them side by side in two windows and lock their scrolling so that you can peruse both at one time. Here's how to accomplish such a trick:

1. **Open both documents.**

2. **On the View tab, in the Window group, click the View Side by Side button.**

   Word instantly arranges both documents in vertical windows, with the current document on the left and the other on the right.

   When more than one document is open, you have to choose the second one from a list.

3. **Scroll either document.**

   Scrolling one document also scrolls the other. In this mode, you can compare two different or similar documents.

You can disable the synchronous scrolling by clicking the Synchronous Scrolling button.

4. When you're done, choose View Side by Side again.

Refer to Chapter 26, which tells how to detect changes made to a document.

Viewing the same document in multiple windows

In Word, you can show one document in two windows. I do this trick all the time, especially with longer documents. Having two windows into the same document is easier than hopping back and forth within the same document window and potentially losing your place.

To open another window displaying your document, click the View tab and, in the Window group, click the New Window button. No, this action doesn't create a new document; instead, it opens a second view into the current document. You can confirm it by noting that both windows have the same document name in their titles: The first window's suffix is :1 and the second window's is :2.

Even though two windows are open, you're still working on only one document. The changes you make in one window are updated in the second. Consider this trick similar to watching the same television show with two different cameras and TV sets.

When you no longer need the second window, simply close it. You can close either window :1 or :2; it doesn't matter. Closing the second window merely removes that view. The document is still open and available for editing in the other window.

- This feature is useful for cutting and pasting text or graphics between sections of the same document, especially when you have an extremely long document.
- You can even open a third window by choosing the New Window command again.
- Another way to view two parts of the same document is by using the old split-screen trick. This feature is discussed — why, it's right here, in the next section.

Using the old split-screen trick

Splitting the screen allows you to view two parts of your document in the same window. No need to bother with extra windows here: The top part of the window shows one part of the document; the bottom part, another. Each half of the screen scrolls individually, so you can peruse different parts of the same document without switching windows.

To split a window, heed these steps:

1. **On the View tab, in the Window area, click the Split button.**

    A gray bar slashes the document window from left to right. That's where the window splits, eventually.

2. **Use the mouse to move the gray bar up or down.**

3. **Click the mouse to split the window.**

    The split falls into place.

Both document views, above or below the split, can be scrolled individually. To edit in one half or the other, click the mouse.

To undo the split, double-click it with the mouse. Poof! It's gone.

- ✒ When the ruler is visible, a second ruler appears just below the split.

- ✒ Another Split button is found just above the Show/Hide Ruler on the vertical scroll bar. Double-clicking that button, or dragging it downward with the mouse, is the fastest way to split a window.

Many, Many Document Types

Word doesn't restrict you to working with only its own documents. You can work with just about any type of word processing or text document in Word. This feature allows you to read in and edit non-Word documents, as well as share your stuff with others. This section explains the details.

Understanding document formats

When you save a document, Word not only places the document's text into a file but also stores other information: formatting, graphics, page layout — everything. To keep it all organized, Word uses a specific *file format* for your document. It's the Word file format that makes a Word document unique and different from other types of files you may store on the computer's hard drive.

The Word document format is popular, but it's not the only word processing document format available. Other word processors (believe it or not) use their own formats. Plus, some popular common file formats are designed to simplify the sharing of documents between incompatible computers. Yes,

Word accepts these formats and allows you to save your documents in those formats, if you want.

The key to opening or saving a document in one file format or another is to use the file type drop-down list in the Open or Save As dialog box, respectively. That list specifies which file format Word uses, for either opening a file or saving a file under a format other than the standard Word document format.

- ✔ The file type list in the Open dialog box has no name. Instead, it appears as a button menu, found just to the right of the File Name text box. Choosing a file type from that list directs the Open dialog box to not only display those specific file types but also open them properly for editing in Word.

- ✔ In the Save As dialog box, the drop-down list is named Save As Type. It lists file formats you can use to save your document in addition to Word's own Word Document file type.

- ✔ Basic document opening and saving information is found in Chapter 8.

- ✔ Later sections explain how to use the file type menus.

- ✔ The standard Word document format is named DOCX, after the filename extension Word applies to documents you save. The older Word document format was the DOC format.

Opening a non-Word document

Word can magically open and display a host of weird, non-Word documents. Here's how it works:

1. **Give the Open command.**

   I prefer the Ctrl+O keyboard shortcut.

2. **From the Files of Type menu button, choose a file format.**

   By choosing a specific file format, you direct Word to narrow the number of files displayed in the Open dialog box. Only files matching the specific file format are shown.

   If you don't know the format, choose All Files from the drop-down list. Word then makes its best guess.

3. **Choose the file from the list.**

   Or, work the controls in the dialog box to find another storage media or folder that contains the file. Chapter 8 explains in detail how it works.

4. **Click the Open button.**

The alien file appears onscreen, ready for editing, just like any other Word document.

Well, the document may not be perfect. It may not even open. But be prepared to fix things or do some tidying up. Word tries its best.

- For some document types, Word may display a special file conversion dialog box that lets you preview the document. Generally speaking, clicking the OK button in this step is your best bet.

- The Recover Text from Any File option is useful for peering into unknown file formats, especially from antique and obscure word processing file formats.

- Word *remembers* the file type! When you use the Open dialog box again, the same file type is already chosen from the Files of Type drop-down list. That means your regular Word document may be opened as a "plain text" document, which looks truly ugly. Remember to check the Files of Type drop-down list if such a thing happens to you.

- Accordingly, when you want to open a Word document after opening an HTML document, or especially by using the Recover Text from Any File option, you *must* choose Word Documents from the list. Otherwise, Word may open documents in a manner that seems strange to you.

- Don't blame yourself when Word cannot open a document. Many, many file formats are unknown to Word. When someone is sending you this type of document, ask them to resend it using a common file format, such as HTML or RTF.

Saving a document in another file format

Word naturally uses the DOCX file format for the documents you create and save. When you need to save a document in another format, use the Save As dialog box to choose a new file format.

- Saving a document in another file format is a part of the document publishing process. Refer to Chapter 9 for specific information on saving a Word document in another file format.

- To save a document in the older Word format known as Compatibility Mode, choose the file type `Word 97-2003 Document (*.doc)` from the Save As Type drop-down list in the Save As dialog box.

- Before saving the file in another file format, be sure to finish it and save it one last time in Word's own document file format. That way, you can retain all the formatting and graphics and other elements that might not work or show up properly in the other file format.

> ✔ When you need to edit the document again, open the original Word document. Avoid working on the document in the alien file format, because you may find that Word features don't work or are unavailable for editing in that format.

Converting an older Word document

Word easily opens documents created by older versions of the program. It even saves them in the older Word formats, so normally nothing goes wrong. Well, except that certain features available to newer Word documents, such as Quick Styles and Themes, aren't available to files saved in older Word formats. To fix the situation, you must update the older Word documents:

1. **Use the Open dialog box to locate an older Word document.**

   Word naturally displays all Word documents, old and new, in the Open dialog box.

2. **Choose the older word document.**

3. **Click the Open button.**

   The Word document opens and is displayed onscreen. You see the text `[Compatibility Mode]` displayed on the title bar, indicating that you're working with a document saved using the older Word document format.

4. **Click the File tab.**

5. **Ensure that the Info command is chosen from the File tab's menu.**

6. **Click the Convert button.**

   A warning dialog box appears.

7. **Click the OK button.**

   The document is updated — but you're not done yet.

8. **Save the document.**

   Now you're done.

Keep in mind that after you convert a document, only folks with newer versions of Word can open it.

> ✔ Word 2010 and Word 2007 use the same document format; their files are compatible.

> ✔ The Convert button appears only when you open an older Word document, one that can be converted to the Word 2007 document format.

> ✔ To save a document in the older Word document format, see the previous section.

Chapter 25

Word for Writers

In This Chapter

▶ Creating an outline in Word

▶ Adding topics, subtopics, and text topics

▶ Promoting and demoting topics

▶ Rearranging topics in an outline

▶ Printing an outline

▶ Creating a master document

▶ Using the thesaurus

▶ Pulling a word count

▶ Avoiding writer's block

The word processor is the best tool for writers since the ghost writer. Seriously, I don't need to explain to anyone the horrors of using a typewriter. The mere dawn of the word processor, back in the primitive, steam-powered era of computing, was a welcome relief. Heck, I remember being overjoyed at being able to backspace and erase text, ecstatic at the concept of word wrap, and floored by the miracle of on-the-fly spell checking.

Writing words in a word processor doesn't make you a writer any more than working with numbers in a spreadsheet makes you a mathematical genius. Even so, beyond its basic word processing abilities, Word comes with an armada of tools for making a writer's job easier. Whether you're writing your first guest piece for the church newsletter or crafting your 74th horror-thriller, you'll enjoy Word's features for writers.

Organize Your Thoughts

All writers I know use an outline to organize their thoughts. In the old days, it was a stack of 3-by-5 cards. Today it's a computer, which is far easier to use and will never get mixed in with grandma's recipes.

Word's outline feature allows you to group ideas or plot elements in a hierarchical fashion. You can then shuffle the topics around, make subtopics, and just toss around notions and concepts to help get your thoughts organized. Even if you're not a writer, you can use Word's Outline mode to create lists, work on projects, or look busy when the boss comes around.

Entering Outline view

An outline in Word is just like any other document. The only difference is in how Word displays the text; to use Word as an outliner, you must activate Outline view.

To enter Outline view, click the teensy Outline view button found on the status bar, as shown in Figure 25-1.

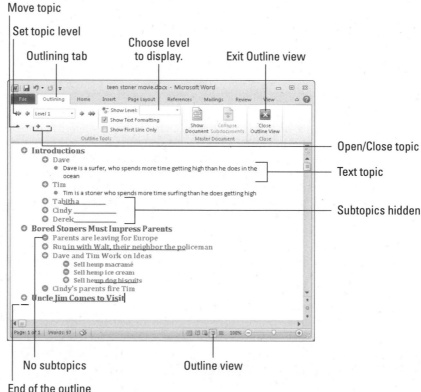

Figure 25-1:
A typical
outline.

Figure 25-1 illustrates Outline view in Word, showing you what an outline looks like. Also visible is the Outlining tab, which appears after you activate Outline view.

All the outlining details are covered in the next few sections. In the meantime, I offer some general tidbits:

- ✔ To leave Outline view, you can choose another document view, such as Print Layout or Draft, or just click the big honkin' Close Outline View button on the Ribbon's Outlining tab.

- ✔ That thick, short, horizontal line marks the end of your outline. It also appears in Draft view for the same reason.

- ✔ All basic Word commands work in Outline view. You can use the cursor keys, delete text, check spelling, save, insert oddball characters, print, and so on. Don't worry about formatting the text.

- ✔ Word uses the Heading 1 through Heading 9 styles for your outline. Main topics are formatted in Heading 1, subtopics in Heading 2, and so on.

- ✔ The Body or Normal styles are used in an outline for making notes and such. See the section "Adding a text topic," later in this chapter.

Putting Topics in the Outline

Outlines are composed of topics and subtopics. The topics are your main ideas, with the subtopics describing the details. You should start your outline by adding the main topics. To do so, just type them out.

In Figure 25-2, you see several topics typed out, each on a line by itself. Each topic, as well as any subtopics, sports a gray circle. The circle acts as a handle for the topic; you can use the circle to expand or collapse the topic, as well as move it around. Later sections in this chapter explain the details.

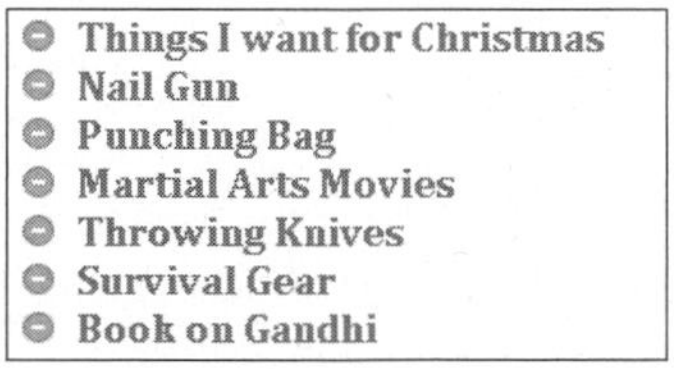

Figure 25-2:
Level 1
topics.

⊖ Things I want for Christmas
⊖ Nail Gun
⊖ Punching Bag
⊖ Martial Arts Movies
⊖ Throwing Knives
⊖ Survival Gear
⊖ Book on Gandhi

By the way, that black bar below your list simply shows you where the end of the document is located. The bar doesn't go away in Outline mode, so don't try to delete it.

- Press Enter at the end of each topic. This creates another topic at the same *level* as the first topic.

- See the next section for information on creating a subtopic.

- Main topics should be short and descriptive, like in a book's table of contents.

- Use the Enter key to split a topic. For example, to split the topic Pots and Pans, first delete the word *and,* and then with the insertion pointer placed between the two words, press the Enter key.

- To join two topics, put the insertion pointer at the end of the first topic and press the Delete key. (This method works just like joining two paragraphs in a regular document.)

- It doesn't matter whether you get the order right at first. The beauty of creating your outline with a word processor is that you can rearrange your topics as your ideas solidify. My advice is just to start writing things down now and concentrate on organization later.

Demoting a topic (creating subtopics)

Outlines have several levels. Beneath topics are subtopics, and those subtopics can have their own subtopics. For example, your main topic may be Things I Regret, and the subtopics would be what those things actually are.

To create a subtopic, simply type your subtopic at the main topic level, but don't press Enter when you're done. Instead, click the Demote command button, found in the Outlining tab's outline tools group and shown in the margin.

The keyboard shortcut to demote a topic is Alt+Shift+→.

Demoting a topic has these effects in Outline mode:

- The topic is shifted over one notch to the right in the outline.

- The text style changes from one heading style to the next-highest-numbered heading style, such as from Heading 1 to Heading 2.

- The Level item in the Outline Tools group changes to reflect the new topic level.

- The parent topic's circle grows a + symbol. That's the sign that subtopics exist, or that the topic can be expanded.

You can continue creating subtopics by typing them and then pressing the Enter key at the end of each subtopic. Word keeps giving you subtopics, one for each press of the Enter key.

 - You don't really *create* subtopics in Word as much as you *demote* main topics.

 - Not only does the Level drop-down list, found in the Outlining tab, tell you a topic's level, but you can also use the list to instantly promote or demote the topic to any specific level in the outline.

 - Unlike when you're creating main topics, you can get a little wordy with your subtopics. After all, the idea here is to expand on the main topic.

 - According to Those Who Know Such Things, a subtopic cannot exist on its own. If a topic is to have a subtopic then there must be more than one subtopic. Otherwise you don't really have a subtopic, but rather a text topic. See the later section "Adding a text topic" for information.

Promoting a topic

Moving a topic to the right demotes it. Likewise, you can move a topic to the left to promote it. For example, as you work on one of your subtopics, it grows powerful enough to be its own main-level topic. If so, promote it:

 - To promote a subtopic, put the insertion pointer in the topic's text and click the Outlining tab's Promote command button. You can also press Alt+Shift+← on the keyboard.

 - Promoting a topic changes its heading style.

 - To instantly make any topic a main-level topic, click the Promote to Heading 1 button.

Adding a text topic

When you feel the need to break out and actually write a paragraph in your outline, you can do so. Although it's perfectly legit to write the paragraph on the topic level, what you should do is stick in a text topic by using the Demote to Body Text button. Here's how:

1. **Press the Enter key to start a new topic.**

2. **Click the Demote to Body Text button.**

   Or, you can press Ctrl+Shift+N, the keyboard shortcut for the Normal style.

What these steps do is change the text style to Body Text. Changing the text style to Body Text in your outline allows you to write a bit of text for your speech, some instructions in a list, or a chunk of dialogue from your novel.

Rearranging topics

The beauty of creating an outline on a computer is that you can not only promote and demote topics but also shuffle them around and reorganize them as your thought process becomes more organized. To move a topic, click the mouse so that the insertion pointer is blinking inside that topic. Then choose one of these techniques to rearrange it:

- ✔ Click the Move Up button (or press Alt+Shift+↑) to move a topic up a line.
- ✔ Click the Move Down button (or press Alt+Shift+↓) to move a topic down a line.

The mouse can also lug topics around. The secret is to drag the topic by its circle. When the mouse is positioned just right, the mouse pointer changes to a four-way arrow (see the margin). I recommend using this trick only when you're moving topics around a short distance; dragging with the mouse beyond the current screen can prove unwieldy.

Expanding and contracting topics

Unless you tell Word otherwise, it displays all topics in your outline, from top to bottom — everything. That's fine for the details, but as your outline grows, you may want to see just part of the picture — perhaps a grand overview of only the main topics or just Level 2 topics. That's done by expanding and contracting portions of the outline.

A topic with subtopics has a plus sign in its circle. To collapse that topic and temporarily hide subtopics, choose the Collapse button or press Alt+Shift+_ (underline). You can also double-click the plus sign with the mouse to collapse a topic.

To expand a collapsed topic, choose the Expand button or press Alt+Shift++ (plus sign). Again, you can also click the plus sign with the mouse to expand a collapsed topic.

Rather than expand and collapse topics all over, you can view your outline at any level by choosing that level from the Show Level drop-down list. For example, choose Level 2 from the list so that only Level 1 and Level 2 topics are displayed; Levels 3 and higher are hidden.

> ✔ When a topic is collapsed, you see a fuzzy line extend over the last part of the topic text. That's a second hint (along with the plus sign) that the topic has subtopics and is collapsed.
>
> ✔ To see the entire outline, choose Show All Levels from the Show Level drop-down list on the Outlining tab.
>
> ✔ If you have wordy topic levels, you can direct Word to display only the first topic line by clicking to put a check mark by the Show First Line Only option.

Printing an outline

Printing your outline works just like printing any other document in Word. But because it's an outline, there's one difference: Only the topics visible in your outline are printed.

For example, if you want to print only the first two levels of your outline, choose Level 2 from the Show Level drop-down list. To print the entire outline, choose All Levels from the Show Level drop-down list. Whatever option is chosen determines how many levels are printed.

The outline isn't printed with any indents, although it's printed using the heading styles of each topic level.

See Chapter 9 for more information on printing documents in Word.

Large Document Organization

Try to keep your documents small when you work in Word. Small documents make for a stable, happy Word, which keeps you from losing your sanity. When the time comes to create a large document, such as a multichapter book or an extremely long paper (more than about 100 pages), you can take advantage of Word's large-document features, which are described in this section.

Setting up for a large document

A Word document can be a zillion pages long. I recommend avoiding the temptation to prove that statement. Instead, organize your large projects by creating smaller documents, and then chain the documents together by using Word's Master Document feature.

The outline shortcut-key summary box

I'm a keyboard freak, and I like using short-cut keys whenever possible. You may be the same way, in which case you'll enjoy using the following keyboard shortcuts when you're dealing with an outline:

Key Combo	What It Does
Alt+Shift+→	Demotes a topic
Alt+Shift+←	Promotes a topic
Alt+Shift+↑	Shifts a topic up one line
Alt+Shift+↓	Shifts a topic down one line
Ctrl+Shift+N	Inserts or demotes a topic to body text
Alt+Shift+1	Displays only top topics
Alt+Shift+2	Displays first- and second-level topics
Alt+Shift+#	Displays all topics up to a number you specify
Alt+Shift+A	Displays all topics
Alt+Shift+plus (+)	Displays all subtopics in the current topic
Alt+Shift+_ (underline)	Hides all subtopics in the current topic

For example, when you're writing a novel, you create each chapter as its own document. Make the Preface its own document. When you're ready, you can weave all documents together by creating a master document.

When you have a master document, you can assign continuous page numbers to your work to avoid having to manually number each chapter. Headers and footers are applied throughout the entire project. Plus, you can take advantage of Word's Table of Contents, Index, and other listing features.

✔ When creating a large document, keep all individual documents — the "chapters" — in a single folder. Further, use document filenames that help you see how they're organized. For example, I name chapters using numbers: The first chapter is 01, the second is 02, and so on.

✔ Ensure that you're completely done with the individual documents — the chapters in your novel or parts of a large report — before you move forward with the master document. Otherwise, creating the master document will involve too much effort.

Creating a master document

To create a big, whopping document out of several smaller documents — a master document — obey these steps:

1. **Start a new, blank document in Word.**

   Press Ctrl+N to quickly summon a new, blank document.

2. **Save the document.**

   Yeah, I know: You haven't yet written anything. Don't worry: By saving now, you get ahead of the game and avoid some weird error messages.

3. **Switch to Outline view.**

   Choose the Outline View button from the status bar to quickly get to Outline view.

4. **On the Outlining tab in the Master Document group, click the Show Document button.**

   By clicking the Show Document button, you open up more choices in the Master Document group. One of those choices is the Insert button, used to build the master document.

5. **Click the Insert button.**

6. **Use the Insert Subdocument dialog box to hunt down the first document to insert into the master document.**

   The documents must be inserted in order. I hope you used a clever document naming scheme, as recommended in the preceding section.

7. **Click the Open button to stick the document into the master document.**

   The document appears in the window, but it's ugly because Outline view is active. Don't worry: It won't print out ugly! Word has set itself up for you to insert the next document:

   If you're asked a question about conflicting styles, click the Yes to All button. It keeps all subdocument styles consistent with the master document.

8. **Repeat Steps 5 through 7 to build the master document.**

9. **Save the master document when you're done.**

At this point, the master document is created. You can edit the headers and footers, create a table of contents, and work on other items that affect the entire document.

> ✔ When you're ready, you can publish the master document just as you publish any individual document. See Chapter 9 for information on publishing a document.

✔ Editing a document included in the master document automatically updates the master document. So, if you need to brush up Chapter 3 in your novel, you don't need to worry about reinserting it into the master document.

✔ Use the Collapse Subdocuments button to instantly hide all subdocument text. That makes it easier to build a table of contents or work on the master document's headers and footers.

✔ See Chapter 21 for more information on creating a table of contents.

✔ Use Word's Full Screen Reading mode to peruse the master document. (This option doesn't work when subdocuments have been collapsed.)

Splitting a document

Splitting a document isn't really a part of creating a master document, but it might be if you mistakenly start out with a humongous document. To split any document into smaller documents, you basically have to cut and paste; no specific Word command splits a document.

Here's how to split a document:

1. **Select half the document, the portion you want to split into a new document.**

   Or, if you're splitting a document into several pieces, select the first chunk you want to plop into a new document.

2. **Cut the selected block.**

   I press Ctrl+X to cut the block.

3. **Summon a new, blank document.**

   Ctrl+N does the trick.

4. **Paste in the portion of the first document you cut in Step 2.**

   Press Ctrl+V to paste.

5. **Save both documents.**

You now have two documents where you started with one.

Improve Your Word Power

A good writer uses the best word. For example, is it *right,* or is it *correct?* Is something *hard,* or is something *difficult?* It all depends on the context, of course, as well as on your knowledge of the English language, your writing experience, and your ability to cheat by using some handy tools: the Thesaurus, the Translator, and the Research features in Word.

Finding the best word

When two words share the same meaning, they're said to be *synonyms;* for example, *big* and *large*. Synonyms are helpful in that they allow you to find better, more descriptive words and especially to avoid using the same tired old words over and over. Obviously, knowing synonyms is a handy skill for any writer.

To find the synonym of any word, right-click the word in your document. From the pop-up menu, choose the Synonyms submenu to see a list of words with a similar meaning (see Figure 25-3).

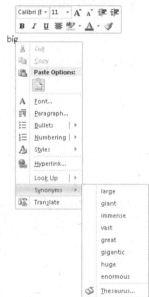

Figure 25-3:
Synonyms
for *big.*

The Synonyms submenu displays eight synonyms for the word *big,* as shown in Figure 25-3. To replace the word in the document with a synonym, just choose it from the submenu.

Antonyms, or words that mean the opposite of the selected word, might also appear in the list.

Not all words have synonyms. If so, the Synonyms submenu displays (No Suggestions). Oh, well.

Using the Research task pane

A good way to play with words, as opposed to just right-clicking and looking up a synonym, is to use the Research view pane in Word. Summon it with these commands:

1. **Select a word in your document.**

2. **From the Review tab, in the Proofing group, click the Research button.**

   The Research task pane appears in the document part of the window.

3. **Click the green Start Searching button — the one with the rightward-pointing arrow.**

   Word uses vast resources to look up factual tidbits about the word in question. The results are displayed in the list.

4. **To choose a replacement word, point the mouse at the word and choose the Insert command from the menu that appears.**

   Or, if the word intrigues you, choose Look Up from the drop-down menu to see more variations.

5. **Close the Research task pane by clicking the X in its upper right corner.**

   Or, you can click the Research button again on the Ribbon.

Be sure to check out other options in the Research view pane's drop-down list, such as foreign translations as well as other various and rich sources for finding that perfect word.

Sadly, this feature is made less handy because, to work best, it requires full-time, broadband Internet access. Also, don't be too disappointed by the translation features: My copy of Word came with only French and Spanish translations. Funny, but I can't seem to find the often-ridiculed but necessary Klingon translator.

Dan's Writing Tips

Nothing beats advice from someone who's been there and done that. As a professional writer, I'm excited to pass along my tips, tricks, and suggestions to any budding scrivener. That's why I wrote this section.

Writing for writers

Here is a smattering of tips for any writer using Word:

- Thanks to AutoFormat, you'll notice that Word fixes ellipsis for you. When you type three periods in a row, Word inserts the ellipsis character: . . . Don't correct it! Word is being proper. When you don't use the ellipsis character, be sure to separate the three periods with spaces.

- You can format paragraphs by separating them with space or by indenting the first line of each paragraph. Use one or the other, not both.

- Keep the proper heading formats: Heading 1, Heading 2, and so on. Or, create your own heading styles that properly use the Outline Level format. That way, you can easily create a table of contents as well as use other Word features that display headings in your documents.

- Use Outline mode to collect your thoughts. Keep filling in the outline and organizing your thoughts. When you find yourself writing text-level topics, you're ready to write.

- Use the soft return (Shift+Enter) to split text into single lines. I use the soft return to break up titles and write return addresses, and I use it at other times when text must appear one line at a time.

- Word is configured to select text one word at a time. That option isn't always best for writers, where it sometimes pays to select text by character, not by word. To fix that setting, from the File tab menu, choose Options. In the Options dialog box, click the Advanced item and then remove the check mark by the item When Selecting, Automatically Select Entire Word. Click OK.

Making every word count

You pay the butcher by the pound. The dairyman is paid by the gallon. Salesmen are paid by a percentage of their sales. Writers? They're paid by the word.

If you're lucky enough to be paid for your writing, you know that "word count" is king. Magazine editors demand articles based on word length. "I need 350 hilarious words on tech support phone calls," an editor once told me. And, novel writers typically boast about how many words are in their latest efforts. "My next book is 350,000 words," they say in stuffy, nasal voices. How do they know how many words they wrote?

The best way to see how many words dwell in your document is to view the status bar. The word count appears after the Words label, and the count is updated as you type.

When the status bar word count isn't enough for you or isn't visible, you can click the Review tab and then, from the Proofing group, click the Word Count button. A detailed Word Count dialog box appears, listing all sorts of word-counting trivia.

Click the Close button to banish the Word Count dialog box.

Also see Chapter 23 for information on inserting a Word Count field into your document.

Avoiding writer's block

I don't get writer's block. I don't even know what it is, though I can imagine. That's because I know the secret to getting rid of writer's block. Like all deep truths and wisdom, foolish people will scoff at this advice. They'll mock it. But the wise writer will understand the meaning and press on to write more and more stuff.

The secret to getting rid of writer's block? *Lower your standards.* If you can't get the words on the page, you're shooting higher than you need to.

Don't think it's for a lack of talent that you have writer's block; it's merely that you haven't yet learned to exploit your talent at the level it works best. Therefore, lower your standards. You'll find that you will not only be more prolific, but your stuff with read better as well.

It's all in your head, right?

Chapter 26

Let's Work This Out

*W*riting isn't considered a team sport, but it can be. Eventually writers encounter collaboration, welcome or not. Often it comes in the form of an editor, but occasionally others chime in. To assist in that task, Word gives you some work-it-out-together tools. They help you share ideas, point out issues that need attention, and even see who has done exactly what to your precious text.

Comments on Your Text

The silly way: You type a comment (something you don't intend to be part of the final document) in ALL CAPS. Or you color the text red or blue. You put parentheses or square brackets around the text. These are all desperate acts.

The best way: You use Word's comment feature, as described in this section.

Adding a comment

To shove a comment into your document, follow these steps:

1. **Select the chunk of text you want to comment on.**

   Be specific. Although you may be tempted to select the entire document, just the first few words of a longer chunk are all that's necessary.

2. On the Review tab, click the New Comment button in the Comments group.

Immediately, the document shrinks a tad to make room for the *markup area,* which appears on the right side of the page. Your selected text is hugged by red parentheses and highlighted in pink. Off to the right, in the markup area, appears a comment *bubble,* inside of which is the comment number and your initials.

3. Type your comment.

The bubble expands to contain all your comment text. Comments can be endless, although short and to the point is best. Figure 26-1 illustrates several comments in a document.

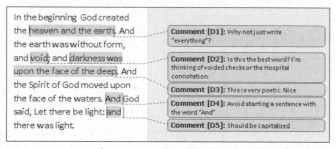

Figure 26-1: Several comments are noted in this text passage.

4. Click the mouse back in your text or press the Esc key to stop typing the comment.

The comments and the markup area stay visible until you hide them; hiding comments is covered in the next section.

- In Draft view, comments appear highlighted and numbered in the text; to see comments, however, you must show the Reviewing pane. Click the Reviewing Pane button to see the comments; click the button again to hide them.

- Comment numbers are sequential, starting with 1 for the first comment in a document.

- When new comments are inserted, the numbering changes so that they're always sequential.

- When someone else reviews your document and makes comments, their initials are used. Furthermore, their comments appear in a different color.

- You can edit the comments the same as you edit any text in Word.

- Comment text has its own style: *Comment Text.* Refer to Chapter 15 for more information on styles.

✔ The initials you see next to a comment are supposed to be your initials, which you entered when Word was first configured. To change the initials, choose Options from the File tab's Button menu to display the Word Options dialog box. Choose the General category on the left side of the window (if necessary). Enter your username and initials in the Personalize Your Copy of Microsoft Office area. Click OK.

Hiding comments

Sure, you'll probably want to ignore comments in your document. That's a given. Better than ignoring them is deleting them, which is covered later in this chapter. In the meantime, you can hide comments if they prove distracting.

To get rid of the markup area, follow these grief-relieving steps:

1. **Click the Review tab.**
2. **Click the Show Markup button to display its menu.**
3. **Choose Comments.**

   By choosing Comments, you remove the check mark there and hide all comments made in the document.

To restore the blasted comments, repeat these steps. By doing so, you add a check mark to the Comments item on the Show Markup button's menu and, lo and behold, comments return.

A quick way to restore comments is to click the Next or Previous buttons, as described in the next section.

Reviewing comments

Peruse comments by using two commands in the Comments group:

 Choose the Next Comment button to jump to the next comment in your document.

 Choose the Previous Comment button to jump to the previous comment in your document.

 To see all comments in a document at one time, click the Reviewing Pane button. A special frame opens to the left of or beneath the document window, listing all comments in sequence for easy review. (To locate a comment from the Reviewing pane in the document text, just click the comment with the mouse.)

Close the Reviewing pane by clicking the Reviewing Pane button again.

Printing comments (or not)

Perhaps you love the comments made on your text, and you love them so much that you want to print them as part of the document.

The truth is more likely the opposite: The comments print and you don't want them to. Either way, printing or not, you control whether a document's comments appear on paper by following these steps:

1. **Choose the Print command from the File tab menu.**

   Or, if you're in a hurry, press Ctrl+P.

2. **Click the Print All Pages button to display what I call the "print what" menu.**

   The Print All Pages button is the first button beneath the Settings heading; it may not always say Print All Pages.

   At the bottom of the menu, you see a set of options, the first of which is Print Markup. That setting controls whether comments, as well as other text markup covered in this chapter, print with the rest of the document. Additionally, you should see comments in the print preview (on the left side of the window).

3. **Choose the Print Markup command.**

   When that command has a check mark by it, the comments print. When no check mark appears, you're directing Word not to print comments (and other text markup).

   Use the Print Preview window to confirm whether comments will print.

4. **Make any other settings in the Print window as needed.**

5. **Click the big Print button to print the document.**

The change made by these steps isn't permanent. You must follow these steps every time you print the document or else the comments print as well.

See Chapter 9 for more information on printing documents in Word.

Deleting comments

To delete a comment, point at it and click the right mouse button. Choose Delete Comment from the pop-up menu. That's the cinchy way.

You can also use the Delete button in the Comments group on the Review tab to remove the current comment. That button is available only when the insertion pointer is blinking inside commented text.

To delete all comments from your document at one time, use the Delete button's menu; choose Delete➪Delete All Comments in Document.

Whip Out the Yellow Highlighter

Word comes with a digital highlighter pen that lets you mark up and colorize the text in your document without damaging your computer monitor. To highlight your text, abide by these steps:

1. **Click the Home tab.**

 2. **Click the Text Highlight button in the Font group.**

   The mouse pointer changes to a, well, I don't know what it is, but the point is that Word is now in Highlighting mode.

3. **Drag the mouse over the text you want highlighted.**

   The text becomes highlighted — just like you can do with a highlighter on regular paper, but far neater.

4. **Click the Text Highlight button again to return the mouse to normal operation.**

   Or, you can press the Esc key to exit Highlighting mode.

The highlight doesn't necessarily need to be yellow. Clicking the menu button to the right of the Text Highlight button displays a palette of highlighter colors for you to choose from.

To remove highlighting from your text, you can highlight it again with the same color, which erases it. Or, you can choose None as the highlight color and then drag the mouse over any color of highlighted text to unhighlight.

✔ Highlighting isn't the background color. It is its own text format.

✔ You can also highlight a block of text by first marking the block and then clicking the Highlight button that appears on the Mini toolbar.

 ✔ The highlighted text prints, so be careful with it. If you don't have a color printer, highlighted text prints in black or gray on hard copy.

Look What They've Done to My Text, Ma

You should be elated when someone makes comments on your text. You can be thrilled with text highlighting. The worst, however, is when your critics — nay, your mortal enemies of the pen — descend upon your text with their viperous scissors and cruel word choices. Sometimes those who change (they say "edit") your text are vicious; their modifications are odiously obvious. At other times, the modifications are satanically subtle. Either way, it helps to employ Word's revision-tracking tools to know what truly is yours and what isn't.

Comparing two versions of the same document

You have the original copy of your document — the stuff you wrote. You also have the copy that Barbara, the vixen from the legal department, has worked on for a week or so. Both documents have different names, of course. Your job is to compare them to see exactly what's been changed from the original. Here's what to do:

1. **Don't open the original document just yet.**

   If you've already opened the original document in anticipation of what I was about to write here, go ahead and close the thing. Don't ever again let me catch you trying to guess my steps!

2. **Click the Review tab.**

3. **From the Compare group, choose Compare⇨Compare.**

   The Compare Documents dialog box shows up.

4. **Choose the original document from the Original Document drop-down list.**

5. **Choose the edited document from the Revised Document drop-down list.**

    In either case (Step 4 or 5), when you cannot find the original or revised document, click the wee folder icon (shown in the margin) to browse for the documents you want to open.

6. **Click OK.**

Word compares the two documents and notes all changes. Then it displays a list of changes, the compared document with changes marked, plus the original and revised documents, laid out as shown in Figure 26-2.

Click an X button to close its pane.

Show/hide Reviewing pane

Compare button menu

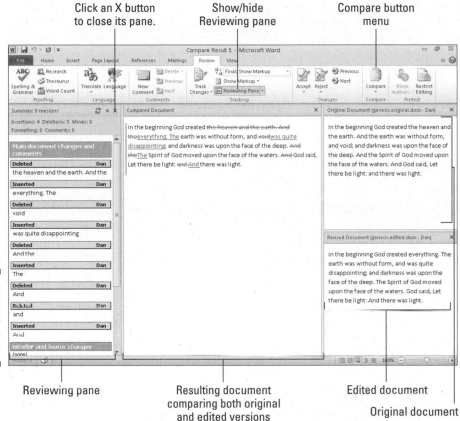

Figure 26-2: The shameful changes show up here.

Reviewing pane

Resulting document comparing both original and edited versions

Edited document

Original document

If your screen doesn't look like Figure 26-2, click the Compare button again, and from its menu choose Show Source Documents➪Show Both.

Look it over! Peruse the changes made to your pristine prose by the barbarian interlopers; use the Reviewing pane to witness each change individually. You can click a change in the Reviewing pane to quickly see which part of your document was folded, spindled, or mutilated.

TIP

✔ It helps to use unique filenames for each document. I strongly recommend that you choose filenames carefully. In fact, I name my originals using the word *org* or *original,* as in chapter1.org or, often, chapter1.dan. The person reviewing your document should follow suit, appending their name or the word *edited* or *draft,* for example to the end of the filename. That helps keep straight the different versions of a document.

✔ Scrolling is synchronized between all three documents: original, edited, and compared.

✔ Each reviewer is given his own color on your screen. For example, on my screen, I see revision marks in red. Had a second person reviewed the text, those comments would appear in a second color, and so on, for other reviewers.

Tracking changes as you make them

Comparing documents after they're edited is the defensive way to locate changed text. A more friendly way to do things is simply to direct your editor to activate Word's revision-tracking feature. That way, changes are noted on the screen as they're made.

 Turn on Track Changes by clicking the Review tab and then clicking the Track Changes button. The keyboard shortcut is Ctrl+Shift+E.

After Track Changes is on, the Track Changes button becomes highlighted. Other changes also happen as you edit text:

✔ All new text you add appears in red underline.

✔ Text you delete is colored red with strikethrough.

✔ A line or bar appears on the left side of the page, indicating where text has been changed. (The bar helps you find formatting changes that don't show up in red onscreen.)

The text colors and strikethrough applied by Track Changes aren't text attributes. Instead, they're the markers Word uses to show you where text has been changed.

Word keeps track of changes and edits in your document until you turn off Track Changes. To do so, click the Track Changes button again.

 It's common for Word users unfamiliar with revision tracking to be frustrated by seeing text unexpectedly underlined in red. When you're done using Track Changes, turn it off.

If you forget to use Track Changes, you can always use the document comparison tools covered in the preceding section.

Reviewing changes

Of course you want to scrutinize every change made to your document. Word makes the task easy, thanks to commands in the Changes group, found on the Review tab. Here's how things go:

1. **Press Ctrl+Home to start at the top of a document with revision marks.**

   Revision marks are added by comparing two documents or by using the Track Changes command on a document being edited. Refer to the preceding two sections.

2. **Click the Next button to locate the next change in your document.**

3. **Click the Accept button to approve a change or click the Reject button to keep your text the way it was originally.**

   You move to the next bit of modified text after clicking either the Accept or Reject button.

4. **Save the final document.**

   When you find the last change and fix it (or not), a dialog box explains that your quest is over.

The document has been reviewed. You should now save it: Be sure to give it a new name so that you know it's the result of combined efforts.

✔ Completing this process removes all revision marks from your document.

✔ Use the X buttons to close various task panes that are open for the reviewing process.

✔ When you're in a real hurry, you can use the drop-down menus beneath either the Accept or Reject command button to choose either the Accept All Changes in Document or Reject All Changes in Document command, respectively.

✔ When you goof, you can choose Edit⇨Undo, just as you can undo any other boo-boo.

✔ You can also right-click any revision mark to accept or reject it.

Chapter 27

Mail Merge Mania

· ·

In This Chapter

▶ Understanding Mail Merge

▶ Building the main document

▶ Conjuring up a recipient list

▶ Making records

▶ Inserting fields into the main document

▶ Merging (the final act)

· ·

Here's a little quiz: What do these things have in common? Rocket science. Nuclear physics. Brain surgery. Levitation. The answer: They're all a lot easier to accomplish on your own than using mail merge in Word. I'm not saying that mail merge is impossible. True, it's an ancient word processing tradition, something that just about everyone toys with at one time or another. Yet the way Word handles mail merge has been traditionally and consistently frustrating. That's why I've written this chapter.

About Mail Merge

The term *mail merge* is given to the process of opening a single document, stirring in a list of names and other information, and then combining *(merging)* everything. The result is a sheaf of personalized documents. Sounds useful, right? Peruse this section before making up your mind.

Understanding Word's mail merge terminology

Before taking the mail merge plunge, you should understand three terms used throughout the mail merge process:

Main document: This document is just like any other document in Word, complete with formatting and layout and all the fancy stuff you can put into a document. The big difference is that the main document contains the various fill-in-the-blanks items used to create form letters.

Recipient list: This list contains the information you use to create customized documents. It's a type of *database file* — basically, names and other information organized in rows and columns. It's that information that's merged with the main document to create customized documents.

Fields: Each of these fill-in-the-blanks items inside the main document is a placeholder that will be filled in by information from the recipient list. Fields are what make the mail merge possible.

Getting these three elements to work together is the essence of mail merge. You'll use the Mailings tab in Word to make it all happen, as explained throughout this chapter.

✔ The main document need not be a form letter. It can be an e-mail message, an envelope, a set of labels, or anything else that can be mass produced.

✔ The key to mail merging is the recipient list. If you plan to create a mail merge as part of your regular routine, build a recipient list that you can use repeatedly.

✔ A mail merge document can have as many fields as it needs. In fact, any item you want to change can be a field: the greeting, a banal pleasantry, gossip, whatever.

✔ Fields are also known as *merge fields*.

✔ Mail merge fields are just like other fields in Word. See Chapter 23 for more information on how Word uses fields.

✔ You can use information from the Outlook program, also a part of Microsoft Office, to work as a recipient list for a mail merge in Word. This trick works best, however, when you're in a computer environment that features Microsoft Exchange Server. Otherwise, making Outlook and Word cooperate with each other can be a frustrating endeavor.

Reviewing the mail merge process

The typical mail merge involves five steps:

1. **Build the main document.**

   You can create several types of mail merge documents:

   Letter: The traditional mail merge document was a letter, which is simply a document in Word.

   E-Mail Messages: Word can produce customized e-mail messages, which are sent electronically rather than printed.

   Envelopes: You can use mail merge to create a batch of customized envelopes, each printed with its own address.

   Labels: Word lets you print sheets of labels, each of which is customized with specific information from the mail merge. (This topic is covered in Chapter 28.)

   Directory: A directly is a list of information, such as a catalog or address book.

2. **Decide which fields are needed for the main document.**

   You need to know what kind of information is necessary for the recipient list before you create it. This chapter explains how to do that so that you don't end up having to repeatedly modify the recipient list after it's created.

3. **Create the recipient list, the data for the mail merge.**

   The recipient list is a database, consisting of rows and columns. Each column is a field, a fill-in-the-blanks part of the document. Each row is a record in the database, representing a person that will receive her own, custom copy of the document.

4. **Insert fields specified in the recipient list into the main document.**

   The fields are placeholders for information from the recipient list.

5. **Merge the information from the recipient list into the main document.**

   The final mail merge process creates the customized documents. They can then be saved, printed, e-mailed, or dealt with however you like.

The rest of this chapter covers the specifics. You can also use the Word Mail Merge Wizard to help you work through each mail merge step. See the sidebar "Chickening out and using the Mail Merge Wizard."

Chickening out and using the Mail Merge Wizard

If all this mail merge malarkey is just too intense for you, consider using Word's Mail Merge Wizard: On the Mailings tabs, choose Start Mail Merge⇨Step by Step Mail Merge Wizard. You see the Mail Merge task pane appear on the right side of the document's window. Answer the questions, choose options, and click the Next link to proceed. That's all I need to write about using the wizard.

The Main Document

Mail merge begins with a document, or what I call the *main document*. It's the prototype for all the individualized documents you eventually create, so it contains only common elements. The specific stuff — the items that change for each document after the mail merge — are added later.

Creating a mail merge letter

The most common thing to mail-merge is the standard, annoying form letter. Here's how you start that journey:

1. **Start a new, blank document.**

   Press Ctrl+N.

2. **On the Mailings tab, from the Start Mail Merge group, choose Start Mail Merge⇨Letters.**

3. **Type the letter.**

   You're typing only the common parts of the letter, the text that doesn't change for each copy you print.

4. **Type the fields you need in ALL CAPS.**

   This step is my idea, not Word's. Type in ALL CAPS the text to be replaced or customized in your document. Use short, descriptive terms. Figure 27-1 shows an example.

   I inserted a PrintDate field in the document shown in the figure. See Chapter 23 for more information on the PrintDate field.

5. **Save the main document.**

   I hope you already saved the document as you were writing it. If so, give yourself a cookie.

Work with
recipients

Start
here

Mailings
tab

Insert
fields

Browse merged
documents

Preview

All done!

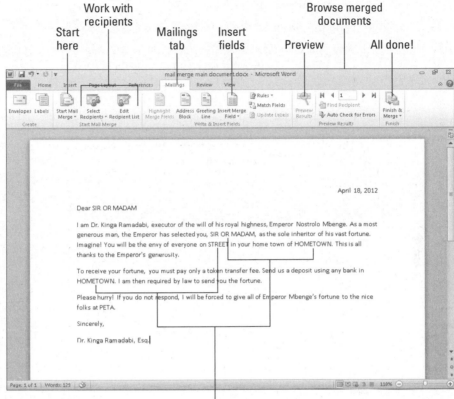

Figure 27-1:
A mail
merge main
document.

Field placeholders

After you create your letter, the next step is to create or use a recipient list. Continue with the section "The Recipient List," a little later in this chapter, for more information.

Creating mail merge e-mail messages

Word lets you spew out custom e-mail messages using the E-Mail option for mail merge. This option works only when you've configured the Microsoft Outlook program on your computer. After that's done, you start the main document for your e-mail merge by obeying these steps:

1. **Press Ctrl+N to create a fresh document.**

2. **On the Mailings tab, choose Start Mail Merge⇨E-Mail Messages.**

   Word changes to Web Layout view, used for creating Internet documents in Word. (I don't write much about that option.)

3. **Create your mail message.**

4. **Type the fields in the message using ALL CAPS.**

   Now you can easily find the parts of the message to be customized, such as someone's name and location and other info.

5. **Save your document.**

Fields are commonly omitted from e-mail merge messages. Even so, you still need a recipient list, which contains all recipients' e-mail addresses. You can't e-mail merge without that field. Continue your mail merge adventure in the later section "The Recipient List."

Creating mail merge envelopes

To create a stack of mail merge envelopes, which is far more classy than using peel-and-stick mailing labels, abide by these steps:

1. **Start a new document.**

2. **On the Mailings tab, choose Start Mail Merge⇨Envelopes.**

   The Envelope Options dialog box appears. You can set the envelope size and font options, if necessary.

3. **Click OK.**

   Word's window changes to reflect a typical envelope, a size specified in the Envelope Options dialog box.

4. **Type the return address.**

   Normally, an envelope mail merge doesn't use different return addresses for each envelope. So type the return address where the insertion pointer is blinking in the upper left corner of the envelope.

   Press Shift+Enter at the end of a line in the return address. The soft return you set keeps the lines in the return address tightly together.

5. **Click the mouse in the text box found in the center of the envelope.**

   Word stuck a text box in the middle of the envelope, which is where you place the recipient's address.

6. **If necessary, type any unchanging text in the recipient's address.**

   Odds are good that each recipient has a different address, so you probably don't have to type anything for this step. Instead, the information from the recipient list — the fields — is inserted here.

7. **Save the envelope.**

Your next task is to use the recipient list to gather the information for your mailing. The later section "The Recipient List" is where you need to continue reading.

Creating a mail merge directory

The steps required for creating a mail merge directory are the same for creating a mail merge letter. Refer to the earlier section "Creating a mail merge letter" but choose Directory after clicking the Start Mail Merge button.

The Recipient List

To make mail merge work, you need a database, a list of information to place into the fill-in-the-blanks part of each document. In Word's mail merge ordeal, that database is the recipient list, the topic of this section.

- ✔ Using a recipient list is the second step in a mail merge, after creating the main document.

- ✔ Each main document must have its own recipient list. You can create a new recipient list, use an existing one, borrow one from the Microsoft Office Outlook program, or steal one from a database server, which is an option too scary for me to write about in this book.

Creating a recipient list

Unless you already have recipient lists built and saved (see the next few sections), you need to make one from scratch. That process involves setting up the list, removing unneeded fields that Word annoyingly preselects for you, adding the fields you truly need, and, finally, filling in the list. It's quite involved, so follow along closely.

Start by creating the new recipient list:

1. **Create and save the main document.**

   Refer to the section "The Main Document," earlier in this chapter. Creating the recipient list works the same no matter what type of mail merge document you created.

2. **On the Mailings tab, in the Start Mail Merge Group, choose Select Recipients⇨Type New List.**

If this option isn't available, you haven't properly created the main document. Start over with the section "The Main Document." Otherwise, you see the New Address List dialog box, shown in Figure 27-2.

Records   Fields   Click to sort the list.

Figure 27-2:
Making a
recipient
list.

Add/Remove
fields

Word assumes that you need a dozen or so fields for your mail merge, which is silly yet a number you must deal with. So the next set of steps removes the fields you don't need in your document and replaces them with the fields your document requires.

3. Click the Customize Columns button.

The Customize Address List dialog box appears, displaying fields that Word assumes you need. Such foolishness cannot be tolerated.

4. Select a field that you *do not* need.

Click it with your mouse.

5. Click the Delete button.

6. Click Yes in the confirmation dialog box.

The keyboard shortcut for the Yes button is the Y key.

7. Repeat Steps 4 through 6 for each field you don't need.

After removing the excess fields, the next step is to add the fields you need — if any.

You need the Email_Address field when you're merging an e-mail message. You need that field whether it appears in the message or not; Word must have the address so that it knows where to send the message. Don't delete that field!

Rather than delete all fields, you can rename some fields to match what you need: Select a field and click the Rename button. For example, I renamed First Name to just First; Last Name to Last; and so on.

8. **To add a field that's needed in your document, click the Add button.**

   The teeny Add Field dialog box pops into view.

9. **Type the field name and click the OK button.**

   Here are the rules for naming fields:

   - Name the field to reflect the kind of information in it; for example, Shark Bite Location.

   - No two fields can have the same name.

   - Field names can contain spaces but cannot start with a space.

   - Field names can be quite long, though shorter is best.

   - The following characters are forbidden in a field name: . ! ` [ ]

10. **Repeat Steps 8 and 9 for each new field you need in your main document.**

    When you're done, review the list. It should match up with the list of ALL CAPS fields in your document (if you chose to create them). Don't worry if it doesn't — you can add fields later, though it takes more time.

11. **Click OK.**

    You now see customized fields appear as column headings in the New Address List dialog box (refer to Figure 27-2).

In the final set of steps, you fill in the recipient list. You need to input *records,* one for each document you plan to create:

12. **Type the first record's data.**

    Type the information that's appropriate to each field: a name, a title, a favorite sushi spot, or planet of origin, for example.

13. **Press Tab to enter the next field.**

    After filling in the last field, you probably want to add another record:

14. **To add a new record, press the Tab key after inputting the last field.**

    When you press the Tab key on the last field in a record, a new record is automatically created and added on the next line. Keep filling in data!

15. **Review your work when you're done.**

    You can edit any field in any record by selecting it with the mouse.

If you accidentally added a blank field at the end of the list, click to select it and then click the Delete Entry button. (Blank records are still processed in a mail merge, which can result in wasted paper.)

16. **Click OK.**

    A special Save As dialog box pops up, allowing you to save the recipient list.

    The recipient lists dwell in the folder named My Data Sources, found in the Documents or My Documents folder. Word automatically chooses (or creates) this folder.

17. **Type a name for the address list.**

    Descriptive names are best. After all, you might use the same recipient list again.

18. **Click the Save button.**

    You return to your document.

The next step in your mail-merge agony is to stir the fields from the recipient list into the main document. Refer to the section "Fold in the Fields," later in this chapter.

Using an already created recipient list

To use an existing recipient list for your mail merge, follow these steps after creating the main document:

1. **From the Mailings tab, choose Select Recipients⇨Use Existing List.**

    The Select Data Source dialog box appears. It works like an Open dialog box, though it's designed to display recipient lists that Word can use or that you've previously created and saved.

2. **Choose an existing recipient list from the files displayed.**

    I hope you used a descriptive name when you first saved the recipient list, which I recommend in the preceding section.

3. **Click the Open button.**

That's it: The recipient list is now associated with the main document.

 ✔ You can tell that a recipient list is associated with the main document when the Insert Merge Field button (on the Mailings tab, in the Write & Insert Fields group) is available.

 ✔ Refer to the later section "Fold in the Fields" for information on inserting fields into your document, which is the next step in the mail merge nightmare.

Making a recipient list document

Here's a secret: You can create a document in Word and use it as a "data source" for a mail merge. The document contains a single element: a table. The table must have a header row, formatted in bold text, which identifies all the fields. Each row after that becomes a record in the recipient list database.

Using a table as a recipient list provides an easy way to import information into Word and use it for a mail merge. For example, you can copy information from the Internet or a PDF file and then paste that information into Word. Edit the information into a typical Word table, add a table heading row, save the thing, and you have a recipient list.

Follow the steps outlined in the section "Using an already created recipient list" to use the table-document as your recipient list. Also see Chapter 19 for more information on tables in Word.

Grabbing a recipient list from Outlook

Assuming that you use Microsoft Outlook as your e-mail program or contact manager, and assuming that it contains information you want to use for a mail merge, you can follow these steps to create a recipient list:

1. **On the Mailings tab, Start Mail Merge group, choose Select Recipients➪Select from Outlook Contacts.**

2. **If necessary, choose your profile from the Choose Profile dialog box.**

3. **Click OK.**

4. **In the Select Contacts dialog box, choose a contact folder.**

   Contact folders are created in Outlook, not in Word.

5. **Click OK.**

6. **Use the Mail Merge Recipients dialog box to filter the recipient list.**

   The simplest way to do this, if the list isn't too long, is simply to remove the check marks by the individuals you don't want in the list. You can also click the Filter link in the dialog box to do more advanced filtering, which I'm loathe to describe right now.

7. **Click OK when you're done culling the recipient list.**

The next step in the painful experience known as Word mail merge is to insert fields into the master document. Keep reading in the later section "Fold in the Fields."

Editing a recipient list

If you're like me, you sometimes have One Of Those Days and forget to add a record or field to your recipient list. When that happens, you need to edit the recipient list. Such torture involves these steps:

1. **On the Mailing tab, in the Start Mail Merge group, click the Edit Recipient List button.**

   The button isn't available unless you're working on a main document and it has been associated with a recipient list.

2. **Select the data source.**

   In the lower right corner of the Mail Merge Recipients dialog box, click the data source filename.

3. **Click the Edit button.**

   You can now use the Edit Data Source dialog box to edit each record in the recipient list or add or remove columns and perform other chaos. The Edit Data Source dialog box looks and works just like the New Address List dialog box (refer to Figure 27-2).

   Click the Delete Entry button to remove a record.

   Click the New Entry button to create a new record.

   Click the Customize Columns button to delete, add, or rename fields.

4. **Click the OK button when you're done editing.**

5. **Click the OK button to dismiss the Mail Merge Recipients dialog box.**

This technique doesn't work when you create a recipient list from a Word document. (See the earlier sidebar "Making a recipient list document.") In that case, you must open the document and edit the list by using Word's table tools. See Chapter 19.

Fold in the Fields

A main document and a handy recipient list are two separate things. To make them work together, and make the mail merge happen, you must mix the two. That step involves inserting fields from the recipient list into the main document. Here's how it works:

1. **Select some ALL CAPS text from a field placeholder in the main document.**

I'm assuming that you followed my advice from the earlier section "Creating a mail merge letter" and used ALL CAPS placeholders to insert fields in your document. If not (if you're creating an envelope, for example), click the mouse to place the insertion pointer wherever you want to insert the field.

2. **Use the Insert Merge Field menu to stick the proper field in the document.**

   Clicking the Insert Merge Field command button displays a menu of fields according to the recipient list associated with the main document. Choose the proper field to insert into your text.

   For example, if you're replacing the text FIRST in your document with a First field, start by selecting FIRST in your document. Then choose the First field from the Insert Merge Field menu. The field is inserted into your document and replaces the ALL CAPS text.

3. **Continue adding fields until the document is complete.**

   Repeat Steps 1 and 2 as necessary to stick all fields into your document.

   When adding fields to an envelope, you can press Shift+Enter and use a soft return to keep the recipient's address from looking too spaced out.

4. **Save the main document.**

   Always save! Save! Save! Save!

The next step in your journey through mail merge hell is the merging of the recipient list with the main document and its fields. See the next section.

✔ When the Insert Merge Field button isn't available, a recipient list isn't associated with the document. See the earlier section "The Recipient List."

✔ Fields appear with double angle brackets around their names, such as <<Name>>.

✔ To delete an unwanted field, select it with the mouse and press the Delete key.

✔ A tad of editing may be required after inserting the field. I typically have to add spaces, commas, or colons after fields as Word inserts them.

Mail Merge Ho!

The final step in the mail merge process is to create personalized documents. The gizmo that handles this task is the Finish & Merge button, the sole item in the Finish group on the Mailings tab. Clicking this button reveals a menu with three options:

Edit Individual Documents: This choice creates a new Word document, one containing all merged documents, one after the other. This option is ideal for long mail merges that may get screwed up during printing; it's easier to print from the merged documents than to repeatedly merge until you get the printing right.

Print Documents: This choice is best for short mail merges: Choosing this option prints your documents and completes the process.

Send E-Mail Messages: This option processes all documents through Outlook, sending each one as an e-mail message. Each document's recipient list must have an Email_Address or similar field in it, filled in with a valid e-mail address.

The following sections detail how each of these procedures works.

Previewing the merged documents

By using the Preview Results command, you can ensure that each document looks good without having to merge them. Here's how to work things:

1. **On the Mailings tab, in the Preview Results group, click the Preview Results command button.**

   The fields in the main document vanish! They're replaced by information from the first record in the recipient list. What you see on the screen is how the first customized mail-merge document appears. Hopefully, everything looks spiffy.

2. **When things don't look spiffy, click the Preview Results button again and then edit the main document. Start over.**

   Otherwise:

3. **Peruse the records.**

   Review every merged document to ensure that everything looks right. Use the record-browsing buttons in the Preview Results group to move forward or backward through the records (refer to Figure 27-1). Look for these problems:

   • Formatting mistakes, such as text that obviously looks pasted in or not part of the surrounding text

   • Punctuation errors and missing commas and periods

   • Missing spaces between and around fields

- Double fields or unwanted fields, which happen when you believe that you deleted a field but didn't

- Awkward text layout, strange line breaks, or margins caused by missing or long fields

To fix any boo-boos, you must leave Preview mode and then go back and reedit the main document.

4. Click the Preview Results command button again to exit Preview mode.

You're now ready to perform the merge, covered in the following sections.

Merging to a new set of documents

When you want to save merged documents and print them, follow these steps:

1. Choose Finish & Merge⇨Edit Individual Documents.

The Merge to New Document dialog box appears.

2. Ensure that the All option is chosen.

3. Click OK.

Word creates a new document, a huge one that contains all merged documents, one after the other. Each document copy is separated by a Next Page section break.

4. Save the document.

At this point, you can print the document, close it and edit it later, or do anything you like.

See Chapter 14 for more information on section breaks.

Merging to the printer

The most common destination for merged documents is the printer. Here's how it works:

1. Choose Finish & Merge⇨Print Documents.

A dialog box appears, from which you can choose records to print.

2. Choose All from the Merge to Printer dialog box to print your entire document.

Or, specify which records to print.

3. **Click OK.**

   The traditional Print dialog box appears.

4. **Click the OK button to print your documents.**

5. **Save and close your document.**

See Chapter 9 for more information on printing documents in Word.

Most printers require special feeding for envelopes. A printer usually has an envelope slot, into which you can stack a few envelopes. You may have to monitor the printer to insert them.

Merging to e-mail

To send out multiple e-mail messages, abide by these steps:

1. **Choose Finish & Merge⇨Send Email Messages.**

   The Merge to Email dialog box appears.

2. **Choose the e-mail address field from the To drop-down list.**

   Your document's recipient list must include an e-mail address, whether that address appears in the document or not. If not, edit the recipient list to include the address.

3. **Type a message subject line.**

4. **Click OK.**

   It looks like nothing has happened, but the messages have been placed in the Outlook outbox.

5. **Open Outlook.**

   After you open Outlook, the messages you queued are sent (assume that Outlook is configured to send pending messages when it's opened).

Unsolicited e-mail that's sent to people is considered spam. Sending it may violate the terms of your Internet service provider's agreement and can terminate your account. Send mass e-mail only to people who have cheerfully agreed to receive such things for you.

Chapter 28

Labels of Love

· ·

In This Chapter

▶ Understanding labels

▶ Printing a sheet of identical labels

▶ Merging an address list onto mail labels

▶ Adding graphics to your labels

· ·

One of the more esoteric Word features is its ability to print sheets of labels. The labels can all be the same or be produced as the result of a mail-merge operation. Word's label feature works because the labels are, at their core, merely cells in a table and, unlike most teenagers, Word has no problem setting a table. You won't either, after you peruse the delightful options for creating labels that are presented in this chapter.

The Label Thing

Word isn't a label-making program. Although it can produce labels, as shown in this chapter, it's not your best choice. For those times when you plan to print labels, I highly recommend that you use a label-design program, one specifically geared to print labels — perhaps even some type of database program that lets you manage simple lists as well.

Word prints on labels just as it prints on any sheet of paper. Basically, Word puts a table on the page, making each cell the same size as the sticky labels. Word then fills the cells with information, which fits snugly on each label. When the sheet emerges from the printer, you have a bunch of labels for your peeling-and-sticking pleasure.

✔ Labels can be found wherever office supplies are sold. Labels come in packages thin and thick, with various label layouts and designs.

✔ You must buy labels compatible with your printer. Laser printers need special laser printer labels. Some inkjet printers require special, high-quality paper to soak up the ink.

TIP

✔ Of all the label brands available, Avery is the one I recommend. Its stock numbers are standard. So, if you buy Avery stock number 5160 or a similar number, your software and printer know which type of label you have and which format it's in.

✔ I use the Avery DesignPro software to create labels on my PC. You can download this free program from www.avery.com; follow the Software links.

Here's a Sheet of Identical Labels

One thing Word does easily and reliably is print a sheet of identical labels. Just follow these steps:

1. **Click the Mailings tab.**

2. **Click the Labels button (in the Create group).**

   The Envelopes and Labels dialog box appears, with the Labels tab ready for action, as shown in Figure 28-1.

Figure 28-1: The Labels side of the Envelopes and Labels dialog box.

Pull in an address from Outlook.

Label address/contents.

Click here to choose label format.

Envelopes and Labels
Envelopes   Labels
Address: ☐ Use return address
Santa Claus 1 Workshop Lane North Pole, 00000
Print   Label
⦿ Full page of the same label   Avery US Letter, 5160 Easy Peel Ad... Easy Peel Address Labels
○ Single label
Row: 1   Column: 1
Before printing, insert labels in your printer's manual feeder.
Print   New Document   Options...   E-postage Properties...
Cancel

3. **Use the Address box to type the text you want printed on the label.**

   Keep in mind that you have only so many lines for each label and that each label is only so wide.

Press the Enter key at the end of each line.

You can apply some simple formatting at this stage: bold, italic, underlining. If you right-click in the Address box, you can choose Font or Paragraph from the pop-up menu to further format the label.

4. **In the Print section of the Envelopes and Labels dialog box, select the Full Page of the Same Label radio button.**

5. **In the Label section, choose the type of label you're printing on.**

If the stock number that's displayed doesn't match up, click the sample label to display the Label Options dialog box, from which you can choose the proper stock number or design of your labels.

For some weird and unexplained reason, Microsoft appears as the label vendor in the Label Options dialog box. Choose Avery from the list when you use Avery (or similar) labels.

6. **Click the New Document button.**

By placing the labels in a new document, you can further edit them, if you like. You can also save them so that you can use the same document when you need to print a batch of labels again.

7. **Print the labels.**

Ensure that the sheet of labels is loaded into your printer, proper side up. Use the Ctrl+P command to print the labels as you would any document.

I have a whole folder on my PC full of label documents I print from time to time. For example, one document is my return address, and another has my lawyer's address. They come in quite handy.

   ✔ When you elect to save the labels to a new document, avoid the temptation to mess with the table, because it's perfectly aligned to the labels. Neither should you adjust the page margins or paragraph formatting.

   ✔ You can edit the labels. Sure, they all look the same, but if you like, you can type a few new names or other information in several of the little boxes.

Print That Address List

Word can take a list of names and addresses and print them all, or a selected few, on a sheet of labels. This trick is more of a mail-merge feature than a true label-making ability; therefore, I highly recommend that you read about the Word mail-merge process (see Chapter 27) before following these steps:

1. **Start a blank, new document in Word.**

2. **Click the Mailings tab.**

   All action in the remaining steps involves command buttons on the Mailings tab.

3. **From the Start Mail Merge button's menu, choose Labels.**

   A Label Options dialog box appears.

4. **Choose the label vendor and product number representing the sheet of labels on which you're printing.**

   For example, to print on a sheet of standard Avery address labels, use Avery catalog number 5160.

5. **Click OK.**

   Word builds a table on your document, one with cells perfectly aligned to match the labels on the sheet you selected. (The table's gridlines may be hidden, but it's still there.)

   Do not edit or format the table! It's perfect.

6. **Use the Select Recipients button's menu to create a recipient list for your labels.**

   If you've read the section "The Recipient List" from Chapter 27, it pays off here.

   After creating or choosing a recipient list, Word fills in all but the first cell (label) in the table with the <<Next Record>> field. That field is how Word can duplicate the label layout from the first label onto the remaining labels on the page. Before that can happen, though, you need to build the first label.

7. **Use the Insert Merge Field button to insert fields to help create and format the first label.**

   Clicking the Insert Merge Field command's menu button displays a list of fields associated with the address list you chose in Step 6. Choose a field from the list, such as First Name. Then type a space and insert the Last Name field from the list. Use the fields, as well as your keyboard, to build the first label. Figure 28-2 shows an example.

   Use the Shift+Enter key combination at the end of each line in label. Shift+Enter inserts a soft return, which keeps the lines in the label tight together.

8. **Check the layout.**

   Ensure that you have spaces between the fields that need them, and also commas and other characters.

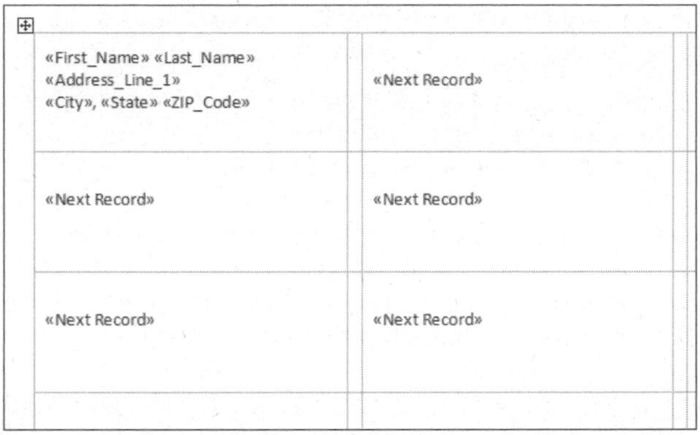

Figure 28-2:
The first label dictates how the other labels are formatted.

9. **From the Write & Insert Fields group, click the Update Labels button.**

   Word populates the remaining cells in the table with the same fields. This is why you check the layout in Step 8: If you find a mistake now, you have to fix every dang-doodle label rather than a single label.

10. **Choose the proper command from the Finish & Merge button's menu:**

    To save the document and print, choose Edit Individual Documents.

    To just print, choose Print Documents.

11. **Click OK in the Merge to Print or Merge to New Document dialog box.**

12. **Save. Print. Whatever.**

    If a new document opens, save it. You can then use it over and over and print it any time you like.

    When you've chosen to print the labels, click OK in the Print dialog box to start printing. (Be sure that the printer is loaded with as many sheets of labels as you need.)

A Label Trick with Graphics

It's possible to add a graphical image to a mailing label. You can do it to a sheet of labels that are all identical or when you're merging names from an address list. I recommend reading Chapter 22, on using graphics in Word, before you proceed.

To stick a graphical image into your list of labels, work through Steps 1 through 5 from the preceding section. What you do next depends on whether you're merging an address list or just making a sheet of identical labels.

- ✔ When you're merging in an address list, follow Steps 6 through 8 from the preceding section.

- ✔ When you're creating a sheet of identical labels, simply type and format the label you want in the table's first cell, such as your own name and address to be used for return address labels.

After making your label, either from an address list's Merge fields or by just typing plain text, you're ready to add the graphical image: Click the Insert tab and use the Picture button to insert the image — or use any of the techniques covered in Chapter 22 for sticking graphics into a Word document.

Right-click the image, choose Wrap Text⇨Square. Resize, and position the image so that it's *completely* within the first cell in the table, as shown in Figure 28-3.

Figure 28-3:
Creating a
label with
an image.

George Washington
1600 Pennsylvania Ave.
Washington, DC 20500

When everything looks just right, click the Update Labels button on the Mailings tab. This action populates the entire sheet, duplicating exactly what you've placed in the first cell — including graphics.

Unfortunately, this graphical trick involves fooling Word's mail-merge function. And, before you can save or print your document, you need to get rid of those <<Next Record>> fields. Here's my suggestion:

1. **Carefully select the text <<Next Record>>, including the angle brackets on either side.**

   You have to select the whole thing; clicking just the field turns it gray. That's not selecting! Drag the mouse over the entire thing to select it.

2. **Press Ctrl+C to copy that text.**

3. **Press Ctrl+H to conjure up the Find and Replace dialog box.**

4. **Click the mouse in the Find What box and then press Ctrl+V to paste.**

   This step pastes the text <<Next Record>> into the box.

   Leave the Replace With box blank.

5. **Click the Replace All button.**

   At this point, Word may replace only the selected text. That's fine: Click the Yes button to continue replacing throughout the entire document.

   Also click the Yes button if you're asked to continue searching at the beginning of the document.

   Click OK when the search-and-replace operation has been completed.

6. **Close the Find and Replace dialog box.**

   All those annoying <<Next Record>> chunks have disappeared from the labels.

Now your labels are ready to save and print.

Chapter 29

A More Custom Word

*I*t's human nature to mess with things. Got a bump on your arm? Odds are good that you'll pick at it. Ever rearrange a room? How about jamming a puzzle piece into a spot where it doesn't fit? Heck, Home Depot wouldn't exist if this innate idea to mess with it yourself didn't exist. The same can be applied to Word: You can change the way Word looks, by customizing it to the way you like. This chapter explains what you can do.

My, What Big Text You Have!

When the information in Word's window just isn't big enough, don't enlarge the font! Instead, whip out the equivalent of a digital magnifying glass, the Zoom tool. It can help you enlarge or reduce your document, making it easier to see or giving you the Big Picture look.

You have several ways to zoom text in Word, as described in this section.

✔ Zooming doesn't affect how a document prints — only how it looks on the screen.

✔ When zooming moves too far out, your text changes to shaded blocks, or *greeking*. Although zooming out that far isn't keen for editing, it gives you a good idea, before printing, of how your document will look on the page.

✔ If you have a Microsoft IntelliMouse (or any other type of wheel mouse), you can zoom by pressing the Ctrl key on your keyboard and rolling the wheel up or down. Rolling up zooms in; rolling down zooms out.

Working the Status Bar Zoom control

For quick-and-dirty zoom madness, use the main Zoom control. It's on the far right end of the status bar. (Refer to Figure 1-1, in Chapter 1.)

The percentage value displayed to the left of the gizmo is the approximate ratio between the size of your document on the computer's monitor versus its size when printed.

You control the document zoom by using the Zoom control: To make the document appear larger, slide the gizmo to the right (toward the plus sign). To make the document appear smaller, slide the gizmo to the left.

Using the Zoom commands

For more specific zoom control, use the commands found in the Zoom group on the View tab, illustrated in Figure 29-1. Here are the various things you can do there:

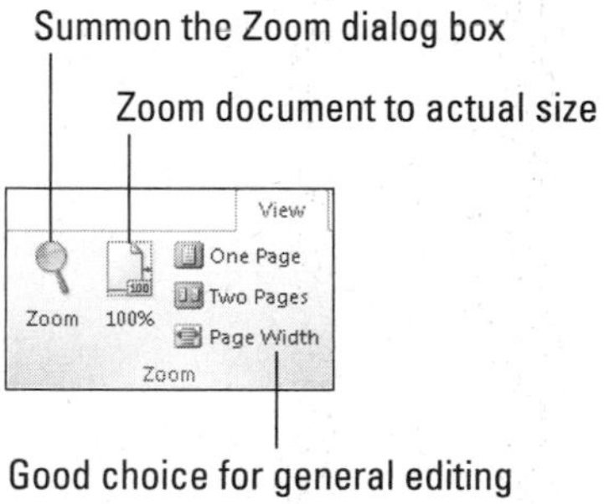

Summon the Zoom dialog box

Zoom document to actual size

Figure 29-1: The Zoom group.

Good choice for general editing

- Click the Zoom button to display the Zoom dialog box. It gives you specific control over how large your document appears in the window.

- Click the 100% button to display your document at 100 percent magnification, basically the same size on the screen as the document when it prints.

- Use the One Page command to zoom out so that you can see the entire page on the screen. The text is too tiny to see or edit, but you can get a good grasp on the page layout.

- Use the Two Pages command (like the One Page command) to zoom out and show two pages on the screen at one time. You can see more than two pages at a time by using the Many Pages button in the Zoom dialog box.

TIP

- Using the Page Width command, set the zoom level so that you see your entire document from its left to right margins; it's my favorite setting.

- You can also display the Zoom dialog box by clicking the zoom percentage (100%) on the status bar.

A Better Status Bar

Word's status bar is an extremely useful gizmo, lurking at the bottom of the Word window. Chapter 1 introduces the status bar but only hints at its potential. Now it's time to reveal all: Right-clicking the status bar produces the helpful Status Bar Configuration menu, shown in Figure 29-2.

Customize Status Bar		
	Formatted Page Number	1
	Section	1
✓	Page Number	1 of 6
	Vertical Page Position	0.5"
	Line Number	1
	Column	1
✓	Word Count	3,136
✓	Number of Authors Editing	
✓	Spelling and Grammar Check	Errors
✓	Language	
✓	Signatures	Off
✓	Information Management Policy	Off
✓	Permissions	Off
	Track Changes	Off
	Caps Lock	Off
	Overtype	Insert
	Selection Mode	
	Macro Recording	Not Recording
✓	Upload Status	
✓	Document Updates Available	No
✓	View Shortcuts	
✓	Zoom	120%
✓	Zoom Slider	

Figure 29-2:
The Status Bar Configuration menu.

The Status Bar Configuration menu does two things: controls what you see on the status bar (informational tidbits as well as certain controls) and lets you turn on or off certain Word features. Here are my thoughts:

- Choosing an item from the menu doesn't cause the menu to disappear, which is handy. To make the menu go away, click the mouse elsewhere in the Word window.

✔ The menu options are on when a check mark appears next to them.

✔ The eight topmost items on the menu display information about your document. You can also choose to have that information displayed on the status bar by choosing one or more of those options.

✔ The Selection Mode option directs Word to display the text *Extend Selection* on the status bar when you use the F8 key to select text. See Chapter 6 for more information on selecting text.

✔ The last three items on the menu control whether the View buttons or Zoom shortcuts appear on the status bar.

Word's Changing Interface

Back in the old days, you could mess with the Word program, adding and remove buttons from toolbars and even creating your own toolbars and buttons. Though Word isn't quite as flexible now, it still allows you to control a few specific parts of the program window, as described in the following sections.

Finding the Quick Access toolbar

The Quick Access toolbar — it's a small strip of command buttons dwelling near the document window's title bar, as shown in Figure 29-3. That territory is yours, free to modify at your whim and according to your needs, as covered in this section.

✔ The Quick Access toolbar is preset to dwell above the Ribbon, just to the right of the Office Button (refer to Figure 29-3).

✔ You can change the Quick Access toolbar location, by switching between above and below the ribbon. To make the move, choose the command Show Below the Ribbon from the toolbar menu (refer to Figure 29-3). To move the Quick Access toolbar back atop the Ribbon, choose the command Show Above the Ribbon.

✔ Put the Quick Access toolbar below the Ribbon when it contains so many custom buttons that it begins to crowd into the document's title.

✔ Three command buttons naturally reside on the toolbar: Save, Undo, and Redo. You're free, however, to remove them.

✔ Beyond the toolbar's curved right end, you find its menu button, which displays a handy menu, illustrated in Figure 29-3.

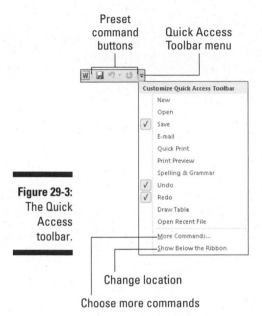

Preset command buttons

Quick Access Toolbar menu

Figure 29-3: The Quick Access toolbar.

Change location

Choose more commands

Customizing the Quick Access toolbar

You control the icons that appear on the Quick Access toolbar, by adding or removing them at your whim. It's quite easy to do, if you know how to right-click the mouse.

To add a command to the Quick Access toolbar, locate that command button anywhere on the Ribbon. Right-click the command and choose Add to Quick Access toolbar from the shortcut menu that pops up.

To remove a command from the Quick Access toolbar, right-click that command button and choose Remove from Quick Access toolbar.

You can also add a command to the Quick Access toolbar by using its menu (refer to Figure 29-3): Choose a common command from that menu, such as the Quick Print command (also shown in the figure) to add it to the toolbar.

Likewise, choosing a command with a check mark by it removes that command from the toolbar.

For vast control over the Quick Access toolbar, you summon the Quick Access toolbar portion of the Word Options dialog box, shown in Figure 29-4. That window not only lets you add any of the bazillion Word commands to the toolbar (including several not found on the Ribbon) but also lets you change the command button's order.

Category list

Add/remove commands

Move the selected command up or down.

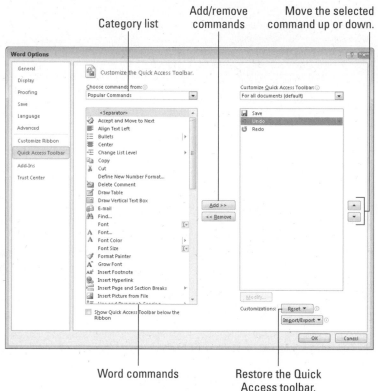

Figure 29-4:
Adjusting
the Quick
Access
toolbar.

Word commands

Restore the Quick
Access toolbar.

When you're done making changes, click the OK button to close the Word Options dialog box. There, you can view and treasure your new Quick Access toolbar.

✔ Word remembers which commands you add to the toolbar. Those same commands will be there the next time you start Word, in every document window.

✔ Choose the All Commands item from the Choose Commands From menu to view every possible command in Word. Sometimes, a missing command that you think could be elsewhere ends up being available in the All Commands list — for example, the popular Save All command or the Tabs command, which quickly displays the Tabs dialog box.

✔ Some commands place buttons on the toolbar, and others place drop-down menus or text boxes.

- ✔ When your command list grows long, consider organizing it. Use the `<Separator>` item to help group similar commands. The `<Separator>` appears as a vertical bar on the Quick Access toolbar.

- ✔ Yes, some items lack specific graphics on their buttons; they show up as green spheres. And, sometimes the button graphics don't make sense.

- ✔ My personal Quick Access toolbar contains these commands: Save, Save All, Open, Quick Print, Undo, Redo, Page Setup, and Small Caps.

- ✔ I don't recommend removing the Undo or Redo commands from the toolbar, unless you've truly committed the Ctrl+Z and Ctrl+Y keyboard shortcuts to memory.

- ✔ To return the Quick Access toolbar to the way Word originally had it, choose Reset➪Reset Only Quick Access toolbar from the Word Options window (refer to Figure 29-4).

Adding stuff to the Ribbon

Word doesn't let you alter the basic groups it places on the Ribbon, but you can add your own, custom groups to existing tabs and create your own tabs. This activity is something I recommend only for experienced Word users, or for those just desperate to customize the way Word looks. Here's how that operation works:

1. **Click the File tab.**

2. **Choose Options.**

3. **In the Word Options window, choose Customize Ribbon.**

   The Word Options window changes, looking similar to the Quick Access toolbar window (refer to Figure 29-4). The purpose is the same: to customize Word.

   Your limitation with customizing the Ribbon is that you can add command buttons only to groups you create yourself. Or, if you create a new tab, you can add command buttons anywhere on that tab. But you cannot alter any of Word's existing tabs or groups or their commands.

4. **When you're done messing with the Ribbon and creating a custom group or tab, click the OK button.**

The changes you make to the Ribbon hold for every Word window you open; they aren't tied to a specific template or document.

- ✔ The tabs and groups on the Ribbon are shown in the right side of the Word Options window, using a hierarchical menu system: Click the [+] plus sign to expand a tab or group; click the [-] minus sign to collapse it.

- ✔ New groups can appear on the standard Word tabs, but note that there often isn't room for all the commands buttons to show up unless you have one of those fancy, wide-screen monitors.

- ✔ To restore the Ribbon to normal, click the Reset button found in the lower right corner of the window (refer to Figure 29-4). Choose the command Reset All Customizations.

Part VI
The Part of Tens

The 5th Wave   By Rich Tennant

"Needlepoint my foot! These are Word fonts. What I can't figure out is how you got the pillow cases into your printer."

In this part . . .

1'm a big fan of trivia, especially trivia in lists. For example, "Ten ways to relax while babysitting toddlers" or "Ten snacks you can make and eat without your spouse knowing about it," or "Ten things you don't want to see when you pull back the covers of a hotel room bed." Of course, the lists don't always have to contain ten items. After all, if there's one additional item you don't want to see under the hotel room bed covers, why not add it to the list?

This part of the book wraps things up with some Word trivia, tips, and suggestions. I've organized the information into lists of ten items. It's my way of drawing this fat, fact-filled book to a fun and fancy finish.

Chapter 30

The Ten Commandments of Word

I'll admit that I don't look anything like Charlton Heston. Though I'm only guessing, I probably don't look anything like Moses, either. Still, I feel compelled to return from Mount Sinai with some basic codes for word processing. I call them my Ten Commandments of Word.

Thou Shalt Remember to Save Thy Work

Save! Save! Save! Always save your stuff. Whenever your mind wanders, have your fingers dart over to the Ctrl+S keyboard shortcut. Savest thy work.

Thou Shalt Not Use More Than One Space

Generally speaking, you should never find more than one space anywhere in a Word document. The appearance of two or more spaces in a row is a desperate cry for a tab. Use single spaces to separate words and sentences. Use tabs to indent or to align text on a tab stop.

- ✔ Refer to Chapter 12 on setting tabs.
- ✔ Refer to Chapter 19 for creating tables, which is a great way to organize information into rows and columns.

Thou Shalt Not Press Enter at the End of Each Line

Word automatically wraps text. As you type and your text approaches the right margin, the words are automatically advanced to the next line. Therefore, there's no need to press the Enter key unless you want to start a new paragraph.

- ✔ For one-line paragraphs, pressing the Enter key at the end of the line is okay.
- ✔ When you don't want to start a new paragraph but need to start a new line, use Shift+Enter, the *soft* return command.

Thou Shalt Not Neglect Thy Keyboard

Word is not Windows. Windows is a graphical operating system. Graphics means using the mouse. So, although you can get lots done with the mouse, some things in Word are done faster by using the keyboard.

For example, when I'm working on several documents at a time, I switch between them by pressing Alt+Tab. Stab the Ctrl+S key combo to quickly save a document. Ctrl+P to print works better than fumbling for the mouse. You don't have to learn all the keyboard commands, but knowing the few I outline in this book helps.

Thou Shalt Not Manually Number Thy Pages

Word has an automatic page-numbering command. Refer to the section in Chapter 13 that talks about where to stick the page number.

Thou Shalt Not Use the Enter Key to Start a New Page

When you need to start text at the top of a new page, you use the *manual page break* command. The keyboard shortcut is Ctrl+Enter. That's the best and most proper way to start a new page. Also see Chapter 13.

The worst way to start a new page is to brazenly press the Enter key a couple of dozen times. Although that may look okay, it doesn't guarantee anything; as you continue to edit your document, the page break moves back and forth and ends up looking ugly.

Thou Shalt Not Forget Thy Undo Command

Just about anything that happens in Word can be undone by choosing the Undo command from the Quick Access toolbar or pressing the popular and common keyboard shortcut Ctrl+Z.

Honor Thy Printer

The biggest printing problem anyone has is telling Word to print something when the printer isn't on. Verify that your printer is on, healthy, and ready to print before you tell Word to print something.

Never (or at least try not to) keep trying the Print command when a document doesn't print. Word tries to print once every time you use the Print command. Somewhere and sometime, those documents will print, unless you do something about it.

Thou Shalt Have Multiple Document Windows Before Thee

In Word, as in most Windows applications, you can work on more than one document at a time. In fact, you can have as many document windows open as you can stand (or until the computer runs out of memory). Word even lets you view a single document in multiple windows. Refer to Chapter 24 to see how things are done.

✔ You don't have to close one document to open and view another document.

✔ You don't have to quit Word to run another program either. In Windows, you can run multiple programs at a time. So don't quit Word when you plan on starting it again in just a little while.

Neglecteth Not Windows

Word is not Windows. Word is an application, designed for productivity. Windows is a computer operating system, designed to control a computer and to interface with a human being. These two different computer programs work together.

Windows is used to help keep files (the documents you create in Word) organized. You cannot do that in Word by itself. Therefore, verily I say unto you, don't feel that just because you're using Word that you can utterly skip out on Windows. You need them both in order to control your computer system.

Chapter 31

Ten Cool Tricks

*W*hen it comes down to it, just about everything Word does can be considered a cool trick. I still marvel at how word wrap works and at how you can change margins after a document is written and all the text instantly jiggles into place. Everything in this book can be considered a cool trick, but when it came down to the wire, I found ten cool tricks barely (or not) mentioned anywhere else and stuck them in this chapter.

Automatic Save with AutoRecover

Word's AutoRecover feature will save your butt someday. What it does is periodically save your document, even when you neglect to. That way, in the event of a computer crash, Word recovers your document from a safety copy that it has secretly made for you. That's a blessing.

Ensure that AutoRecover is activated: From the File menu, choose Options. In the Word Options dialog box, choose Save on the left of the window. On the right side, ensure that a check mark appears by the item Save AutoRecover Information Every 10 Minutes. Click OK to close the window. Whew! You're safe.

Most of the time, you never notice AutoRecover. But when a computer crashes and you restart Word, you see the Document Recovery pane displayed and any files listed that you didn't save before the crash. To recover a document, point the mouse at its name. Use the menu button that's displayed to open and recover the document.

 ✔ When AutoRecover is disabled (deselected), Word's draft recovery feature is disabled. See Chapter 8 for more information on recovering unsaved drafts.

 ✔ The best way to avoid accidentally losing your stuff is to *save now* and *save often!*

Keyboard Power!

You can use the keyboard in Word to do just about anything the mouse can do. Specifically, you can use the keyboard to work the Ribbon interface.

Each tab on the Ribbon has its own keyboard shortcut. To see the shortcut, you press one of two magical keys: Alt or F10. After you press either key, a tiny bubble appears, telling you which key to press next to choose a tab on the Ribbon.

After you press a tab's shortcut key, additional shortcut keys appear for each command or group on the tab. Sometimes one character appears as a shortcut, and sometimes two characters appear. Either way, pressing those keys one after the other activates the command or displays further keyboard shortcuts.

For example, to change the page orientation to Landscape mode, you press Alt, P, O to display the Orientation menu and then press the down-arrow key to choose Landscape. Press Enter to choose that menu item.

After you press Alt or F10 to activate keyboard control over the Ribbon, your keyboard is used to manipulate the Ribbon, not to write text. Press the Esc key to cancel this mode.

Build Your Own Fractions

Word's AutoCorrect feature can build common fractions for you. Actually, it doesn't build them as much as it pulls them from a set of existing fraction "characters." Sadly, Word has only a few of those fraction characters. When you need your own, specific fraction, such as ¾₄, you can create it this way:

1. **Press Ctrl+Shift+= (the equal sign).**

   This keyboard shortcut creates the superscript command.

2. **Type the *numerator* — the top part of the fraction.**

   For example, type **3** for ¾₄.

3. **Press Ctrl+Shift+= again to turn off superscripting.**

4. **Type the slash mark (/).**

5. **Press Ctrl+= to turn on subscripting.**

6. **Type the *denominator* — the bottom part of the fraction.**

7. **Press Ctrl+– to turn off subscripting.**

There's your fraction.

Electronic Bookmarks

Word allows you to stick electronic bookmarks into your document. They not only help you set your place in a document but also flag specific tidbits of text for other commands, such as Go To, or the Browse buttons. Bookmarks can prove quite handy — better than trying to use the Find command to locate places in your text where the text itself may not reflect what you're searching for. For example, your bookmark might say, "Here's where you stopped reviewing the text."

To set a bookmark, place the insertion pointer where you want to insert the bookmark. From the Insert tab, click the Bookmark button in the Links group. Type a name for the bookmark in the Bookmark dialog box. Press the Enter key or click the Add button.

Bookmarks don't show up on the screen; they're invisible. But you can use the Go To command to find them: Press the F5 key to summon the Go To tab in the Find and Replace dialog box. Choose Bookmark from the Go to What list and then select a bookmark name from the drop-down list on the right side of the dialog box. Click the Go To button to visit that bookmark's location. (Close the Find and Replace dialog box when you're done with it.)

Lock Your Document

When you really, *really* don't want anyone messing with your document, you can apply some protection. The key is to lock your document. Several levels of protection are available, but you start the journey by following these steps:

1. **From the File tab menu, choose Info.**

2. **Click the Protect Document button.**

   You have five choices, several of which require more technical expertise than I have room to write about in this book. I recommend these options:

   Mark As Final: The document is flagged as *final,* which means that editing is disabled. Still, you can easily override it by clicking the Edit Anyway button that appears.

   Encrypt with Password: The document is encrypted and a password is applied. To open the document in Word, you must enter the password. You cannot remove a password after it's applied.

   Restrict Editing: You can limit whether a user can edit a document or whether all changes are tracked or restrict that person to make only comments.

3. **Choose an option and answer the appropriate dialog boxes that appear.**

4. **Click OK.**

   The document protection you've chosen is applied.

 Locking your document is a serious decision! I cannot help, nor can anyone else, if you forget a password or are otherwise unable to remove the restrictions you've applied to your document.

The Drop Cap

A *drop cap* is the first letter of a report, article, chapter, or story that appears in a larger and more interesting font than the other characters. Figure 31-1 shows an example.

Figure 31-1:
A drop cap.

> **B**y the 15ᵗʰ of the month I'd finally sobered up enough to find the dead body on the couch.

To add a drop cap to your document, select the first character of the first word at the start of your text. For example, select the *O* in "Once upon a time." From the Insert tab, choose a drop cap style from the Drop Cap button's menu, found in the Text group. And there's your drop cap.

- ✔ It helps if the drop cap's paragraph is left justified and not indented with a tab or any of the tricky formatting operations discussed in Part III of this book.

- ✔ You can undo a drop cap by clicking it and then choosing Drop Cap➪None.

- ✔ Drop caps, like other fancy elements in your text, show up best in Print Layout view.

Map Your Document

The Navigation pane can be used to not only find text but also help you get the big picture on your document. The pane replaces an older feature, beloved by many Word users — the Document Map.

To see the big picture, click the View tab and put a check mark by the item Navigation Pane, found in the Show group. You see a document summary listed by heading style, as shown in Figure 31-2.

Figure 31-2: The Navigation pane document map.

- ✔ Click a heading inside the map to instantly jump to that part of your document.

- ✔ Remove the check mark by Navigation Pane to close that little window, or just click its X close button.

Add an Envelope to Your Letter

A quick way to print an envelope with every letter you create is to attach the envelope to the end of the document. After typing your letter, click the Envelopes button on the Mailings tab. When your document already has an address in it, Word magically locates that address and places it in the Delivery Address box in the Envelopes and Labels dialog box. Click the Add to Document button and you're done.

When Word doesn't find the address, manually type it in the Envelopes and Labels dialog box. Remember to click the Add to Document button to return to your document.

It may not be obvious on the screen, but the first page of your letter is now an envelope. When you're ready to print the letter, the envelope is printed first and then the letter. All you have to do is stuff the letter into the envelope and seal it and then apply the increasingly costly postage.

✔ Most printers prompt you to manually enter envelopes if that's what they want you to do. After doing so, you may have to press the Ready, On-line, or Select button for the printer to continue. (My LaserJet printer just says "Me Feed!" and, for some reason, it knows when I insert the envelope because it just starts working.)

✔ Check the envelope as you insert it into your printer to ensure that you didn't address its backside or put the address on upside down — as so often happens to me.

✔ If you have trouble remembering which way the envelope feeds into your printer, draw a picture of the proper way and tape it to the top of your printer for reference.

Sort Your Text

Sorting is one of Word's better tricks. After you understand this feature, you go looking for places to use it. You can use the Sort command to arrange text alphabetically or numerically. You can sort paragraphs, table rows, and columns in cell tables and in tables created by using tabs.

Save your document before sorting. It's just a good idea.

Sorting isn't difficult. First, arrange whatever needs to be sorted into several rows of text, such as

```
Lemon
Banana cream
Apple
Cherry
Rhubarb
Tortilla
```

 Word sorts by the first item in each paragraph, so just select all the lines as a block. Then click the Sort button in the Home tab's Paragraph group. Mess around in the Sort Text dialog box if you want, but most of the time, clicking OK is all you need to do to sort your text alphabetically.

Text That Doesn't Print

One of the stranger text formats is *hidden text,* which seems bizarre until you realize how useful it can be. For example, rather than cut a swath of your text, you can just hide it, maybe to revive it later.

You hide text by first selecting the text and then choosing the Hidden attribute from the Font dialog box. To display the Font dialog box, click the Dialog Box Launcher in the lower right corner of the Font group on the Home tab. Choose Hidden from the list of effects in the Font dialog box.

Hidden text is made invisible in your document. There's no blank spot where the text was; things just appear as though the text was never written.

 To see the text, use the Show/Hide button, found in the Home tab's Paragraph group. In addition to seeing spaces, paragraph marks, and tabs, you see hidden text show up in your document with a dotted underline.

Chapter 32

Ten Bizarre Things

*1*f Word were only about word processing, this book would end at Chapter 17. Fully half the book talks about things I would consider to be along the lines of desktop publishing or even graphics, tasks that can be done far better by using other applications. But beyond those strange abilities are things I consider even more strange and unusual. Welcome to the *Twilight Zone,* the chapter where I list ten bizarre things I've found in Word.

Equations

Here's a feature that everyone demands, as long as everyone graduated from college with a degree in astrophysics or mathematics. It's Word's Equation tools, which you need whenever you're desperate to stick a polynomial equation into your document and don't want to endure the tedium of building the thing yourself.

You can pluck a premade equation from the Insert tab's Equation button menu, as long as the equation you need is shown there. Otherwise, just click the button by itself (not the menu triangle) and two things happen: An equation *content control* is inserted into your document at the insertion pointer's location, and the Equation Tools Design tab appears on the Ribbon. Creating equations was never easier! Well, creating them is easy, but knowing what they mean is a different story altogether.

No, Word won't solve the equation.

Math

Equations are merely graphical decorations in your text. When you need Word to do math for you, it can — not the "Taylor series expansion of *e* to the *x*" type of equations, although some simple math isn't beyond Word's reach.

Word's math is primarily done in tables, and it's basically a subset of some simple math formulas found in Excel worksheets. After creating a table, click the Table Tools Layout tab and locate the Formula button in the Data group. Clicking that button displays the Formula dialog box, from which you can paste into the table various functions that do interesting things with numbers in the table.

For example, to calculate the total of a column of numbers, click in the bottom cell in that column, choose the Formula command, and insert the `=SUM(ABOVE)` function. Word automatically calculates the total. If the values change, right-click in the cell and choose Update Field from the pop-up menu.

Make a Macro

Too many people want to know about macros in Word, but it's such a big topic that I continually avoid it, unable to do it justice in such scant space. Well, anyway. Here goes: A macro is a teensy program you can write in Word that automates things, such as repetitive keystrokes or tasks.

You start making a macro by recording it. Here are some steps:

1. **In the View tab, choose Macros⇨Record Macro.**
2. **Give the macro a name in the Record Macro dialog box.**

3. **Click the Keyboard button to assign a keyboard shortcut to the macro.**

   I recommend using this approach over choosing the Button option, which is more work.

4. **Type a keyboard shortcut combination.**

   Most of the good combinations are already used by Word, though many of the Ctrl+Alt+*letter* combinations are not. One shortcut key I like is Ctrl+Alt+Z because the keys are close together.

5. **Click the Assign button.**

6. **Click the Close button.**

   You're now recording a macro in Word. Everything you do is recorded, from typing text to choosing commands and setting options.

   If you're just testing the waters, type some text. That's good enough.

7. **To stop recording, choose Macros⇨Stop Recording.**

   The macro is saved.

To play back the macro, press the keyboard shortcut you assigned. Word repeats all actions taken while the macro was being recorded, playing them back as though you just issued the commands or typed the text yourself.

✔ To review macros you've made, choose Macros⇨View Macros. You can manually run a macro from the Macros dialog box, or you can rename, edit, or delete the macros. You know the drill.

✔ Macros in Word broach on the arena of computer programming. If you want to dig into macros, find a book or resource on the Microsoft Visual Basic for Applications programming language.

✔ Macro is short for macroinstruction. Yeah, whatever.

The Developer Tab

Word's advanced, creepy features lie on a tab that's normally hidden from view: the Developer tab. To display the Developer tab, choose the Customize Ribbon command from the File tab's Option menu. On the right side of the window, place a check mark by the Developer Tab item. Click OK.

The Developer tab is aptly named; it's best suited for people who either use Word to develop applications, special documents, and online forms or are hell-bent on customizing Word by using macros. Scary stuff.

Hyphenation

Hyphenation is an automatic feature that splits a long word at the end of a line to make the text fit better on the page. Most people leave this feature turned off because hyphenated words tend to slow down the pace at which people read. However, if you want to hyphenate a document, click the Page Layout tab and then the Page Setup group and choose Hyphenation⇨Automatic.

Hyphenation works best with paragraph formatting set to full justification.

Document Properties

When your company (or government agency) grows too big, there's a need for too much information. Word happily obliges by providing you with a sheet full of fill-in-the-blanks goodness to tell you all about your document and divulge whatever information you care to know about who worked on what and for how long. These tidbits are the *document properties*.

To eagerly fill in any document's properties, click the File tab and choose the Info item. Document properties are listed on the far right side of the window. Some information cannot be changed, but when you click the lighter-colored text, you can type in your own stuff.

The document's property information can be inserted into your text: From the Insert tab's Text group, choose Quick Parts⇨Properties to insert various property text information tidbits into a document.

Cross-References

The References tab sports a bunch of features that I don't touch on in this book, not the least of which is the Cross-Reference button in the Captions group. The Cross Reference command allows you to insert instructions such as "Refer to Chapter 99, Section Z" into your document. This feature works because you absorbed excess energy from the universe during a freak lightning storm and now have an IQ that would make Mr. Spock envious. Anyway, the Cross-Reference dialog box, summoned by the Cross-Reference command, is the place where cross-referencing happens. Page 653 has more information about this feature.

Smart Tags

The Smart Tags feature was introduced back when literally four people were clamoring for that type of feature. Fortunately, it now comes disabled in Word. When it's enabled, though, it underlines names, dates, places, and similar contact information with a dotted purple line. Pointing the mouse at any text underlined with purple dots displays a Smart Tag icon, from which you can choose a menu full of options that work only when you have Microsoft Outlook on your computer and everything is configured by an expert.

Enabling Smart Tags involves some clever decision-making processes in the Word Options dialog box, in both the Advanced and Add-In areas. On the remote chance that you're in an office situation where Smart Tags can make a difference in your life, odds are that the thing is already configured and ready for you to use. Otherwise, I've wasted as much text as I care to on the silly subject of Smart Tags.

Click-and-Type

A feature introduced in Word 2002, and one that I don't believe anyone ever uses, is *click-and-type*. In Print Layout mode, in a blank document, you can use it to click the mouse anywhere on the page and type information at that spot. *Bam!*

I fail to see any value in click-and-type, especially when it's easier just to learn basic formatting. But click-and-type may bother you when you see any of its specialized mouse pointers displayed; thus:

$$I^{\vDash} \quad I^{\dashv} \quad \underline{I} \quad {}^{\equiv}I$$

That's click-and-type in action, with the mouse pointer trying to indicate the paragraph format to be applied when you click the mouse.

The best news about click-and-type is that you can disable it: Choose Options from the File tab menu. In the Word Options dialog box, choose Advanced from the left side. On the right side, in the Editing Options area, remove the check mark by Enable Click and Type. Click the OK button to rid yourself of this nuisance.

Word and the Internet

Microsoft went kind of kooky in the 1990s when Bill Gates suddenly realized that his company was behind the curve on the Internet. In response, many Microsoft programs, including Word, suddenly started to bud various Internet features, whether the features were relevant to the software's original intent or not. For example, Word has — even to this day — the ability to create Web pages or send e-mail.

Word is an excellent word processor. Word is a lousy e-mail program. Word is even worse at creating Web pages. Still, these features exist, and even more were added in this version of Word, including the ability to create an online Web log, or *blog*. Word also sports tools for collaborating with others on the same document by using some Internet let's-work-together feature that's more a part of Microsoft Office than of Word itself.

Yes, I cover none of that stuff in this book. This book is about *word processing*. If you want software for e-mail, making Web pages, using an Internet fax, creating a blog, or finding pictures of famous celebrities in compromising poses on the Internet, you just have to look elsewhere.

Chapter 33

Ten Avuncular Suggestions

*J*ust like Mom wouldn't let you run off to school without ensuring that you wore a sweater (especially when she was cold) and had your books, homework, lunch, and money for milk, I don't want you to march forth with your word processing efforts without reading at least ten more pieces of loving, Word-friendly advice. This chapter is where you can find that advice.

Keep Printer Paper, Toner, and Supplies Handy

The electronic office is a myth. Along with your word processor, you need some real-world office supplies. Keep them stocked. Keep them handy.

✔ When you buy paper, buy a box.

✔ When you buy a toner cartridge or printer ribbon, buy two or three.

✔ Keep a good stock of pens, paper, staples, paper clips, and all other office supplies handy.

Get Some References

Word is a writing tool. As such, you need to be familiar with, and obey, the grammatical rules of your language. If that language just happens to be English, you have a big job ahead of you. Even though a dictionary and a thesaurus are electronic parts of Word, I recommend that you keep a few references handy:

- ✔ Strunk and White's *Elements of Style* (Allyn & Bacon) is also a useful book for finding out where to place apostrophes and commas.

- ✔ Any good college or university dictionary is helpful. Plenty of good electronic copies of dictionaries are available now. Use one.

- ✔ Find a good thesaurus. (I love a good thesaurus. The one I use is from 1923. No electronic thesaurus I've seen has as many words in it.)

- ✔ Books containing common quotations, slang terms and euphemisms, common foreign words and phrases, and similar references are also good choices.

If you lack these books, visit the reference section of your local bookstore and plan to invest some good money to stock up on quality references.

Keep Your Computer Files Organized

Use folders on your hard drive for storing your document files. Keep related documents together in the same folders. Properly name your files so that you know what's in them.

One of the biggest problems with computers now is that millions of people use computers who have no concept of basic *computer science.* You can get a good dose from my *PCs For Dummies,* but also consider taking a class on computer basics. You'll enjoy your computer more when you understand how to use it.

Add the Junk Later

Write first, then format, then edit. Keep writing and editing. Save your stuff. Only when you truly finish writing should you go back to insert a picture or a graphical doodad. Doing those tasks last keeps you focused on *writing,* which is the main part of your document. Also, Word behaves better when a document doesn't have a lot of graphics or fancy junk in it. Write first, add the junk later.

Back Up Your Work

You should have two copies of everything you write, especially the stuff you value and treasure. You keep the original copy on the computer's main storage device (the hard drive); this book tells you how to save that copy. A second copy, or *backup,* should also be made, one that doesn't live on the same disk drive as the original.

To back up your work, use an optical disc, a USB thumb drive, a flash drive, an external hard drive, or a network drive. You can back up files by simply copying them in Windows, though using a traditional backup program on a schedule is the best method. Refer to my book *PCs For Dummies* for more information.

Use AutoCorrect

As you work in Word, you soon discover which words you enjoy misspelling the most. These words appear on the screen with a red zigzag underline. The common thing to do is to right-click the word and correct it by choosing a proper replacement from the pop-up list. I suggest that you go one step further and choose the AutoCorrect submenu and *then* choose the replacement word. With your oft-misspelled word in the AutoCorrect repertoire, you never have to fix the misspelling again. Well, either that or just learn how to spell the dumb word properly in the first place!

Use Those Keyboard Shortcuts

You should have a repertoire of keyboard shortcuts, representing many of the commands you use often. Though it may not seem so at first, using the keyboard is much faster than getting by with the mouse. (Refer to this book's Cheat Sheet at www.dummies.com/cheatsheet/word2010.)

Try New Things

In Word, as in life, people form habits and repeat the same behaviors. Rather than fall into that trap, consider trying new behaviors from time to time. For example, consider using tables rather than tabs to organize your stuff. If you're an ancient Word user from days gone by, try out some of the Quick Styles or mess around with themes. Try to explore as much of Word as possible. You may learn a new trick or discover a faster way to get something done.

Let Word Do the Work

Word does amazing things. In fact, any time you feel that you're doing too much work in Word, an easier, faster way to get the same job done is probably available. Use this book's index or the Word Help system to peruse the various tasks you undertake. You may be surprised that a shortcut exists, one that saves you time and makes your stuff look good.

Don't Take It All Too Seriously

Computers are about having fun. Too many people panic too quickly when they use computers. Don't let them get to you! And *please* don't reinstall Word to fix a minor problem. Everything that goes wrong has a solution. If the solution isn't in this book, consult your computer guru. Someone is bound to be able to help you out.

Index